Expanding the Circle

Essays in Honor of Joan E. Hemenway

Catherine F. Garlid,
Angelika A. Zollfrank,
George Fitchett (Editors)

Journal of Pastoral Care Publications, Inc.
Decatur, Georgia
2009

Journal of Pastoral Care Publications, Inc. Decatur, Georgia 2009

ISBN: 978-0-929670-03-4

Library of Congress Control Number: 2009920827

PRINTED IN THE UNITED STATES OF AMERICA

CONTENTS

BIOGRAPHICAL INFORMATION

Joan E. Hemenway was born in Philadelphia, Pennsylvania, on March 14, 1938. Her father, Seymour Hemenway, was an engineer and her mother, Katherine McKeown Hemenway, was a social worker. Joan and her sister, Marion, were raised in Swarthmore, Pennsylvania. When Joan was a child her family attended the local Presbyterian church.

Joan graduated in 1960 from Connecticut College, where she majored in American History. After college she went to work in Philadelphia for *Youth* magazine, a publication of the United Church of Christ. In the fall of 1965 Joan began a Ph.D. program in theology at the University of Chicago Divinity School, but within three months she returned home to care for her mother who had terminal breast cancer. Joan attended Union Theological Seminary, New York, and graduated in 1968. After seminary she worked in the Promotion Department of the Lutheran Church in America, and again for *Youth* magazine. She was ordained an Elder in the United Methodist Church in 1976 and for several years was Associate Minister of the First United Methodist Church of Germantown, Philadelphia, Pennsylvania.

Joan's first unit of CPE was taken in the summer of 1966 at Haverford State Hospital, a new psychiatric hospital in suburban Philadelphia that had opened in 1964. Bill Jackson was her supervisor. She completed her first Residency (2 units, one Basic, one Advanced) in 1973-1974 at Philadelphia State Hospital with Bill Wykoff as her supervisor. This was followed by three advanced units in 1974-1975 at The Presbyterian Medical Center in Philadelphia with Dan DeArment as her supervisor. The following year, 1975-1976, she completed three units of supervisory education with DeArment. She was certified as an Acting Supervisor in 1976 and as a Full Supervisor in 1981.

Joan's career included employment as Director of CPE at the

Hospital Chaplaincy, Inc. in New York City, Associate Director of the chaplaincy program at Hartford Hospital, Hartford, Connecticut, and Director of the Chaplaincy and CPE program at Bridgeport Hospital, Bridgeport, Connecticut. In 2000, she co-founded a CPE supervisory training program affiliated with the Yale-New Haven Health System, New Haven, Connecticut. Joan was a Fellow in the American Association of Pastoral Counselors and worked at pastoral counseling centers in Philadelphia and Manchester, Connecticut.

Joan's involvement in the organizational life of ACPE was extensive. It began with service on the Eastern Region's Accreditation Committee in the late 1970s. She was Regional Director of the Eastern Region, ACPE, from 1983-1990. Throughout her career she served on many ACPE committees, as well as the Board of Representatives. She was also active in planning several national conferences. Joan was installed as President of ACPE in October, 2005, the third woman to serve in that office. During her year as President-Elect, Joan chaired the ACPE Strategic Planning Task Force, helping create a vision for ACPE that will continue for many years.

Joan lived with Jennifer Allcock, her life partner who is a retired physician, for 19 years. In May, 2005 Joan resigned from her ordination in the United Methodist Church in protest of the denomination's prohibition against the ordination of gay men and lesbians. In June, 2006, Joan was diagnosed with a malignant brain tumor. She died at her home on January 31, 2007.

Curriculum Vitae

Education

1960	Connecticut College, New London, CT
	Bachelor of Arts, major in American history, minor in religious studies
1968	Union Theological Seminary, New York, NY
	Master of Divinity, major in Old Testament, minor in psychology and religion
1994	Andover Newton Theological School, Newton, MA

Doctor of Ministry, with honors, major in pastoral counseling and family systems

Professional Certification
1978	Board Certified Chaplain, Association of Professional Chaplains
1981	Supervisor, Association for Clinical Pastoral Education
1994	Fellow, American Association of Pastoral Counselors

Ecclesiastical Status and Endorsement
1974/76	Ordained Deacon/Elder, Eastern Pennsylvania Conference, The United Methodist Church (retired June 2003)
1979	Endorsement for Hospital Ministry, Division of Chaplains and Related Ministries, The United Methodist Church
1994	Endorsement for Pastoral Counseling, Division of Chaplains and Related Ministries, The United Methodist Church

Employment
1962-1965	Associate Editor, *Youth* magazine, United Church of Christ, Philadelphia, PA
1968-1970	Director, Promotion Department, Lutheran Church in America, Philadelphia, PA
1970-1972	Managing Editor, *Youth* magazine, United Church of Christ, Philadelphia, PA
1974-1978	Pastoral Counselor, Pennsylvania Foundation for Pastoral Counseling, Philadelphia, PA
1974-1978	Staff Chaplain, Presbyterian Medical Center, Philadelphia, PA
1976-1978	Associate Minister, First United Methodist Church of Germantown, Philadelphia, PA
1978-1984	Director of Clinical Pastoral Education Program, The Hospital Chaplaincy, Inc., New York, NY

1983-1990	Regional Director (part-time), Eastern Region, Association for Clinical Pastoral Education.
1984-1994	Associate Director, Anna M. Fulling Chaplaincy, Hartford Hospital, Hartford, CT
1990-1994	Pastoral Counselor, Pastoral Counseling Center, Manchester, CT.
1995-2000	Director, Pastoral Care and Clinical Pastoral Education (CPE), Bridgeport Hospital, Bridgeport, CT
2000-2005	Director (part-time), Pastoral Education Consortium, Yale-New Haven Health System, New Haven, CT

Academic Employment

1979-1983	Adjunct Professor of Practical Theology, Union Seminary, New York, NY
1986-1993	Adjunct Professor of Pastoral Care, Hartford Seminary, Hartford, CT
1995-2004	Adjunct Lecturer in Pastoral Care, Yale Divinity School, New Haven, CT

Awards

1984	Professional Service Award, Association of Professional Chaplains
2000	Distinguished Service Award, Association for Clinical Pastoral Education

Professional Memberships

Association for Clinical Pastoral Education
American Association of Pastoral Counselors
Systems-Centered Training and Research Institute
Association of Professional Chaplains

Publications
Books

     Inside the Circle: A Historical and Practical Inquiry Concerning Process Groups in Clinical Pastoral Education. Decatur, GA: Journal of Pastoral Care Publications, 1996.

Devotional Guide
Holding On...While Letting Go: Reflections in Times of Grave Illness. Cleveland, OH: The Pilgrim Press, 1985. Revised Edition 2004.

Articles and Chapters
"Covenant House in Philadelphia." *The Christian Century*, October 27, 1965, pp. 1316-1319.

"Where Is God?" In O.J.Z. Sahler (Ed.), *The Child and Death*. St. Louis, MO: The C.V. Mosby Company, 1978, pp. 229-237.

Position Paper on CPE Supervision and Learning. *Journal of Pastoral Care*, 1982, 36(3): 194-202.

"Four Faith Frameworks." *Journal of Pastoral Care*, 1984, 38(4): 317-323.

"Some Conceptual Tonic for a Toxic Brew" *Journal of Supervision and Training in Ministry*, 1996, 17: 88-90.

"Beyond Belief." In Lee Hancock (Ed.), *The Book of Women's Sermons: Hearing God in Each Other's Voices*. New York: Riverhead Books, 1999, pp. 144-154.

"The Shifting of the Foundations: Ten Questions Concerning the Future of Pastoral Supervision and the Pastoral Care Movement." *Journal of Supervision and Training in Ministry*, 2000, 20: 59-68.
"Opening Up the Circle: Next Steps in Group Work for in Clinical Pastoral Educators." In Susan P. Gantt and Yvonne M. Agazarian (Eds.) *SCT in Action: Applying the Systems-Centered Approach in Organizations*. Lincoln, NE: iUniverse, 2005, pp. 81-97. Reprinted, with minor editing as, "Opening Up the Circle: Next Steps in Process Group Work in Clinical Pastoral Education (CPE)", *Journal of Pastoral Care and Counseling*, 2005, 59(4):323-334.

Presentations

1987	"Women Leaders in the Association for Clinical Pastoral Education," National ACPE Meeting video interview.
1988	Connecticut Public Radio: Interview on Open Air New England with Faith Middleton on hospital ministry.
1990	"New Perspectives on Pastoral Care and Theology," Care Cassette Series, College of Chaplains.
1992	"Faith Frameworks for Effective Ministry," Tele-medicine University of Toronto.
1993	"A Woman's Journey into Ministry: Heights and Depths Re-examined," Teleconference Network of Texas.
1996	"Group Process in CPE," Workshop, ACPE Annual Conference, Buffalo, NY.
1998	"Group Process in CPE," Southwest Regional Meeting, ACPE, Albuquerque, NM.
1998	"Play and Object Relations," Seminar on Supervision, Northeast and Eastern Regions, ACPE, Madison, CT.
1999	"Women and Power," Women Supervising Women Conference, Northeast and Eastern Regions, ACPE, Madison, CT.
1999	"Group Process and CPE," Workshop, Pacific Regional Meeting, ACPE, Arcadia, CA.
1999	"Future Trends in Pastoral Care and Education," 20th anniversary symposium, Journal of Supervision and Training in Ministry, ACPE Annual Conference, Albuquerque, NM.
1999	"Group Work in CPE," Southeast Regional Meeting, ACPE, Atlanta, GA.
2001	"Group Processes and Supervision," St. Luke's Hospital, Houston, TX.
2001	"Group Work in CPE," Mid-Atlantic Region, ACPE, Orkney, VA.

2002	"Group Work in CPE," East Central Region, ACPE, Heuston Woods, OH.
2003	"Seeing Beyond Inside the Circle," St. Luke's Hospital, Houston, TX.
2004	"Systems-Centered Group Work: Contributions to CPE Group Work," North Central Region, ACPE, Wisconsin Dells, WI.

INTRODUCTION

Catherine F. Garlid, Angelika A. Zollfrank, George Fitchett

Joan Hemenway and Her Contributions to Clinical Pastoral Education (CPE)

It is an unprecedented honor for a festschrift to be published in memory of a CPE supervisor. With roots in the academic community, a festschrift is a collection of articles or essays written by colleagues and admirers that build on the ideas and life work of an honored scholar. While not a scholar in the strictly academic sense, Joan was a scholar nonetheless, a person of expertise, committed to leadership in her field through her lifelong commitment to learning, teaching, and writing. Her contributions to our profession deserve to be honored in this special way; to be shared among her colleagues through the publication of this festschrift and to be passed on to the next generation of CPE supervisors.

Joan Hemenway was a unique and important leader in CPE. Her leadership encompassed her supervision of students and mentoring of junior colleagues, her organizational leadership, and her many "firsts" as a woman in CPE. Throughout her career Joan also contributed and generated theoretical and conceptual knowledge that raised the bar of the standards of our practice as educators and staked the course for the future of the ACPE.

In 2004 Joan accepted her nomination as a candidate for President Elect of ACPE with these words: "I am realizing, as I am standing up here, how my relationship with ACPE has evolved through the years—first as a daughter of the organization learning the ropes and checking out the people, later as a wife and mother helping the organization to govern itself and preparing a great variety of CPE students to enter this unique family. Looking ahead, I guess some sort of unanticipated 'grandmotherhood' may be emerging!" These metaphors reflect the fact that in many ways ACPE was Joan's family.

Joan was first and foremost a dedicated supervisor. Her goal was to educate students for ministry. For Joan this meant accompanying students in the process of becoming more real in their pastoral interactions and clear in their communications. In support and challenge she aimed at freeing her trainees' energy so that they could bring all their inner resources to their pastoral and educational encounters. Students remember her words and the details of her supervision many years later. A quote from Susan Lunning in an article in the newsletter *East by Northeast* celebrating Joan's acceptance of the Distinguished Service Award from ACPE in 2000 captures Joan's unique supervisory style: "It seems to me this vignette took place during a summer when Joan was supervising me in my certification process. I would travel to Bridgeport to meet with her weekly. She would occasionally refer to her own group at this time. It seems this was an uncommonly 'with-it' group. While I was anxiously learning about my own style, an aspect of Joan's struck me. She was such a wise woman of authority and was able to foster such playfulness in a group. They had taken up nick-names and had even the audacity to nick-name Joan—and to her face! They had called her 'Eagle-eye.' I came to see that loving nick-name as a true metaphor for Joan's supervision with me. At times feeling small and exposed in my unconscious attempts to hide from the process, Joan could find me with her super-vision, not to over-power me but to bring me out of the underbrush into the light. I came to learn the true meaning of 'telling the truth in love.'"

This quality of keen observation and insight was also a supervisory liability. Joan took up significant space in a seminar room. She had gravitas. Her facial expressions of approval or disapproval easily affected group dynamics. Her clear sense of herself as leader as well as her brilliant theoretical mind aroused authority issues in her students. At times her passion for her conceptual understandings kept her from listening with curiosity to her students' differences or emerging supervisory theories. Although learning to stand up to Joan offered a powerful opportunity to develop one's own authority, students who did not have this capacity or desire felt frustrated or diminished by her strength.

Joan had a profound affect on people beyond those whom she supervised. She was passionate and generous in passing her knowledge and wisdom on to those who followed her, mentoring numerous junior colleagues, many of them women, either through the certification process or as they assumed leadership in ACPE. This included sharing her vision and modeling behaviors and practice in what had been a male dominated professional organization. While a strong feminist herself, she avoided being identified with ideological language and political causes in her leadership. Yet she was uncompromising in the advice she gave to women as they learned to negotiate organizational structures and challenge entrenched assumptions and biases. In her supervisory and collegial relationships as well as in her leadership roles in ACPE she communicated her challenging feedback, criticism, and disagreement as clearly as her affirmation, warmth, love, and protectiveness.

Joan spent her whole life in CPE in the Eastern Region where she began with service on the Region's Accreditation Committee in the late 1970s and soon thereafter became a Regional Representative to the ACPE General Assembly. She served as the Regional Director of the Eastern Region from 1983–2000; she was the first woman Regional Director in ACPE. In this capacity she brought her pastoral heart to the CPE supervisors and centers of the region along with her keen problem solving abilities and her gift in differentiating the "noise" in the system from the work at hand. She was a founding member of Women Supervising Women, a retreat open to women of the Eastern and Northeast Regions. This annual retreat continues to support the next generation of women in taking up their roles as supervisory and clinical leaders.

On the national level she served on and chaired numerous ACPE committees, perhaps most notably the national Personnel Committee through which the General Assembly/Board of Representatives gave oversight to personnel matters in the national office. She also served on the Public Issues Task Force and the Governance/By-laws Task Force. In the mid-1980s and again in the later 1990s, she served on the Board of Representatives. In later years she served on regional and national Certification Committees and chaired the Bi-Regional Conference Planning Committee for the 2004 ACPE Annual Conference in Portland, Maine.

Joan was elected ACPE President-Elect in the fall of 2004. During her year as President-Elect, Joan chaired the ACPE Strategic Planning Task Force, helping create a vision for ACPE that will continue for many years. She was installed as the 20th President of the ACPE in October, 2005, during the ACPE annual meeting held in Honolulu, Hawaii, and assumed her duties as ACPE President on January 1, 2006. She was the third woman to serve as ACPE President.

In conversations with longtime colleagues about Joan's organizational leadership we heard over and over again of their deep admiration for her insight and intelligence. She was sharp, in more than one sense, and innovative in challenging conventions. She could also be cautious and conservative regarding change that she felt would adversely impact the core traditions and identity of the organization. Joan was intense and could give the impression that her way was the only valid way. As a consequence there are those who found her opinionated and divisive. She did not suffer those she considered fools gladly, nor did she shy away from conflict or resolve conflict quickly. However the colleagues who held Joan in the highest regard remember her with great warmth, and acknowledge the underlying shyness that guarded her most vulnerable self.

As much as she loved the organization and her students, perhaps Joan's most significant professional contribution was in the area of group work in CPE. Joan had observed that CPE group work was lacking a consistent theoretical grounding that could maximize the educational use of group supervision in CPE. As a "daughter, a mother, and a grandmother of the ACPE," she never lost touch with the history of the CPE movement. She loved her "family" enough to use her observations to offer encouragement and often also tough feedback. Her doctoral thesis, which became her book, *Inside the Circle*, presented the ACPE community with tough feedback, while affirming the CPE movement by offering ways of working towards solutions to the problem. Through her historical and theoretical analysis Joan concluded that the reason for supervisors' theoretical difficulty in the area of group work was the conflict between humanist psychology and the psychodynamic theories that shaped the origins of the CPE movement. According to Joan this unresolved conflict within the CPE movement became visible in CPE Small Process Group practice. *Inside the Circle* offered both an analysis of Small Process Groups in CPE and of the CPE movement at the same time.

Joan began searching for a viable solution to the problem. Her exploration led her to explore Systems-Centered Training (SCT). Skeptical at first, thoughtful and excited soon after as she made a connection with SCT theory, Joan became convinced that SCT offered a sophisticated meta-theory and an extremely applicable practice. Instead of focusing on the individual psychodynamic, it offered a group/system approach. SCT made sense to Joan, because it was goal-oriented, theoretically sound educationally, and organizationally applicable. At the same time SCT was still emerging and was consistently put to the test. The Systems-Centered Training and Research Institute (SCTRI^{TM}), as a much younger organization, was also mindful of using its theory to examine its own organizational structure. Joan, who had in many ways experienced that organizational structures preach truths of their own, found a sense of possibility in SCTRI^{TM}. Since both organizations share similar enough values, Joan took up a mission. Clear about her personal professional goals, "I will give myself a year and then I want to be able to see systems, not people," she also had goals for ACPE and SCTRI^{TM}. She built a subgroup of CPE supervisors who were interested in SCT and eventually integrated SCT into their practice.

With great thoughtfulness and far-sightedness Joan infused the CPE movement with theory in a way that had not happened for a long time. She saw in SCT the theory that would allow the CPE movement and the organization of ACPE to tackle the challenges formulated in the strategic planning initiative. Joan was delighted about the effects of her many theoretical and practical contributions to the educational practice of future generations of CPE supervisors.

Origins of This Festschrift

Festschrift co-editors Kitty Garlid and Angelika Zollfrank are two of Joan's professional daughters. With Joan, in their supervisory family of origin, they experienced affirmation and respect which also came with a demanding educational agenda and plenty of well-meaning challenge. This honorary publication is a tribute to a beloved teacher, dedicated mentor, generous guide, and empowering mother and colleague in ACPE, whose voice is greatly missed.

Kitty Garlid's relationship with Joan developed over 25 years. Joan was Kitty's CPE residency supervisor from 1981-82 at what was then the Hospital Chaplaincy, Inc. in New York City. Joan and her partner Jennifer became friends to Kitty and to her husband and children. Kitty remembers Joan saying to her when she was in the thick of the pressures related to having three young children and a job, "You are really doing it!" Kitty and Joan served as department head colleagues in partner hospitals within the same health system. As a result of their collaboration with each other and with Peg Lewis at Yale New Haven Hospital, the health system formed a supervisory training alliance and Greenwich Hospital launched a CPE program. Kitty was ready to hire a supervisor-in-training for the new program when Joan asked her, "Are you sure you don't want to do this?" And so, not surprisingly, Joan became Kitty's CPE training supervisor. Of the many contexts and roles they juggled this was by far the most powerful and intimate one for Kitty.

In June 2006, four months after Joan assumed her duties as ACPE President, she was diagnosed with a malignant brain tumor. She was told that the tumor would spread quickly and was unlikely to respond to aggressive treatment. The idea of the festschrift developed out of Kitty's feelings of helplessness in relationship to the looming loss of Joan in her life and the lives of friends and colleagues in ACPE and SCT. Kitty's husband Peter suggested the festschrift. He had witnessed the coming together of Kitty's stepfather's academic colleagues following his retirement and death to publish such a collection in his honor. The idea was intriguing.

Kitty suggested the idea to Angelika Zollfrank, her friend and colleague, hoping she would agree to collaborate on the project. Like Kitty, Angelika had trained to be a CPE supervisor under Joan's supervision.

Angelika's relationship with Joan began with her supervisory training at Yale-New Haven Hospital in September 2001. Originally from Germany, Angelika had completed her CPE residency at Memorial Sloan-Kettering Cancer Center and interviewed with Joan for a position as part-time staff chaplain and supervisory student on Ash Wednesday. "Ash Wednesday seems like a good time for a new beginning," Joan said, "and if you can make it in New York you can make it anywhere."

Angelika's supervisory relationship with Joan was powerful and transformational. Joan's belief in Angelika's growing ability and competence was unwavering. Whenever Angelika struggled with the anxiety of taking up a new role, Joan commented, "You are fussing, just do it." Joan was steadfast in her dedication, affirmation, challenge, and support. Together they enjoyed theoretical reflection on ongoing practice and had to learn to call each other back to the emotional processes involved in the art of supervision. Joan's style could be provocative and stimulating, soothing and reassuring, attuned and visionary. Joan was Angelika's aunt, a coach and guide in a unique training process. The supervisory training group, led by Joan that Angelika participated in, became a holding environment for her, a place to trust the fortunate repetitions of her family dynamics, while keeping the task of applying her whole self to supervision and pastoral care front and center. When Angelika first learned of Joan's diagnosis she was surprised and moved as she realized that she had become part of Joan's ACPE family.

Knowing Kitty's inclination to put her head ahead of her heart, Angelika's first apt response to Kitty's suggestion about the festschrift was, "So is this what you do with your grief?" And yes, in part it was and it continues to be. Thankfully, after a short time thinking it over Angelika threw her wholehearted support and collaboration into the project and the festschrift was underway.

Early in the summer of 2006, friends and colleagues responded to Jennifer's hospitality and growing need for support in caring for

Joan. One Saturday after Kitty had helped with Joan's bedtime routine, she retired early to Joan's study which doubled as the guest room. This meant she had hours alone "with Joan" in her library, with books on topics ranging from Freudian analysis to feminist theology to organizational behavior, leadership development, and group theory. As Kitty had already discovered in her training, the books she borrowed from Joan had all been read. She often found Joan's penciled conversational remarks as interesting as the author's work because they dealt not only with ideas but also with their practical application to CPE.

The next morning Kitty proposed the idea of the festschrift to Joan. Joan loved the idea from the start and began making suggestions for possible contributors. Her list included some of her friends and mentors as well as her students. Kitty and Angelika divided up the list and contacted many of Joan's friends and colleagues, knowing at the time and under the circumstances that the list was not comprehensive. Many of the people with whom they spoke felt honored and inspired by the invitation. For a variety of reasons not all of those asked accepted. Late that summer several of the contributors gathered in a circle in the sunroom in Joan and Jennifer's home in Guilford overlooking their beloved garden. Joan was very much there, leaning back in the recliner where she spent many hours of her day. One last time dear ones and colleagues sat in the circle with Joan. Ideas were shared and thoughts punctuated by Joan's pithy remarks.

That fall at the Annual Conference in Tampa, Florida, where Joan was to have served in her role as President of ACPE, a room was set aside where friends and colleagues could be with her through prayer and quiet reflection. Many wrote notes to her in a journal that she received a few days later. A fund was established by ACPE to which contributions could be made towards the realization of this project. In this way the festschrift has become a gift and a memorial to which many supporters have contributed.

Having received initial encouragement and sufficient interest in the project from the Journal of Pastoral Care Publications, the publisher of Joan's book, Kitty and Angelika began looking for an experienced editor who could guide them. Neither Kitty nor Angelika had the experience they knew they would need to carry the project to its fruition. They approached George Fitchett to inquire about his interest in the project. George first met Joan in the early 1980s when he tried to recruit her to come to work in Chicago. Out of that meeting they developed a collegial friendship and enjoyed conversations with one another at ACPE committee meetings and conventions. Joan served on the College of Chaplains editorial team that helped edit George's book, *Assessing Spiritual Needs*. George knew Joan as a colleague and leader in CPE. He especially appreciated her contributions to our understanding of group work in CPE. George responded without hesitation to Kitty and Angelika's invitation to help with the festschrift. Feeling nothing short of clueless, Kitty and Angelika were ready to hand the task over to him. However, George gently pushed and prodded them to maintain their roles as co-editors in honor of their relationships with Joan and to the work. George proposed to join them as an editorial mentor and co-editor, and they agreed.

During one of Angelika's last visits with Joan, reminiscing about their journey together in Angelika's supervisory training, Joan asked, "Tappenzee... Tappenzee... I wonder what the word means?" Angelika reminded her of the bridge to New Jersey, which they had crossed on their way to a supervisory training meeting twice a year. But Joan shook her head. Much later in the conversation, Joan suddenly said, "I know what it means, Tappenzee stands for transition." In some way this festschrift in Joan's honor has been a transitional object, something for us to hold on to, while letting go of her.

The Festschrift Contents

We have divided the festschrift into three parts. In Part I, Joan's Work and Ministry, we reprint four of Joan's essays along with three essays that describe different aspects of Joan's life and ministry and her impact on the authors. Chapter 1 reprints Joan's 1984 *Journal of Pastoral Care* article, Four Faith Frameworks. In this article Joan describes four authentic ways of being faithful and their implications for pastoral care. Soon after it was first published, it became a popular article to use with CPE groups and we know of colleagues who still value it and use it with every group they supervise. Chapter 2, The Shifting of the Foundations: Ten Questions Concerning the Future of Pastoral Supervision and the Pastoral Care Movement, is Joan's contribution to a symposium in honor of the twentieth anniversary of the *Journal of Supervision and Training in Ministry*. Readers will see her characteristic thoughtful and far-sighted perspective on CPE, the challenges it faced and directions to be considered. Chapter 3, Opening Up the Circle: Next Steps in Process Group Work in Clinical Pastoral Education (CPE), is an essay from 2005 in which Joan begins to link SCT and CPE. It was originally published in a collection of essays about SCT and reprinted, with minor modifications, in the *Journal of Pastoral Care and Counseling*, which is the version we reprint here. This essay is the best written example of Joan making the case for why CPE supervision needs to be informed by SCT theory and practice. Chapter 4 reveals a side of Joan that may be less familiar to those who only knew her in the context of ACPE. The chapter reprints the original sections of *Holding On While Letting Go: Reflections in Times of Grave Illness*, a devotional booklet that Joan first wrote in 1985 for a series published by Pilgrim Press. The chapter is a special revelation of Joan's pastoral heart. A number of Joan's friends looked to it for comfort in her time of grave illness.

Chapter 5, The Joy of Friendship, is a reflection by a former pastor and friend of Joan's, Robert (Bob) Raines. Raines writes about the time in the early 1960s when Joan and Jennifer joined the First United Church of Germantown (Philadelphia). They became part of a small group that established Covenant House, an outreach of the church in a poor area of their community. Raines writes that Joan's experience in this group was influential for her later interest in small group process. Writing in 2006, while Joan is still alive, Raines also expresses his gratitude to Joan and her partner Jennifer for the warm friendship with them that was renewed when they became neighbors. Chapter 6, Over the Years with Joan, is by Ted Loder, who knew Joan for over 40 years as her pastor, co-worker, and friend. In his essay he shares his view about three key attributes of Joan's: her processing integrity, her empathetic realism, and her relational particularity. The final chapter in Part I, Chapter 7, is by Audun Ulland, a pastor and group analyst from Oslo, Norway. It was also written in 2006, while Joan was still alive. Ulland uses the title of Joan's devotional booklet as the title for his essay, which is an account of his first unit of CPE, taken in 1999 under Joan's supervision, and its transformative impact on his life and his work.

Part II, Systems-Centered Training and CPE Supervision, presents a collection of essays that further introduce SCT to the CPE community and build on Joan's leadership in bringing SCT into CPE. The first essay, Chapter 8, by Yvonne M. Agazarian, inventor of SCT and founder of SCT Research Institute (SCTRI™) describes a systems-centered approach to group work focusing on the major SCT concepts of boundary permeability, the process of discriminating and integrating information, functional subgrouping, and phases of system development. In Chapter 9, Susan P. Gantt, Director of the SCTRI™, presents highlights of her work with a pastoral care department. She describes the application of systems-centered methods in an organizational context. The article focuses on the team's growing ability to think systems, to use functional subgrouping, to become aware of phases of system development, and to consciously shift roles, goals, and contexts. The essays by Angelika A. Zollfrank, Peg Lewis, Catherine F. Garlid, and A. Meigs Ross provide examples of integration of SCT into CPE. Angelika A. Zollfrank presents a case study of a CPE summer group in which SCT theory and methods were applied (Chapter 10). In Chapter 11, building on the objectives and outcomes of CPE, Peg Lewis offers an educational methodology based on SCT methods and techniques. In Chapter 12, Finding Life in Personal Story Telling, Kitty Garlid differentiates between functional and non-functional use of personal story telling in CPE. In her contribution, The Mentoring Relationship in the Development of Clinical Pastoral Educators, A. Meigs Ross focuses on the mentoring that occurs in the CPE student-supervisor relationship (Chapter 13). Using a model from SCT, she describes four stages in that mentoring relationship: dependency, authority/autonomy, separation/individuation, and collegiality.

Part III, Reflections on Supervision, consists of essays about chaplaincy and supervision by colleagues and former students of Joan's. In Chapter 14, The Chaplain's Specialty: Relational Wisdom, John Patton describes a capacity that he sees as central to effective pastoral care and counseling. In Chapter 15, CPE and Spiritual Growth, George Fitchett focuses on faith development theory. Using examples from several CPE students he describes how CPE, at its best, can be a profound experience of spiritual development. As the title of her essay indicates, in Chapter 16, Teresa Snorton focuses on The Concept of Circle and Group in the African-American Community. Specifically, she describes the worldview, relational values, and religiosity of the African-American community and notes their importance for pastoral supervisors who work with African-American students. In Chapter 17, Contextualizing CPE: Developing a Jewish Geriatric CPE Program, Mary Martha Thiel describes the CPE program she and her colleagues have developed at Hebrew SeniorLife/Hebrew Rehabilitation Center in Boston, Massachusetts. She shares what it is like for her Jewish students to experience CPE among "their own," and what it is like for her, a Christian, to be their supervisor. Finally, in Chapter 18, The Lost Art of Apology: An Educational Tool in CPE, Paula J. Teague and Stephen L. Dutton, co-authors who are also married, focus on the important place of apology in the supervisory relationship. They review key models of apology, including models from current management literature. Then they apply a five step model of apology to experiences with two CPE students.

Looking Toward the Future

It is our hope that this volume will carry forward and develop the vision and some of the ideas to which Joan devoted her career. In particular, we believe the middle section of the book, devoted to group theory and the application of systems-centered training and practice, would have been a deep source of satisfaction and delight to Joan. She worked hard to bring the ideas of Yvonne Agazarian and SCTRI^{TM} into the theory and practice of CPE supervision. In the process she not only created a bridge between the two organizations, but impacted SCTRI^{TM} as an organization in the process. There are now enough CPE supervisors who are active members of SCTRI^{TM} to have an identity of our own within their training structures.

We edited this festschrift as plans were being made for the Spiritual Care Collaborative Summit of 2009 to be held in Orlando, Florida. At that meeting the six pastoral care cognate groups of North America will gather for a shared conference. The plans for the Summit include having Joan's friend and colleague Susan Gantt, the Executive Director of SCRTI^{TM}, consult with the leadership of the Spiritual Care Collaborative, the group responsible for guiding the ongoing collaboration of the cognate groups. We feel sure that Joan would have been pleased with this development and in the knowledge of the impact she has had on the people and organizations she held so dear.

A quote from Joan's long time friend and colleague, Emily Jean Gilbert, in the article in the issue of the *East by Northeast* newsletter that reported on Joan's 2000 ACPE Distinguished Service Award summarizes much of what made Joan such an important figure in CPE over the past three decades. Emily Jean said, "Joan is the sister who pushes and stands with and encourages and celebrates; the leader who visions and implements and takes risks and receives the resulting affirmation and the resulting critique; the teacher who expands the knowledge base and provokes the mind and stimulates excitement and passion for our art. ACPE would be greatly diminished without her contribution." We are pleased to share this collection of essays in honor of Joan Hemenway. We hope this festschrift will expand the circle of those who benefit from Joan's contributions to our profession.

PART ONE

Joan's Work and Ministry

CHAPTER 1

Four Faith Frameworks[*]
Joan E. Hemenway

Abstract

Describes four faith frameworks—"After the Fall," "Jesus Saves," "God in History," and "The Completion of Creation"—and how such theological themes may be used in CPE as a way of delineating different ethical assumptions and of introducing various approaches to pastoral care and personal growth.

In May of 1981 I agreed to conduct a workshop entitled "Pastoral Care as an Ethical Enterprise" at Union Theological Seminary's Alumni Day. In tackling this subject I was more interested in exploring the inherently ethical nature of pastoral care itself than I was interested in raising some of the specific ethical issues current today. While thinking through this theme in this way I became cognizant once again of the intertwined relationship between who we are, what we do in ministry, and how we are constantly and endlessly living out of the ultimate meanings and beliefs of our lives whether we know it or not.

As I attempted to sort out the various ethical perspectives ranging from the highly moralistic to the loosely situational, it became clear that certain theological assumptions (our meanings) lie behind what we ultimately determine to be both ethical (our values) and pastoral (our actions). In addition, I was aware that to present material about pastoral care and praxis from an ethical perspective to a group of clergy is potentially divisive when differences in

---

[*] Reprinted with the permission of the Journal of Pastoral Care Publications, Inc. from The Journal of Pastoral Care, (1984), 38(4), 317-323.

theological, cultural, pastoral, generational, and personal view-points will inevitably be present and may be deeply held. So I sought a way to enlarge the subject, to open up some new win-dows, arouse curiosity, and combine objectivity with engagement with the material. The "Four Faith Frameworks" described in this article are the result.

Since that workshop I have presented these frameworks to sev-eral groups of basic and advanced CPE students as well as to field education students. Each time participants have found the scheme helpful because it is both simple and easy to remember. Their first and primary use of it has been in examining their own theological orientations and assumptions in order to discover areas of enjoy-ment, growth, inconsistency, blockage, and discomfort. Secondly, as with the original workshop group, presentation of the material has stimulated participants to deal with their differing theological orientations. In the CPE context it has often served to de-personalize or de-fuse potentially volatile relationships and thus begin more creative, dispassionate dialogue with one another. Third, it has helped students sort out some of their own theological history and baggage, thereby making possible some decisions about what to keep, what to discard, what is too heavy, what is too light, what is missing, etc. Fourth, it has given participants an or-ganized way to think about their own pastoral work with patients, families, and members of congregations, particularly in terms of the theological orientation and consequent pastoral needs of others.

In sharing these frameworks I usually draw four columns on the blackboard with a heading for each, and then as the material is pre-sented I urge participants to fill in themes as they recognize their own theological, ethical, or pastoral approaches. In this way I get to know the participants better, learn how they are reacting to the mate-rial, and benefit from the richness of their thinking and experience.

The attitude with which I come to this material is essentially an imaginative, playful one. Since a good deal of stereotyping, brief characterization, and oversimplification about major theological themes is necessary in order to form each framework, it is impor-tant that the task be approached with an open, creative, non-defensive mindset. This is an exercise in curiosity, necessitating a good dose of non-literal thinking. As such, consideration of the frameworks is more an act of faith than a presentation of fact. Secondly, it is important to build each framework separately, but also to realize that the walls are porous between them and that there is an inevitable flow from one to the other. Thirdly, although people tend to find themselves coming down in one particular framework, under certain circumstances (or because of certain theological issues and life experiences), it is often the case that part of a person's belief system may be discovered in a totally different framework from the rest. As a result, thinking about beliefs and attitudes within these frameworks may highlight inconsistencies and serve to identify old and new theological and personal growing edges. In other words, the process can be historic and dynamic, intellectual and emotional.

Framework No. 1: After the Fall

The basic focus for this first framework is the belief that we all live after the fall in the midst of tragedy, sin, and evil. Through an unforeseen act of deception, humankind has left the garden of paradise forever behind and is forced to wander and labor in a difficult and godforsaken world. In this framework God is viewed primarily as a Judge who punishes, as a Power not very amenable to the hopes and needs of humanity. Creation is not good; sin is abundant. Jesus, as a part of the human situation, is "a man of sorrows and acquainted with grief." Death is viewed as inevitable and negative, synonymous with darkness and evil. In this framework there is a great need for rules because human freedom has proven to be disastrous. Theologically it is a view reminiscent of the dark mood of the Middle Ages when rigid ecclesiastical structures held human evil at bay. It also echoes the fire and brimstone of the New England Puritans, as well as the dire predictions of the apocalyptic literature.

Our main religious experience in this model is one of alienation and separation from God and inadequacy before God. We feel guilty for what we have done to ourselves and helpless to do anything substantial about it. We wait for better days to come, perhaps only after death, though we are not sure even about this. Ontologically we live in a state of non-being. Psychologically we are bound by our own repressions and suppressions brought about by trying to protect ourselves from the destructive forces within and without (à la Freud). In our worst moments we tend to feel sorry for ourselves as victims of a power beyond our own reckoning. The Book of Job and the stoicism of the preacher in Ecclesiastes catch the mood of skepticism and hopelessness and the underlying anger. Pastoral care in this model consists primarily of efforts to offer comfort (albeit cold comfort) as we huddle together in the inevitable isolation which is our lot.

Framework No. 2: Jesus Saves

This second framework is based on the central belief that Jesus has saved the world. It is clearly a response and rebuttal to Framework No. 1. By entering into our sinful situation Jesus Christ has redeemed it and us. Therefore, our task in life is to proclaim the Good News that humanity is saved. Through our proclamation of this Word, Jesus' saving work continues alive and operative. God is not so much Judge as He is a Father who sent his only Son, a Redeemer who has given us the Messiah. Death has been overcome, for the promise of eternal life has been received. Though life on earth lived in finite time is not totally good or easy, it is at least fundamentally improved. The cosmic power of evil has been banished and as a result, our alienation from God has been overcome.

If there was a great need for rules in the first model, in this one there is a great need for faith. This viewpoint sets the scientific (secular, humanistic) world clearly over-and-against the religious (faithful) world. If the doctrine of the fall predominated in Number 1, the importance of Christology (and especially the doctrine of the atonement) predominates here. Pastoral care is seen primarily as evangelism, spreading the Good News which heals the breach between God and humanity. The prophecies of second Isaiah are important as well as the Gospel story and the Pauline letters with their emphasis on what Jesus Christ did, or won, for us. Many would say this is the heart, the truth, the crux of the Christian faith. The charismatic movement and television evangelists give new impetus and fervor to this view among many believers today.

Framework No. 3: God in History

The major emphasis in the third framework is the idea that God has intervened in history, making a special covenant with Israel (and later with the Church) to which He remains faithful no matter what. Thus, God continues to intervene in our lives and hearts and history now. As faithful people we live somewhere between the "already" and the "not yet" of salvation history. As there was a great need for rules in the first model and a great need for faith in the second, in this framework the central need is for relationship. In fact, pastoral care is defined primarily as reaching out to friends and strangers in ways which make God's presence known and lively. This is how we are to "keep the promise" of God's love active in the world. Life is a dynamic process within which God is preeminently Sustainer. There is a strong doctrine of the Holy Spirit in this model where even "a still small voice" can be heard and heeded. Interest in developmental psychology (Erikson), stages of faith (Fowler), education (Piaget) and inter-relationships (Sullivan) predominate.

In this model there is a recognized tension between the power of good and the power of evil, and some uncertainty as to which might win out at any given time (both in the believer's heart and in world events). The story of Jesus dramatizes this tension, the best example being the temptation in the wilderness. Death is seen as interruptive of our active participation in the process of salvation history. After death there is the expectation that we might become part of a larger community (the communion of saints). Old Testament biblical theology is very influential, with the Exodus as a primary referential point. The prophet Hosea and the story of the Prodigal Son are two particularly poignant examples of God's constant wooing of us, while Hebrews 11 paints large the canvas of faithful people through the ages. (One student commented that if

God can be seen as a Policeman in the first framework and as a kind of Emergency Medic in the second, then in this model God is certainly a tireless Negotiator and Lover).

Framework No. 4: The Completion of Creation

This framework reflects a radically wholistic outlook in which God and humanity, good and evil, suffering and joy, are intrinsically interconnected one with the other. There is a synchronicity between the human and divine; the one mirrors the other; each weaves a tapestry which is the other. This is a non-hierarchical framework in which the radical potential exists for God to be as affected by us as we are by Him/Her. The need for the incarnation (Framework No. 2) is superseded by the presence of an "I Am" which means "we are." Though evil and sin are powerful, the positive thrust of one-ness between God and creation is more powerful. In fact, because good and evil exist within creation and within God, they are both part of the natural ebb and flow of creation. Likewise, death is a part of life and accepted as such. "From dust to dust" is an affirmation of basic order and therefore an expression of praise—not a sign of defeat. The creation, though filled with unknowns, is nevertheless trustworthy even though we may not necessarily be able to see all of the why's and wherefore's ourselves. God is pre-eminently Creator in this model, and humanity is His/Her highest creative act, and, therefore, blessed. Ecological concerns are in the forefront, for to save our creation is to save ourselves. We are all connected with one another so that family and group therapy, as well as general systems theory, are appealing modalities in the psychotherapeutic realm.

Whereas being in relationship was important in Framework No. 3, in this framework participation and responsibility are key concepts. Coming into one's full being, one's full potential, is the task of a faithful person, and Jesus (along with other prophets within other world religions) is a primary example. Pastoral care involves empowering people, affirming and blessing their personhood as unique, and praising God together for the gift of creation.

There is faith here and in the natural order, that life's processes will carry us towards growth and light if we can but participate fully and not be thrown by the inevitable ambiguities and uncertainties which will crop up. The story of Noah captures the optimism of this point of view. And the Book of Revelation points toward the way things are (nearing completion) and the way they will be finally (complete). Interest in eschatology (a "hope against hope" à la Moltmann) is a subject for theological exploration, but only as a subtheme to the overall thrust of wholeness, participation, synchronicity, and celebration.

Implications

One of the major implications of these frameworks is that where a person lands has a major impact on how he or she conceptualizes the pastoral task. One student who had come out of a heavily liturgical background with a Christological emphasis (Framework No. 2) tended to feel as pastor/priest he had to "save" people (or at least make them feel better). After consideration of all the frameworks, he was able to see his capacity to "bless" (Framework No. 4) as just as important, and therefore began to get greater balance between doing and being in his ministry. A second student's extreme fear of judgmental authority (God, supervisor, Church) was such that he experienced himself as truly a non-entity ("nonbeing" as in Framework No. 1), remaining withdrawn, depressed, and stalled in his ministry. Eventually he was wooed by the persistent concern of his peer group, released some of his anger, and moved towards Framework No. 3 with a more relational, forgiving posture in his pastoral work.

Another student whose theological training heavily emphasized biblical and process theology (Framework No. 3) realized that she was too amorphous in her thinking as a Christian. After exploration of the doctrines of the incarnation, resurrection, and atonement (as emphasized in Framework No. 2), she become more comfortable talking about Jesus as Lord and Savior with her patients and more ready to claim her identity as a minister. Another person was pressed by the new ideas of Framework No. 4 to think about God in less hierarchical, "static," masculine terms but in more androgynous, creative, reciprocal terms. This work not only helped him get in touch with his feminine side, but also to become more collegial and less distant in his peer group work and in his ministry.

In discussions with students it also became apparent that we all move back and forth between these different frameworks depending on the degree of hopefulness, goodness, and self-confidence we feel on any given day. This is also true of our patients. Just as we tend to regress psychologically when faced with crisis or tragedy, so do we regress theologically. For example, a physically healthy person who lives comfortably within the ambiguities and the organic quality of Framework No. 4, when faced with unexpected crisis may move toward Framework No. 2, wanting to hear the more literal and specific story of Jesus the Christ as a means of "holding on." At such times the need for certain beliefs and doctrines and actions—whether these be certain prayers repeated "by the book," or receiving the Eucharist daily, or the desire to have a Bible or one's own chaplain close at hand—will surface. In contrast, one of my patients who was basically charismatic in orientation used the crisis of open heart surgery and his resultant anxiety and helplessness to achieve a breakthrough towards trusting a more process-oriented, less specific, more relational experience in which being part of a greater whole (creation) was more healing and more faithful than holding on to a few theological formulas which no longer seemed relevant. Of greater concern to me was another patient who, when confronted with surgery for cancer, began to recognize that he had been surrounded all his life with a religious culture which said "if you believe in Jesus you will be saved (or healed or happy)" and that in fact he did not believe in this name/person/story. This recognition thrust him into Framework No. 1 with little to hold on to except total despair.

The degree to which the chaplaincy student accepts these shifts and layers within himself or herself will determine the extent to which he or she can be responsive and go with these shifts in others. Being able to name and use these different frameworks, whether their function be corrective or freeing, has provided an accessible and rewarding way into new theological and pastoral territory.

Finally, one danger of outlining these frameworks in this way is the tendency to think of them as developmental in nature, so that a person moves "back" towards No. 1 and "forward" towards No. 4. Thinking in this way would imply a value judgment that some stages are more sophisticated and more healthy than others. This is perhaps inevitable if the model is viewed in a linear, flat fashion. However if it can be viewed multi-dimensionally, perhaps as a spiral, with four inter-related strands varying in color and intensity with different energies and emphases flowing between and through all the strands causing the spiral to move and create ever-new patterns, then we are freer to explore the strengths and weaknesses of each framework within ourselves and others. The goal of such exploration is twofold: first, to recognize and claim our various theological "parts"; and second, to decide what needs further development, what can be discarded, and what can be affirmed and delighted in as is.

Conclusion

This has been a beginning attempt to use theological themes as a way of delineating different ethical assumptions as well as opening up various approaches to pastoral care and personal growth. Though recognizing the pervasive influence of developmental psychology (Erikson, Levinson, Sheehy), the increasing importance of cognitive learning theory (Piaget and Kohlberg *via* Fowler), and the continuing concern about the theological assumptions which lie behind current pastoral praxis (Browning, Lapsley, Way), these four faith frameworks are presented as a preliminary means to consolidate our past thinking in order to prepare the way for working with more sophisticated and complicated material. The presentation is necessarily sketchy, though hopefully provocative enough to plow up the ground so that some new seeds might be planted among those who teach, those who learn, and all who seek to minister.

CHAPTER 2

The Shifting of the Foundations:
Ten Questions Concerning the Future of Pastoral
Supervision and the Pastoral Care Movement[*]
Joan E. Hemenway

R obert Fuller's paper, "Rediscovering the Laws of Spiritual Life," summarizes the ways in which those of us in pastoral care, pastoral counseling, and clinical pastoral education have focused on trying "to jolt the church into a new kind of spirituality." Fuller maintains we have been doing this reformative work through our clinical (or empirical) theology, a theology which grows out of our efforts to understand human experience through the lens of the behavioral sciences. Using psychological rather than theological categories as our primary tool has freed us as clinicians (as well as our students, counselees, and patients) to become open in new ways to the divine transcendent reality which is present at the deepest levels of human experience. Key to our method is our belief in the ongoing correlation between psychology and theology. This process of discovery has made it possible for us to re-experience and re-incorporate the fruits of faithful living into our daily lives, into our clinical practices and, in some cases, into our religious institutions.

Though Robert Fuller's effort to present a retrospective view of where we have been is helpful, my own perspective is increasingly future-oriented, somewhat troubling to me, and full of questions. Two contrasting vignettes illustrate my growing conviction—even

---

[*] Reprinted with permission from the Journal of Supervision and Training in Ministry, (2000), 20:59-68. This article was a response to a paper reflecting on the first 20 years of the Journal, Robert Fuller, Rediscovering the Laws of Spiritual Life: The Last Twenty Years of Supervision and Training in Ministry, Journal of Supervision and Training in Ministry, (2000), 20:13-40. With Volume 27, 2007, the Journal was renamed, Reflective Practice: Formation and Supervision in Ministry.

alarm—that the foundations of our pastoral care and counseling movement are currently shifting, and doing so at a rapid pace.

- Ten years ago there were approximately 160 National Association of Catholic Chaplains certified CPE supervisors. In 1998 there were only 36 people who describe themselves as actively practicing supervision under the NACC CPE standards.
- In 1985 the American Association of Christian Counselors was founded by a Mississippi psychologist and had about 100 members. In 1991, when two professional leaders took over, it had about 700 members. Now, in 1998, AACC has over 17,000 members with a huge variety of sophisticated services and professional resources. In fact I just received one of their mailings this past week offering me a $20 bonus certificate towards its membership fee.

Our Foundational Beliefs

These kinds of contrasts within the world of religious counseling and pastoral education not only make me question the efficacy of my chosen profession with its grounding in clinical theology and liberal Protestantism, they also make me anxious about the future. Whenever I sense a need to re-evaluate where I am in order to know where I need to go, I always start with a historical review. From my point of view, we need to know what is central to our tradition—what we absolutely do not want to lose in our history and our supervisory and counseling practice—as we head into the new millennium. From my practical vantage point, six elements are central to our tradition of pastoral supervision.

First, we take the unconscious seriously and we never forget its psychological influence on all that we are and do in our ministries. Whether this means studying Freud or Jung or Winnicott or Kohut, using parallel process à la Ekstein and Wallerstein, or encouraging our counselors and students to share their dreams or get out from underneath their masks—we honor the unconscious rages and passions, hopes and fears and tremblings that undergird our lives. They keep our clinical work honest and keep us humble as well as amazed at how beautifully we are made!

Second, we focus on the individual person, whether this be the supervisee, the student, the client, or the patient. His or her feelings, sense of self worth, direction in life, family history, and relationship to God, are areas of constant valuing and exploration. This emphasis on the individual is not just a fascination of American culture, but rather it is part of our grounding in the Christian tradition and the one-on-one ministry of Jesus.

Third, as clinicians and educators we use the dynamics of relationship in our pastoral care, pastoral counseling, and pastoral supervision to bring about insight and healing. These dynamics provide the grist for the mill (the "process") to do its work. No matter the names we use—transference, countertransference, projective identification, self-in-relation, good enough mother, basic assumption group—these here-and-now dynamic experiences in our clinical and group relationships help us grow and renew our feeling life in relationship to self, others, and God.

Fourth, we see a way to God or the Divine Energy through human experience. This is the root of our spiritual gifts and the foundation of our empirical theology as accurately emphasized by Fuller's presentation. This point of view is the psychological and theological centerpiece of our tradition. The radical nature of this assertion (and its optimism) is reflected in Anton Boisen's conviction that his own mental illness was the way his soul was trying to find its own healing. Likewise, we view physical illness, and even emotional trauma, as an experience through which a person—with adequate guidance—may glimpse the soul and/or re-discover God.

Fifth, we accept and even celebrate the paradoxes of life. The most cogent and perceptive summary of how this value effects the educational experience of our students was presented by George Fitchett (1982) at the 1982 national ACPE meeting. Fitchett points out the several paradoxes with which every CPE student is confronted: professional vs. student, independent vs. dependent learner, competent vs. caring, relationship building vs. skill development. He also points out paradoxes in our supervisory methods: conflict vs. aggression, empathy vs. mirroring, anxiety vs. hospitality. Efforts to resolve these tensions result in continuing awareness of human limitation and finitude.

Sixth, we forge our identity as people who often live on the margins of our religious communities. While we seek the blessing of organized religion through requirements of theological study and ordination, we tend to prefer secular, non-parochial settings in which to exercise our gifts and graces. Our strong tendency to identify with, and reach out to, other people on the margins is one of the outcomes of this reality. Furthermore, many of us tend to find our true spiritual home, both locally and nationally, in the professional associations which govern our clinical practice rather than in our faith communities which endorse our ministry.

Current Challenges and Opportunities

Out of this thumbnail review of our heritage in the pastoral care movement come the following ten questions.

1. How easy is it going to be to take these hallowed elements of our educational and clinical tradition into a new time and a new place? For example, increasingly I am being asked to supervise field education students and chaplaincy volunteers. It is unusual for individuals from either one of these groups to have any inclination to deal with unconscious elements which affect their ministry efforts. Nor is there much desire to become aware of the depth of the paradoxes which inform the human situation. Do I then let go of these parts of the pastoral clinical tradition and adjust myself to what feels like simpler but less sound supervisory work? What about some of the part-time units of CPE training which involve a maximal number of students and a minimal number of hours per week for verbatim, didactic and interpersonal relations group? Exactly how far can we pare down our training programs and still have students really "get" CPE in all its intended emotional intensity, theological complexity, and professional challenge?

2. Are we really able to make a shift in name and paradigm from pastoral care to spiritual care, from pastoral counseling to spiritual counseling? During the past year, President Jo Clare Wilson of ACPE and Executive Director Joe Driscoll of NACC have each written about their frustration that chaplains and pastoral clinicians are being totally left out of the current conversations about spirituality. Clearly those around us have not understood our clinical method or our clinical theology. In a soon-to-be published article titled "Professional Chaplaincy: An Absent Profession?" Larry VandeCreek points to the continuing gulf between science and religion as one of the causes of the present situation. It seems that we are viewed by those in the so-called scientific world (doctors and nurses) as "religionists" who are tied to specific institutions (churches and synagogues and mosques), hired to perform outdated rites expressive of unnecessarily doctrinaire beliefs. Spirituality, however, belongs to anybody and everybody, including doctors and nurses and administrators. Others outside of pastoral care have authority over how we define our department. For example, four years ago I suggested to my Advisory Committee that we change the name of our department from Pastoral Care Department to Healing and Spiritual Resource Center. This seemed like an obvious thing to do in view of the hospital's shift from an illness-focused to a wellness-focused paradigm. My Advisory Committee, which was made up of a combination of hospital personnel and local clergy, immediately shelved the idea, saying it was "too new age" and "too California." It has never been brought up again!

There are other examples as well: I cannot get out of my mind the story of a chaplain who was recently called up to the floor in order to "teach" the doctors and nurses "how to deliver spiritual care" to their patients. The expectation was that the chaplain would continue to make routine friendly visits and give sacraments, but the health care team would take care of spirituality—both their own and their patients'. In addition to raising my anxiety and anger, this story lifts up my awareness that there is a vast difference between the way I perceive myself as chaplain and the way my hospital perceives me—even though we have always made a point of talking about the "interfaith spiritual care" that we offer to all patients and their families.

One of the outside speakers for my CPE program is an ordained interfaith minister and psychotherapist. She has a strong healing ministry in a local church plus a private counseling practice. She has no official credentials from a mainline denomination or from any of our professional guilds. In addition to her ongoing ministry efforts, she currently visits oncology patients once a week in one of our local hospitals where she regularly receives referrals from doctors to offer therapeutic touch to their patients.

On the other hand, if we do shift the paradigm from pastoral to spiritual care, what happens to our relationship with the religious institutions which we represent and are accountable? What about the deeper issues concerning what we believe in, or are supposed to believe in, as religionists? If we really come clean on some of these issues, how do we maintain credibility and, for some of us, ordination in our respective denominations?

3. To whom we will be ministering in the future, and what type of counseling or pastoral care will we be offering? Is the time now past when we can do one-on-one relationally-oriented ministry by the bedside, or offer insight-oriented pastoral psychotherapy in a private office in a counseling center to one person over a number of months or even years? I now teach my CPE students how to do a one shot 20-minute initial pastoral visit in seven steps: clearly introducing one's self and one's purpose, establishing an empathic relationship, hearing the person's story, making a spiritual assessment, implementing a care plan, noting outcomes, and documenting the visit in the chart. In our counseling offices, we offer brief strategic therapy—three sessions to heal a broken heart or a broken marriage, six sessions to get a patient through major depression, and so on. And are we not also undergoing a paradigm shift here of which we are not yet totally aware—moving away from relationally-focused care and counseling to a more problem-centered model based on narrative therapy and second order change (Capps, 1995)? I predict we will see four major changes in this area:

- We will increasingly be working with people in groups, in both local churches and counseling centers and hospitals. One of our most successful offerings in the hospital setting now is spirituality groups on psychiatric inpatient units. Another success is interfaith worship on Sunday mornings which the chaplain does right on the psych floors and rehab unit. In-services with staff groups is another way to interact both professionally and pastorally. A group approach to ministry is efficient, financially viable, synergistic, and systems-oriented. Our anthropology, as well as our practice, needs to affirm the importance of maintaining a balance between affirming the human person as an individual and as a social being.

- Chaplains, pastoral counselors, and CPE supervisors will continue to find ways to reinvent themselves. A number of CPE supervisors working in large health care organizations are no longer doing CPE supervision or pastoral care. Rather, they basically do administration and recruitment, or writing and research. Pastoral counselors who become Executive Directors of counseling centers focus mainly on fund raising and administrative and (not even clinical!) supervision. There are board-certified chaplains who are now EAP (Employee Assistance Program) specialists. One CPE colleague was re-hired after a downsizing as a Work Life Quality Chaplain—a sort of ombudsmen for the human resources department who helps teams in the workplace improve their relationships and group process so that they can be more productive and focused (Schmidt, 1999)

- There will be more interchange between our profession and other professionals in the health care setting. This is a truly exciting development! It is not focused on the supposedly common ground of "spirituality" but rather on learning and teaching interpersonal care skills and enlarging professional formation. One pastoral counselor in New England specializes in offering interpersonal support groups for physicians. And in the CPE program at Massachusetts General Hospital, several professionals from other disciplines are doing

CPE training along with clergy and seminarians on hospital time while being supported by a special grant.

- The CPE training programs and pastoral counseling centers which survive and grow will be developed in a variety of settings with an increasing emphasis on creating connections between community agencies, churches, counseling centers, half-way houses, mental health and health care institutions, in order to provide "a continuum of care" for clients and enhance health promotion in the community. These new programs will be successful to the degree that they can find a variety of funding sources and increased growth in their contractual relationships.

4. Who will pay to educate our clinical supervisors? Due to the changes wrought by managed care, the formerly hidden expenses of training pastoral counseling and CPE supervisors are no longer hidden and certainly no longer available. And though efforts continue to retain Medicare pass through monies for hospital-based programs, the future is far from certain. So what are we to do to financially support the two to four year mentoring and maturing process necessary for people who aspire to be certified supervisors in ACPE and certified diplomats in AAPC? Increasingly trainees have to work part-time to support themselves, a situation which can lengthen the training period significantly. Will only those willing to live poor or are married to a working spouse be able to enter these fields? And what about the judicatories and seminaries who benefit from our educational and counseling ministries? How might they help support our efforts to pass it on to the next generation?

5. How can we in the fields of pastoral care, counseling, and education manage and sell ourselves effectively in order to survive and grow? Up to now there have been several approaches:

- Chaplains work to become a vital part of the health care team by adapting even further to the institution's way of doing its business. That is, they set up the pastoral or spiritual component for all the major clinical pathways for patients, complete with outcomes and performance indicators.

- Chaplains prove they are making a financially significant contribution to the institution by doing research about pastoral care and how it increases healing powers and decreases length of stay.
- Pastoral Counselors secure state licensure, get on panels, and adapt counseling methods to meet criteria being set by HMOs even though this basically means managing rather than resolving the emotional problems of our clients and their families.
- Pastoral Counselors link up with a national holistic network, such as the Complementary Care system. This guarantees AAPC folks national exposure to a partnered and networked market for referrals. Although this sounds like a wonderful opportunity, can we keep our unique identity when market values push us towards efficiency and product control and alliances with huge health care organizations?

The question remains: Are we in danger of losing the uniqueness of who we are and what we do? Many think so. Certainly one thing which will be needed for future growth is an ability of our professional associations to be flexible, helpful, and supportive in accrediting new places of ministry and training.

6. How will we adjust to, indeed take full advantage of, the information age? How can we use computer technology to work more efficiently and do record-keeping, build in performance improvement, and enhance communication in our professional guilds? The growing acceptance of personal e-mail addresses is only one sign of the revolution that is happening for everyone on the globe. Distance learning is upon us, not only for seminary-based courses but also in our supervisory and pastoral counseling training programs. This could be enormously exciting and bring new resources and students into the process. Increased use of conference calls and e-mail is changing the way the governance of our organizations is working and changing our regional relationships.

Other questions include: Will those of us in pastoral counseling do our work in chat rooms? Might we be hired by particular websites to be chaplains to people visiting these sites and needing help? What effect will the ease of communication have on our relationships both nationally and internationally?

One troubling thought: One of my friends recently commented that she had written so many e-mails in one day and so far had gotten minimal response back so that she couldn't remember what she said to whom. Will the speed of communication cause us to lose track of our real relationships?

7. How can we be good pastoral supervisors, counselors, and educators when we are confronted with an ever increasing list of demands and an ever diminishing amount of time to take care of ourselves as clinical practitioners and our souls as persons of faith? I was shocked to discover the following list of over twenty activities and roles which I take on almost every day: chaplain to patients, counselor to staff, supervisor to students, leader of groups, in-service provider, ethics consultant, fund raiser, marketing and promotional person, theologian, mediator, crisis intervener, recruiter, administrator, secretary, environmental manager, translator, liturgist, grief specialist, entrepreneur, politician, plant waterer, mailperson, and staff coordinator. There are some who think this need to be a Jack or Jill of all trades will be our greatest area of crisis in the new millennium.

8. Can we and our fellow cognate organizations learn how to live together and benefit from each other's wisdom without sacrificing each group's unique identity and function? And can this happen on a regional and state level as well as a national level? Some excellent work is currently being done by a national steering committee which is identifying "do-able cooperative projects" within several of our groups. Further, can such an alliance of cognate groups become an effective lobbying force for pastoral care and counseling in our states as well as in Washington? The National Interfaith Coalition (NIC) is making efforts in this direction, but needs greater focus and clarity if it is to continue. My own recent

experience as a NIC state representative was that I had neither the time nor the energy to gain the expertise and do the networking necessary to understand the legislative world, much less figure out how to influence it.

9. How will we learn to live with difference? There are many questions which cluster around this area of concern. How can pastoral supervision adjust to a multicultural and multireligious world to educate leaders for the 21st century? How open are we to people outside our white, liberal, male, Protestant, American world? How seriously do we take culture and context as an influence in our pastoral and educational work? How flexible are we in our professional standards as we seek to be responsive to different types of students with different values and different learning needs coming from different cultures and countries? How can we genuinely dialogue with folks with whom we disagree, including the different cultures within our own organizations?

A recent meeting of supervisors-in-training and their training supervisors from four different supervisory cluster groups in the Eastern Region focused on "Multi-cultural Supervision" and had over 25% people of color in attendance. During our worship time guided by a Buddhist priest, we heard Psalm 23 read in seven different languages, each of which was native to the speaker. These included Swahili, Dutch, Hebrew, and Spanish.

The new Religious Ethnic Multicultural (REM) Coordinator Teresa Snorton recently wrote, "I believe the greatest challenge [for the future] will be to truly do what REM was initially formed to do—to lift up the needs of those who represent a point of view not always regarded as the norm, to advocate for programs, ministries, policies and procedures, that are inclusive of those often left out or overlooked, and to join hands together to make our ministries, our communities, and our world a better place for everyone...." This goal will call for all of us to change. If we cannot, we risk being in the situation of the bushmen in that wonderful movie "The Gods Must Be Crazy." A coke bottle is discovered in the middle of the Kalahari Desert and the bushmen wonder if it is a device for curing snake skins, a musical instrument, a rolling pin, or a water holder. When one child hurts another with it, they decide it is a source of evil and go to bury it "at the ends of the earth." Hopefully this will not be the fate our of pastoral care movement.

10. What will be the nature of the spiritual or religious communities to which we will hold allegiance in the future? One thing is certain—there will be a huge variety. In the Christian community there will be prayer groups and base communities. The Christian paradigm itself is already being questioned by some Christian feminists who criticize it as too individualistic, patriarchal, hierarchical, and oppressive. They seek a theistic paradigm which sees the self-in-relation and encourages community building and the sharing of power.

In the world of spirituality there will be healing groups and labyrinth walks. In the secular world there will be AA and Birth Mothers and Diabetes Support Groups. In the world of specialized ministries and education there will be professional associations and academic guilds, both locally and nationally. Any of these groups can legitimately become spiritual home for some people, the place where the split between mind and heart, body and soul, past and future begins to be healed. The important bottom line is that everyone needs a spiritual home if nourishing the soul is to be valued within the culture.

Conclusion

It may seem to some that raising all these questions about what is to happen to us in the future is an indication of how much is shifting in front of our very eyes. Such an array of questions is surely a sign that a lot is up for grabs. In response I offer the following story from Annie Lamott's book *Traveling Mercies* (1999) as a source of comfort and hope. It is about a woman traveling to a medical conference in Russia.

> Everything that could go wrong did—flights were canceled or overbooked, connections missed, her reserved room at the hotel had been given to someone else. She kept

trying to be a good sport, but finally, two mornings later, on the train to her conference...she began to whine at the man sitting beside her about how infuriating her journey had been. It turned out this man worked for the Dalai Lama. And he said—gently—that they believe that when a lot of things start going wrong all at once, it is to protect something big and lovely that is trying to get itself born—and that this something needs for you to be distracted so that it can be born as perfectly as possible (p. 107.)

So much for all our questions. Perhaps, instead of calamity, "something big and lovely...is trying to get itself born."

References

Capps, D. (1995). *Living stories: Pastoral counseling in congregational context.* Minneapolis: Fortress Press.

Fitchett, G. (1982). A Coherent Theory of Education Relevant for CPE. *Journal of Supervision and Training in Ministry,* (6),73-108).

Lamott A. (1999). *Traveling mercies: Some thoughts on faith.* New York: Pantheon Books.

Schmidt A. (1999). *Vision* February, 7-8.

CHAPTER 3

Opening Up the Circle:
Next Steps in Process Group Work in Clinical Pastoral
Education[*] Joan E. Hemenway

Abstract

This article applies Systems-Centered Theory (SCT)™
to the small process group experience in Clinical Pastoral Education (CPE) by exploring six key questions: 1)
What is the purpose of the small process group in CPE?
2) Is there an alternative to getting stuck in the "hot seat"
dynamic? 3) Do we (clergy) always have to be nice? 4)
Is there life beyond personal story telling? 5) Does the
authority issue ever go away? 6) How much difference is
too much difference? The article includes vignettes to illustrate theory.

C linical Pastoral Education (CPE) is an educational methodology that combines knowledge of psychology (who we
are) with knowledge of theology (what we believe) with
process education (how we learn) in order to prepare seminarians,
clergy, and qualified lay people to provide effective interfaith spiritual care amidst the religious and social complexities of the modern
world. Similar to other professional practicum, CPE is offered in a
variety of institutional settings—medical centers, nursing homes,
prisons, rehabilitative facilities, hospices, counseling centers, and
local faith communities. Clinical Pastoral Education programs are

---

[*] Reprinted with permission from Journal of Pastoral Care and Counseling,
2005, 59(4):323-334. An earlier version of this paper was published in SP
Gantt and YM Agazarian (Eds.) SCT in Action: Applying the Systems-
Centered Approach to Organizations (Lincoln, NE: IUniverse, Inc., 2005),
pp. 81-97.

supervised by educators (CPE supervisors) who are ordained clergy or ecclesiastically endorsed chaplains trained in psychology, educational theory, and group dynamics. At the present time there are approximately 700 certified CPE supervisors and 400 accredited training centers in the United States.

The CPE educational methodology is based on an action-reflection-action model of learning. It includes weekly teaching seminars with an emphasis on theory combined with student case presentations that emphasize application. A key educational element is the small process group involving anywhere from three to eight participants. Sessions are usually once a week (in a part-time program) and twice a week (in a full-time program) for 1-1.5 hours per session. This group experience, often quite intense and memorable, is a required element of every accredited Clinical Pastoral Education program. By learning how to harness the full potential of the small process group experience, students are better prepared not only to engage in significant human relationships but also to understand organizational and systems dynamics in an increasingly complex world.

It is the purpose of this article to explore the application of the theory and method of Systems-Centered Theory (SCT) group work to group process work in CPE. Though this application is still in its infancy, there is evidence of growing interest among CPE supervisors. Not only can SCT enhance our educational efforts, it can also further the implementation of values that the Association for Clinical Pastoral Education (ACPE) considers fundamental to its educational mission. This article focuses on six specific questions regarding CPE process group work—questions that have been a longstanding focus for conversation among CPE supervisors. The article will demonstrate how SCT group theory and methods can shift the concerns that have elicited these questions from being sources of confusion and misunderstanding to being opportunities for new learning and satisfaction for both CPE students and supervisors.

1. What is the purpose of the small process group in CPE?
This question has persisted among both CPE students and CPE supervisors over the years and has evoked a broad range of

responses. It is "an opportunity to develop interpersonal relationship skills," "a context in which to share personal information and feelings," "a place to create an emotionally supportive community and review our pastoral work," "an opportunity to learn about group dynamics and group leadership," "a context in which to deal with family dynamics and authority issues." No matter what the answer to this question is, or whether the group is highly structured to totally unstructured, a point usually occurs in about the third week of a training unit when an uncomfortably long silence descends on the group with all eyes on the floor. Eventually the most anxious (and courageous) member says (with a short intake of breath and a look of fleeting concern edged with annoyance): "I don't know why we're here."

One supervisory response to this situation is to refer to the Student Handbook where there is usually a brief, generic and not very helpful description of this element of the educational program and its purpose. One student reading this description out loud to the group (and the supervisors—perhaps—responding to questions) may or may not move things forward at this juncture. Another supervisory response is to repeat, perhaps more slowly, whatever words of wisdom were offered at the start of the program about the purpose of process group work in CPE: "We're here to share personally, relate interpersonally, and learn about group dynamics" or some similar version. A third response is to ignore the question and instead comment on the here-and-now dynamics: "I'm wondering how group members are feeling about the long silence in group today?" There is continued discussion in CPE about how to deal with the inevitable increase of anxiety and resistance in the group. In general, a CPE supervisor working out of the psychoanalytic model/Tavistock tradition (less apparent structure and more direct confrontation) will make group-oriented interpretations that focus on the group dynamic and not on individuals in the group: "The group in its silence is acting out its anger towards the authority figure and has appointed one person to be its messenger" said with unreadable facial expression and eyes looking at no one in particular. At the other end of the spectrum, a CPE supervisor working within the humanistic psychology model/T-group tradition (more obviously structured and openly supportive) will demonstrate relationally-available behavior by responding from the perspective of someone inside the group: "I was feeling more anxious as the silence deepened; it would probably be helpful if we each could share how we are feeling" said while looking hopefully around the group at each person. No matter which supervisory approach is taken, or all the variations in between, students basically experience uncertainty and anxiety regarding the small process group, often calling it "group therapy"—a designation that has prompted considerable discussion among CPE supervisors through the years.

SCT has several contributions to make to this conversation. First, SCT's emphasis on role, goal, and context immediately clarifies that CPE is first and foremost a professional education program intended to prepare qualified lay people, seminarians, and clergy to deal with the intricacies and intensity of interfaith pastoral work. Though the group educational element may have some therapeutic and personal benefit to participants (that is, it may result in some degree of emotional and behavioral change), the context is educational, the role of the student is to be a member of the group, the role of the supervisor is to be a facilitator of the group, and the purpose of the group's work is to encourage participation in, and reflective observation on, the group experience. Thus, from the SCT perspective, a response to the student's query "I don't know why we're here" might be: "Would you like to explore what you think the goal of the group is and see who can join you?"

Secondly, SCT has built on Kurt Lewin's concept of the group as a "laboratory for learning" which is an idea familiar to most CPE supervisors. In this theoretical framework, the work of the facilitator is to encourage students to participate in the group (SCT calls it "staying curious on the edge of the unknown") as well as observe and reflect on their participation (SCT calls this "turning on your inner researcher"). Contrary to the early years when CPE supervisors tended to keep the group purpose as mysterious and vague as possible, increasingly it is recognized that students need to learn about group theory and dynamics in order to participate knowledgeably and productively in the group process.

In addition, SCT emphasizes that setting up specific structures including consistent meeting room, chair arrangement, and clear time boundaries is of the utmost importance. SCT also avoids using psychological language that pathologizes; instead it encourages colloquial language that is user-friendly and memorable. In the foundational or beginning SCT group experience, each session often starts with ten minutes of teaching and ends with ten minutes of "surprises, learnings, satisfactions, dissatisfactions and discoveries." CPE supervisors sometimes add "applications to pastoral care" as part of this concluding group time. All of the above suggestions are way "the lab" is provided with sufficient air, light, and equipment to assure a comfortable and trustworthy space for the work of leaning and preparation for ministry to begin.

2. Is there an alternative to getting stuck in the "hot seat" dynamic? This is an all too familiar pattern in CPE groups where the specific troubles or personal needs or learning problems of one student become the focus for the group. In the early days of process group work, putting pressure on one person (repetitively if necessary) was acceptable and expected in CPE. The rationale for this "hot seat" approach became a cliché: "A group can only go as fast as its slowest member." Though there is growing awareness in recent years of the dangers of this dynamic within groups (increasing defensiveness and/or creating an identified patient or scapegoat), it continues to be an all-too-easy trap to fall into. Though CPE supervisors do offer many instances of important role modeling in terms of interpersonal relating when dealing with a "problem student" or a "student problem" in the group, it is also a temptation to be drawn into the pleasure of simply demonstrating one's supervisory skills in front of the group. In addition, students are inevitably drawn towards their own desires "to be helpful and comforting," desires already deeply internalized among those who aspire to the pastoral role.

SCT has made a major contribution to solving this problem through functional sub-grouping. By training group members to say "Anyone else?" after each person has made a contribution, and by expecting group members to respond and build on what has been shared, the focus on one person can be alleviated. This is particularly important in the early stages of the life of the group when CPE students may be unsure of the purpose of the group and feel increasingly ambivalent or suspicious about the whole enterprise. In addition, in SCT there is a simple "Push, Wave, Row Exercise" that helps group participants grasp the difference between keeping distance and really engaging on a feeling level (Agazarian, 1997, pp.57-59). The following example illustrates the application of the exercise in order to begin sub grouping:

> Student A: I am so upset about Mrs. S. dying. She was such a beautiful person. I couldn't even talk with the family afterwards. I just had to leave the floor (crying). I really need help with this. I know I have a problem...(nods of agreement all around the group).

> Student B: When did this happen? [A question is a push.]

> Student A: Earlier this afternoon (more tears).

> Student C: You couldn't even take care of the family? [another push]

> Student B: It's probably because the patient reminded you of your mother. [speculative analysis is also a push]

> Student A: Hmmmm (looking at the floor and disengaging)

> Student D: (concerned) I had a similar experience last year in my parish. [This effort to identify from past experience is a wave from the shore.]

> CPE Supervisor: There is a lot of focus on questions to A or opinions about A, yet the job here is to join A. Has anyone else had a favorite patient die during this time and could you share your feelings and make eye contact with A?

> Student E: (after some silence) Well...I remember Mr. B.

He was such a faithful man. When he died I just couldn't believe it. I went up to the floor and his bed was empty. (looking at Student A). Then I felt an emptiness clear down to the soles of my feet. And a dark sadness sort of took me over... [Sharing a here-and-now experience and the feeling attached to it is getting in the boat and rowing with the person.]

Student A: Sadness, yes. And I also felt helpless and my arms felt limp [Rowing here on several levels!]

CPE Supervisor (prompting by looking toward Student A): Anyone else?

Student A: Oh yeah, anyone else?

SCT makes an important distinction between functional and stereotype subgroups. Based on a dominant/subordinate dynamic, a stereotype subgroup enforces social stability by rejecting, and sometimes even persecuting, differences with some people "in" and others "out." It is this phenomenon that has earned subgrouping a justifiably negative reputation in the group dynamics field. It occurs when two or three of the same people begin to eat together or meet regularly outside of group time, closing off the possibility of changing membership. It also happens when several members within a group band together on a stereotype similarity such as age or sex or ethnicity. A functional subgroup, always working in the context of the group session itself, is constantly integrating differences (taking in new members and new ideas and new feelings), discovering similarities, and creating greater complexity in its emotional life.

Functional sub-grouping also needs to be distinguished from pairing in which only limited differences can come into the group due to the role locks between people. Role locks (often unconscious) happen when two people are caught in repeating a significant relationship from the past. In one CPE group, a female student and a male student had both gone through recent divorces. Unfortunately they each reminded the other of their former spouses. As a result, they kept the group repeatedly "entertained" for many weeks during group sessions by constantly nit-picking and criticizing each other whenever the group's anxiety went up because the next piece of work was not clear and the waiting within the silence became uncomfortable. In contrast, functional sub-grouping would require anyone feeling the impulse to criticize or nitpick to explore the impulse together in the same subgroup in order that the information contained in the impulse could be integrated into the group-as-a-whole. In this example, the two role-locked students, and likely others, would end up exploring in the same subgroup together.

3. Do we (clergy) always have to be nice? The pastoral or religious role carries the burden of a vast array of introjections and projections, and the strong tendency on the part of those who carry these to "take things personally." SCT sees the issue of personalizing as a significant human challenge and an important one for groups to work with. For the CPE student, it is usually introjected parts of significant relationships (including with a personal or impersonal Higher Power) that have most influenced the desire to enter a profession focused on providing spiritual guidance to others. CPE training involves helping students become aware of what kind of introjected material is shaping both their internal motivation for ministry and their external style of doing ministry. Integration of the professional demands of the role with personal congruency and satisfaction in the role is a crucial step in the educational process.

Of course those in a pastoral role also continually receive whatever projections people in a particular context may decide to express, either indirectly or directly. It is a common experience for a new chaplain intern to approach a nursing station and suddenly all of the staff milling around behind the desk stop talking. Several weeks later, after the chaplain has gotten to know the staff, someone may give voice indirectly to the feelings behind the (now former) silence: "Okay everybody, let's hold up on the dirty jokes because the chaplain is here!" An important part of CPE training focuses on helping the student accept and work with the richness of such projective material aimed at religious authority. Learning how to contain the feelings generated in these relationships may eventually lead to help exploration of the underlying assumptions.

Work in the small process group includes the students becoming aware of the ongoing introjective and projective processes within themselves and others. Actively becoming conscious of the fantasies about one's peers (SCT call these "mind reads") as well as fears about one's self (these often take the form of what SCT calls "negative predictions") is the first step. Being able to literally digest and metabolize this new information (feedback) establishes increased relational reality with others. Further, as competitive behavior (rather than finger pointing) surfaces in the group, the strong feelings that are generated can be explored in functional subgroups, thus releasing new energy into the system. In these ways individuals are encouraged to join others in exploring the full potential of their emotional life. This includes accepting the "not-so-nice" parts along with the "so-nice" parts and thus becoming more real.

One group struggled with their negative feelings about another student who was consistently late for group sessions. In this example Student A is twenty minutes late. She enters the room hurriedly, sits down, and addresses the group.

> Student A: (hangs her head and addresses the group): I'm really sorry that I'm late. My floor is really busy and that same nurse wanted to talk to me. I just couldn't say no... (voice trails off as her role lock takes over).

> Student B: (face flushed, right hand in a fist, leaning forward): I was really concerned. I care a lot about you and was worried something was wrong to make you late...again.

> Student C (to Student B): You look angry. Are you?

> Student B: No, I just care about her.

> Student C: Well, I'm angry. My body feels tense. I might get into trouble for saying this, but I feel like I could just explode.

Student D: (leg is tapping the floor) I'm with you. I feel very frustrated. This will probably keep happening at the beginning of every group session.

Student B: I guess I am a little angry, now that you mention it.

Student E: I don't think it's right to get angry. If we can't be understanding and patient   with each other, how can we be real ministers out there?

Student A: (to student D) I agree with you. As a chaplain intern I want to always be responsive to people's requests and love them no matter what.

CPE Supervisor: Today we have a Make Love subgroup and a Make War subgroup. (To Student F who tends to stay on the sidelines): Which subgroup do you want to join?

The next steps in this work would involve the supervisor helping each subgroup continue to reality test their negative predictions and their mind reads as well as explore the array of deeper feelings around expressing or inhibiting their feelings of frustration. This work would lead to beginning to realize the extent to which the students have introjected their own and others' expectations about how they are to feel and act in the pastoral role.

Recent theoretical work in SCT has distinguished between stereotype roles (a role we are locked into from the past) and functional roles that are more appropriate to the immediate context and expressive of the spontaneous self (Agazarian, 2003). Stereotype roles are the result of adaptation to frustration experienced in previous early attachment relationships and in important growing-up experiences. Such compromised roles allowed us to stay in relationships despite experiencing the distress of mis-attunement (McCluskey, 2002a). SCT is particularly helpful in highlighting the split-second induction of a role lock through noticing even the smallest of physical changes: head bent slightly to one side, one finger tapping, feet shifting on the floor, eyes averted, face drained of color, slumping position, and so on. Such physical changes are often habitual and thus emblematic of an old role. For CPE students it can be freeing to discover that the professional role of pastoral care giver is not limited to, or even bound by, the stereotype roles learned long ago. Being sensitive to those times when the clergy role has actually inducted a patient or parishioner into a stereotype role can be extremely useful when this can be named and worked through in order to create a more real pastoral relationship.

4. Is there life beyond personal story telling? One of the most highly valued aspects of CPE supervision is learning about each student's personal history and faith journey. Initial material required for application to a program includes a lengthy autobiographical essay. The personal interview prior to acceptance into a CPE program often focuses on examining more thoroughly the texture of a student's relationship to parents, siblings, and influential teachers and spiritual mentors. During the training itself, dynamics with patients are often highlighted in verbatim sessions as being part of the "parallel process" reflected within the student's personal story. For example, a male student whose mother recently died may be overly attentive to the son of a female patient who is dying, spending extra time without realizing the degree of identification activated in his pastoral work until this is pointed out.

In terms of the actual verbal sharing of personal story, the CPE process group usually provides the main stage. CPE Supervisors working out of the humanistic psychology tradition often begin the first session by telling their own story and thereby modeling "how to do it" for the students. Some programs then devote the next few sessions to each student telling his or her lebenslaufe (life story) in order to discern new meanings in these stories and allow for deeper relating. Students who have already done therapeutic work often bring hard-won insights about family dynamics as well as current personal problems. Other students, more hesitant, struggle with exactly how to deal with this initial up-close-and-personal experience. As this process unfolds, the group atmosphere becomes increasingly cohesive and intimate. However, when personal story time is concluded, the group is still confronted with trying to figure out how best to use the process group time.

The systems-centered approach of SCT uses neither the content of each individual's story, nor his or her professional niche, as the main identifier for the person's presence in the group. Taking up one's role as a group member depends less on personal autobiography and more on being able to respond emotionally to whatever phase of development the group is in and whatever material one of the subgroups is exploring in the here-and-now. Moving out of the "person system" into the "member system" in order to "do the work" of the group-as-a-whole marks a critically important shift within one's self and in relationship to the other group members. The crucial first step in this process involves reducing anxiety by training students to use the "fork-in-the-road" method (Agazarian, 2002a, pp. 122-123) to distinguish between "explaining" and "exploring" their feelings. As this work progresses, each person's emotional experience is expanded beyond historic roles and long-embedded expectations.

A middle-aged woman, eldest of two girls, had grown up with a mother who suffered frequent bouts of depression resulting in periodic hospitalizations. As a result, this woman found herself as a teenager caring for her father and younger sister in both practical and emotional ways. Having learned a clear and much-needed role in her family of origin, she was strongly drawn towards the caring and helpful aspects of ordained ministry. However, underneath her responsible and proud self-image was identification with her mother that included deeply held fears of becoming emotionally ill herself.

When this woman first joined an SCT training group, she tended to be seduced into a stereotype role lock whenever any member of the training group became emotionally upset. She would immediately reach out to calm and reassure. Her work in the SCT group was to let go of this immediate emotional response and, instead, access less familiar parts of her feeling life by joining the ongoing work of one of the subgroups. Her success at doing this was not only satisfying and emotionally expanding, but also led to the growing realization that her mother, though ill at times, was in fact a very accomplished professional person. This data from her past significantly eased her fears about her own present and future mental health.

The exciting aspect of SCT for CPE supervisors and students is that this approach frees people from the constructions and constrictions that they have created for themselves through the life-long formulation of their personal story with its stereotype roles. By staying in the emotional reality of the present moment, rather than relying on formulations about the meaning of past hurts and disappointments or fleeing to the irreality of future hopes and fears, group members begin to get to know themselves and each other in more satisfying ways. By no longer taking things "just personally" individual group members working in subgroups see how they are contributing to the group-as-a-whole and the larger living human system that is striving to "survive, develop and transform" itself on many levels (Agazarian, 1997, pp. 17-40). For some CPE students this approach may be experienced initially as a loss, denying them some of their personal satisfactions for entering ministry in the first place; for others this approach may be a relief that actually frees them to commit more deeply to a pastoral vocation.

5. Does the authority issue ever go away? The brief answer to this question is No! Yvonne Agazarian (1999), the founder of SCT, writes: "[The authority issue] is as old as the human race and it fuels revolutions and wars. It never sleeps; a leviathan, it stirs restlessly in the depth of human experience and is easily aroused" (p. 241). Whether, and exactly how, to deal with the leviathan is one of the biggest challenges for CPE supervisors when leading process groups. Initially, this issue seems to be more accessible for those working in the psychoanalytic tradition than it is for those working in the humanistic psychology tradition. And while students are strongly encouraged to exercise pastoral authority in their ministry with patients and in their relationships with other professional staff,

they are often given mixed messages in the group—both about initiating confrontation among themselves as well as in relationship to the supervisor.

Occasionally the process group work in CPE will be videotaped for the supervisor's peer review, supervisory training, or student learning. The presence of the camera provides an excellent opportunity to surface the authority issue, an opportunity some students assiduously avoid while others take up with enthusiasm.

Student A: I don't like having the camera here. It makes me nervous.

Student B: I agree. I don't see why it's necessary. Did we do something wrong?
Student C: It doesn't affect me.

Student D (glancing anxiously around): Me neither. What shall we talk about?

Student E: I just had a wonderful visit with one of my patients.

CPE Supervisor: We have two subgroups, one that is Camera Ready and one that is Camera Shy.

Student B: Well, I don't feel particularly "ready" but I do feel angry.

Student A: Me too. It's like someone with a Big Eye watching us all of a sudden.

Student B: Spying on us...maybe getting ready to hurt us.

Student A: I'd like to hurt it, just kick it and knock it down.

Student C: I don't know why you're making such a big deal of the camera.

CPE supervisor (to Student C): You are probably in the
Camera Shy subgroup. For the moment let's allow the Camera
Ready group to do some work together before you come in.

Student D: I don't know which group I'm in.

It is extremely helpful as well as comforting to learn the seriousness with which SCT takes the authority issue. Exploration of this issue is key to the work of the group and results in increased integration of personal self and professional functioning—a central aspect of the learning task and ministry experience for students in Clinical Pastoral Education.

In SCT the authority issue is carefully enumerated in the many sub phases of group development within the Authority Phase (understanding phases of group development is key to understanding SCT (Agazarian, 1997, Chapter 4)). It is only by working through the defenses in the Authority Phase that a group is then ready to move to the defenses of the Intimacy Phase. Still later comes the emergence of an Interdependent Work Group that has flexibility to explore more deeply specific aspects within any of the sub phases. SCT understands defenses as actually restraining forces specific to each phase of group development. They mark the many ways people learn to cope (that is, maintain attachment) despite the inevitable mis-attunements experienced initially in relationship to primary caregivers and later in relationships with significant others. Though the term "defenses" may sound too psychological or psychoanalytic for many CPE supervisors, the way SCT works with defenses (that is, everyday coping mechanisms) provides a useful framework within which to understand the parallel process between human emotional development and the phases of group development.

It is easy for CPE process groups, with the help of the supervisor, to create an initial milieu of interpersonal closeness. From an SCT perspective, this behavior is one way the process group avoids dealing with social defenses, ignores potential conflict, and creates a pseudo-community to shelter themselves from what they fear might be (or in fact, is) a stressful training situation. In contrast, CPE supervisors who in the initial interview have explored what SCT calls "the social defenses against communication" as well as the "cognitive defenses against anxiety" exhibited by the student applicant, will have begun the process of preparing their students for a different kind of work in CPE and in the process group. Examples of the above include such interventions as: "Do you realize you are smiling as you are talking about the death of your brother?" or "Is your uncertainty about CPE because you have already made a negative prediction about what it will be like?" or "You are at a fork in the road between explaining your reasons for choosing CPE or exploring what you don't know yet about your choice. Which way do you want to go?"

In terms of group work, when the CPE supervisor stays relatively separate from the student group and comments consistently on the here-and-now group dynamics, strong feelings about authority will be elicited. This supervisory stance opens the way for the group to begin to move through social and cognitive defense towards the role locks inherent in compliant/defiant feelings. Underneath this material resides the primal rage at authority expressed in sadism and masochism. This work, though emotionally draining for everyone when engaged directly, can also be indirectly—and sometimes playfully—addressed:

> One CPE group created a nickname for everyone. A tall attractive African American male was "King Tut." An outspoken Episcopal woman was "Miss Piss and Vinegar"; a Roman Catholic Sister who was unerringly kind and always dressed in a habit was "Snow White." The leader of the group, an Episcopal laywoman, came to be known as "The General." And the CPE supervisor was named "Old Hawkeye." In this particular group, the supervisor sat in a swivel chair that was the best chair in the room. One day the Roman Catholic Sister sat in the supervisor's chair just before the process group meeting was to begin. Her peers responded to her daring with considerable laughter and encouraging remarks. When the supervisor walked in, "Snow White" was politely asked to move (which she did). The group expressed their appreciation for her boldness by changing her nickname to "Sister Act II"!

An approach to CPE group work that consistently and creatively deals with the authority issue requires leadership that is grounded in theory, has undergone sufficient training, and is able to stay self-confident and curious. It also requires ongoing support from colleagues who are engaged in similar group leadership work. Wilfred Bion left the group dynamics field because he became emotionally worn out with having to sit "behind his face" day after day and contain the projections of his patients (and presumably the staff as well) at the Tavistock Clinic. Experiencing one's own essential loneliness while receiving, but not taking personally, both impassioned idealizations and/or rebellious feelings of hatred from group members requires discipline, considerable experience, and at times pure grit. Being able to effectively work with projections requires good timing and accurate attunement. The goal here is to help CPE students give up the defense of externalization (being a victim to the perceived negative influence of parents, upbringing, religious group, culture, etc.). In this way the path is cleared for taking greater responsibility for one's self and one's engagement in the CPE learning process.

6. How much difference is too much difference?

It is currently a high value in the Association for Clinical Pastoral Education to see itself as a provider of training for ministry that is multi-faith and multicultural. This commitment marks a shift in emphasis from the more personal and individualistic approach of former years to a broader social and contextual framework "spiritual care and the teaching of it should *not* be viewed as a simple matter of practice by well-intentioned individual practitioners. Rather, it must be seen as a complex cultural practice that has implications for individuals, organizations and society at large" (Lee, 2003, p.5). The seriousness with which this issue is being taken is reflected in the 2005 revision of ACPE Accreditation and Certification Standards to reflect this larger framework.

A systems-centered understanding of group dynamics (and indeed of the other educational elements in CPE as well) makes a major contribution in terms of supporting this shift and developing its implications. Systems-centered thinking makes explicit the inter-dependent relationship within the living human system between the group-as-a-whole system, the subgroup system, and the member (individual) system. Not only does this approach help students understand their own emotional life more fully (that is, the subsystems within themselves) and contribute to the subgroup work (places where they can be joined by others), but it also helps them "see" the various larger systems (group-as-a-whole, hospital, faith group, local community) in which they seek to do ministry. Further SCT emphasizes that the subgroup work is always focused on "exploring differences in the apparently similar and the similarities in the apparently different." In this way, groups (systems, organizations, societies) survive, develop and transform themselves in increasingly complex ways.

A CPE group of students had just begun a full-time summer unit of training. There were two male and two female students from a mainline Protestant seminary, plus a female Jewish rabbi, and a Hispanic Pentecostal man in the group. On the third day of the program, when the group was still in its infancy, the rabbi turned to the Pentecostal and said: "Do you believe that the only way to God is through Jesus Christ?" Immediately the group went silent. The Pentecostal, ruffled but able to recover, responded: "Do you believe that Jews are the Chosen People?" Both locked eyes while the rest of the group held its breath.

Could the group hold this much difference so early in its life together? Or, would either the rabbi or the Pentecostal (or both, in which case they would form a subgroup) move into a barrier experience of shame and be cut off from his or her spontaneous self and from the group-as-a-whole? Agazarian (2003) writes: "System response to the too different is to contain it in a subsystem behind impermeable boundaries which keep it split away from the system-as-a-whole, unless or until the system as-a-whole develops the capacity to recognize and integrate it" (p.4). This is the well-known elephant-in-the-room phenomenon, the secret no one wants to talk about, which can stall all efforts to do the sub-grouping work and cause the group to become depressed and go dead-in-the-water.

The story of the group described above that was working with their differences actually had a happy, somewhat unexpected, resolution. Though they did some good work in the process group as part of the educational program, the real turning point came when they discovered that they could sing in four-part harmony together. Because of obvious religious differences, they initially compromised by singing Broadway songs. However, eventually they developed a repertoire of semi-religious songs in Spanish, Hebrew, Latin, and a few old favorites in English such as "Amazing Grace." Every Friday afternoon the "Singing Chaplains" went to the floors to serenade patients, families and staff with their beautiful music—discovering a creative way to integrate their differences and in the process pleasing themselves, their supervisor and the hospital!

This exploration of the foregoing six key questions demonstrates some substantial ways in which SCT theory and practice can inform and enrich CPE group process work. One of the most appealing aspects of SCT for those of us involved in Clinical Pastoral Education is its integration of a wide variety of theoretical approaches: general systems theory, communication theory, developmental psychology, cognitive and behavioral psychology, as well as the psychoanalytic tradition. This comprehensive approach is appreciated by the CPE supervisors who both enjoy a wide variety of psychological and educational theories and also seek ways to bring them all together.

A second appeal of SCT is its emphasis on the integration of the apprehensive (intuitive, emotional) and comprehensive (cognitive) self. Such integration of head and heart lies at the center of both the theory and practice of Clinical Pastoral Education. Increased permeability between these two basic aspects of the human personality results in the ability to mobilize and release one's many resources for ministry. Learning how to fully "use the self" is exciting work! A sign of this achievement is the ability to access one's common sense (an ego free of defenses) in managing day-to-day living as well as major decision-making. As this work takes place in the subgroup, the outcome is greater flexibility, creativity and energy within the self, in relationships with others, and in the group-as-a-whole.

A final appeal of SCT is its emphasis on empathic attunement as the basis for work in the subgroup. Attunement in this case is defined as "an interpersonal process that takes place between two people based on the communication of verbal and non-verbal signals" (McClusky, 2002b, p.2). The importance of eye contact, physical posture, skin tone, facial expression, and emotional availability all contribute to effective relating with other people. The small process group experience in CPE provides opportunity for individuals to become aware of previous mis-attunements and the defensive emotional maneuvers that have grown out of these early experiences and then try out new behaviors. From an SCT perspective, this new work reverberates throughout the living human system that both holds the work and is changed by it as well. Such healing relational work, which is both personal and system-wide, lies at the very center of pastoral care and Clinical Pastoral Education.

References

Agazarian, Y. (1997). *Systems-centered therapy for groups*. New York, NY: Guilford Press.

Agazarian, Y. (2002). *A systems-centered approach to group psychotherapy*. London and Philadelphia: Jessica Kingsley.

Agazarian, Y. (2003). Roles. (Unpublished paper)

McCluskey, U. (2002a). The dynamics of attachment and systems-centered group psychotherapy. *Group Dynamics: Theory, Research and Practice, 6*(2), 131-142.

McCluskey, U. (2002b). Workshop material.

Samuel, L.K. (2003). A prolegomena to multi-cultural competencies in clinical pastoral education. (Unpublished paper)

CHAPTER 4

Holding On...While Letting Go:
Reflections in Times of Grave Illness[*]
Joan E. Hemenway

Preface

No one enjoys being in the hospital. It is an alien environment, a scary place filled with strange smells and sounds and people. We count the days, fear the pain, try to understand the diagnosis, are courageous in undergoing tests and treatments and examinations, welcome visits from family and friends—and most of all, wait expectantly to have it all over with and return home.

I have made numerous visits to people in the hospital both as a hospital chaplain and as a local pastor. I have also been hospitalized. These experiences have made me more aware of the gap between the hospital bed and the world, the sick and the healthy, being comforted and being the comforter. Support from family and friends as well as professional help from doctors and nurses are wonderful, necessary gifts in the face of illness, the threat of pain, and even death. But when all is said and done, each person in the bed is finally left alone to withstand and understand the rigors of what is happening to his or her body and soul.

Faith, at such a time, is crucial. One's faith may be expressed in daily prayer and Bible reading, or simply in muffled, uncertain cries in the still of the night. God is listening for both, and more. How we make sense of what is going on during such critical hard times is primarily the work of faith. And often, it is the crisis of

[*] Selections from Holding On...While Letting Go: Reflections in Times of Grave Illness, revised edition. Cleveland Ohio: The Pilgrim Press, 2004. Reprinted with permission.

illness or unexpected tragedy that marks the real beginning of this work in our lives. During such a time we may be forced to wonder more deeply than ever before where God is; why this is happening to us; what we did wrong; why the world is so unfair; and whether we will find strength to go on.

The prayers and poems and scripture reading in this book are ones I have found to be helpful both in my ministry and during my hospitalization. They are shared here in a spirit of openness and encouragement.

> Come and be with me:
> All you who would believe but feel doubtful,
> All you who do believe and feel thankful,
> All you who want to believe and feel curious,
> All you who disbelieve but are not satisfied.

Holding On While Letting Go

I remember when my niece was learning to swim, she never seemed quite able to let go. At first, she always held on to me or the edge of the pool. As she got more sophisticated, she was careful to keep the big toe of her right foot in contact with the bottom of the pool as she splashed vigorously on the top. I was not convinced, and she knew it!

Learning to swim is a lot like learning to have faith in a God who loves us but does not control or protect us. We are free to make our own mistakes, hold to the sides when necessary, and even on occasion, feel like we are drowning. Yet all the while, we are surrounded by the waters of God's love, if we would but trust and let go. This is hard enough to do when everything is going smoothly, but in time of crisis, it can be almost impossible. Sometimes I need a great deal more than one toe on the bottom to convince myself that I won't drown. I am grateful that God's love does not depend on my faith!

My Daily Prayer

When we are scared, like my niece, it is important to hang on to the sides. This prayer is one of my ways of doing this. Sometimes it even helps me to let go.

> Almighty God, by whose will it is that we walk by
> faith and not by sight in the mysterious universe you
> have created, increase now my faith in you that in the
> midst of things which pass my understanding, I may not
> doubt your love, or miss your joy, or fail in my
> thanksgiving.
> Through Jesus Christ our Lord. Amen.

God's Promise to Us

The following verses from the prophet Isaiah foretell the coming of the Savior, Jesus Christ. For me, they are broader than that. I believe that we are each sent forth with a promise we will not return empty. This kind of purposefulness provides the framework for faithful understanding of all that happens to us in a lifetime.

> For as the rain and the snow come down from heaven,
> and do not return there until they have watered the
> earth, making it bring forth and sprout,
> giving seed to the sower and bread to the eater,
> so shall my word be that goes out from my mouth;
> it shall not return to me empty,
> but it shall accomplish that which I purpose,
> and succeed in the thing for which I sent it
> (5:10-11).

A Prayer for Difficult Days

O God, some days are simply difficult. The breakfast is late, the doctor is early, visitors stay too long, flowers wilt, tests are not done, promises are broken, and discouragement sets in. I know who I really am by how I respond to these frustrations and disappointments. Sometimes I am patient and can see beyond them. Sometimes they just do me in. Help me to be steadfast, O God, and hang in with both the good and the bad. Amen.

A Prayer about Friendship

Thank you, God, for all the friends who have reached out to me while I've been here in the hospital. Thank you for the cards and calls and flowers, for the gentle touch of hands and hearts and voices. They have helped me to feel alive and whole when I needed them most. They have helped me to find myself again. Thank you especially for the laughter and tears shared these past days, for our memories, and for all our hopes for one another. Bless my friends, O God, and keep them safe and close to you. Amen.

God the Protector

Some habits from our everyday routines can be carried over into our time in the hospital, when they may become newly meaningful. Saying grace at mealtime provides an opportunity to recognize God's gifts of daily sustenance at a time when we may be aware of how much we have been taking for granted. Sometimes saying grace with a chaplain or visitor can deepen our sense of connectedness and nurture, both physically and spiritually. Or saying grace silently and alone can act as a constant reminder that all we receive is given to us. And when we are not hungry but need to eat, saying grace can help us focus on the hard task ahead.

The Bread We Need

Often times new words can bring new life to our old, familiar prayers, and ways of praying. Jesus said,

> "And whenever you pray, do not be like the hypocrites; for they love to stand and pray in the synagogues and at the street corners, so that they may be seen by others. Truly I tell you, they have received their reward. But whenever you pray, go into your room and shut the door and pray to your Father who is in secret; and your Father who sees in secret will reward you." (Matthew 6:5-6)

A hospital stay can be a perfect time to go into the secret place of prayer, perhaps with some new words, and find the bread you need.

Coping with Anxiety

> O God, there is so much to be anxious about in the hospital! Will I be all right? What will the doctors do? What if the nurses don't like me? I wonder if I'll ever get used to it here—this funny hospital gown, the hard bed, this fear of embarrassing myself, no snacks between meals, strangers who don't know me but are trying to help. O God, I am so uncomfortable. But you are my friend, my helper, my comforter. Be with me now and soothe my worries. Amen.

> Therefore I tell you, do not worry about your life, what you will eat or what you will drink, or about your body, what you will wear. Is not life more than food, and the body more than clothing?...And can any of you by worrying add a single hour to your span of life? (Matthew 6:25, 27)

Thoughts on Confession

To make our confession means to draw near to God by coming clean and clear within ourselves. It means recognizing that we are human and not divine, fallible, needing to be forgiven. Confession is the path into deeper prayer. It involves a kind of intimacy and honesty that is hard, humbling, and well worth the effort.

A Prayer on a Dark Night

O God, I feel alone, frightened, and angry.
I'm afraid I won't get well.
My body hurts all over, and my spirits are so low.
I remember Jesus on the cross crying out:
"My God, my God, why have you forsaken me?" (Matthew 27:46).
I feel forsaken, but I don't want to give up.
I feel so weak and tired and discouraged. The night is long and dark.
Are you there?

A Prayer before an Operation

God is our refuge and strength,
a very present help in trouble. (Psalm 46:1)

Dear God, be with me now as I wait and try to prepare for surgery. Help me to feel your caring embrace and be strengthened by your love for me. Be with the surgeon and the nurses and all who will take care of me in the days ahead. Help my family and friends to accept this time as necessary for me. I know there will be some pain and with your presence near me I will endure as best I can, knowing it will be good enough. Amen.

If I Should Die

> If it is now time, O God, let my spirit join with yours. My body is tired, and I know you have promised eternal rest. If I feel doubt and uncertainty, fill me with your love. If I fear entering the unknown, help me to trust in your goodness. I pray for my family and friends that they may not so much mourn my absence as celebrate the memory of my presence and rejoice in my living. If I am to enter a new time and a new journey, I ask for peace, O God, and a deepening sense of your mighty grasp of me. Amen.

A Benediction

> May the strength of God guide us,
> May the power of God preserve us,
> May the wisdom of God instruct us,
> May the hand of God protect us. Amen.

CHAPTER 5

The Joy of Friendship
Robert Raines

T he week after the May 1963 civil rights demonstrations exploded in Birmingham, Alabama, a group of residents of Germantown (Philadelphia) invited the Reverend Andrew Young, Martin Luther King's right-hand man in the Southern Christian Leadership Conference, to address a public rally in our sanctuary (The First United Methodist Church of Germantown) on what was happening in Birmingham. I was one of the Co-Ministers of the Church. In the diverse crowd that gathered that night, many of whom had no relation to our church and some of whom were not Christian, were two young women. One was Joan Hemenway, 25, Associate Editor of *Youth* Magazine, a publication of the United Church of Christ. She came to cover the event for her magazine. She brought with her a friend, Jennifer Allcock, an English doctor in the United States for a year of pediatric training. Neither had ever been to First Methodist; neither had a significant relation to any congregation at the time. But intrigued that a church would hold a civil rights rally in its sanctuary, they came back on Sunday mornings to see what made us tick. They were drawn deeply into the life of the church, and in December of that year, became members, though both of them thought they would be gone from Philadelphia within six months. Jennifer was considering an offer to teach medicine in a Nigerian hospital, and Joan had made application to the Peace Corps. However, they found themselves discussing with friends in the church the possibility of engaging in some form of mission in the poverty stricken Wister area of Germantown. The wild idea came to them of renting an apartment there with the hope of helping to serve whatever human needs should manifest themselves. Jennifer had long dreamed of some day starting a medical practice in such a poverty area. Things jelled in March 1964 when both turned down their opportunities to serve abroad, and with eight other church friends committed themselves to seek some form of mission in Wister. We covenanted together to search for the shape and substance of the mission to which God would call us by committing ourselves to daily prayer and Bible study, and to meeting weekly to share insights and make decisions. At the second meeting Joan jolted the group. She had been talking with a friend about the apartment idea. The friend said, "You shouldn't rent. If you really mean business and aren't just going there to look around, you should buy a house and put your roots down." Joan said, "That would be great but we don't have any money." Her friend replied, "I'll loan you five thousand dollars." Believing that we were not likely to get more convincing leading of the Spirit than that, the ten of us decided to borrow the money and start looking for a house to buy. On August 1, 1964, Joan and Jennifer moved into the house on Bringhurst Street and began an "apostolate of being," which in the coming years would result in a medical practice for poor families and whose healing ministries brought hope to a neighborhood without hope. Initially supported by churches, individuals, and foundations, its budget eventually was in the millions. The Kingdom of God is like two women who went to live in a house on Bringhurst Street....

Covenant House was born out of the Covenant Group. In an article titled "Covenant House in Philadelphia," published in *The Christian Century* (October 27, 1965), Joan wrote "For our little gathering, those first few months were very special. Seeds were sown, fruits were realized, shared, and [the seeds] re-sown. It was glorious time when faith burst forth into so many crystals it seems that not even the heavens [were]able to contain their bounty and beauty. Meeting once a week, in Bible study, prayer, and discussion, we came to know and love one another: two ministers, a businessman, a newspaper reporter, the wives of the four, and Jennifer and me." Indeed, the first two years of the Covenant group evoked the most fruitful Bible study of which I have ever been a part and opened the door to a joyous friendship. The mutual discovery of the mission and of each other as new friends took us by surprise. It was sheer gift, like finding a pearl of great price or a treasure in a field (Matthew 13:44-45). It was a transformative experience for each of us, and, I believe, opened Joan to the possibility of ordained ministry with an eventual focus on the healing power of small group process. In addition, I entered into a friendship with Joan and Jennifer that would endure through decades of living in different cities and be renewed and deepened in these last eleven years in Guilford, Connecticut. During those decades apart, Joan kindly served as an editor for a number of my books. I watched with admiration as she went to Union Theological Seminary, was ordained, and came back to serve as an Associate Minister at First United Methodist Church of Germantown. She went on to become an ACPE supervisor, a leader in that organization, and eventually its president. She wrote a landmark book on group process, *Inside the Circle*. Along the way she resigned from the United Methodist Church in courageous protest against its discriminatory policy against gay people. In recent years she expanded her intellectual research exploring new systems of group process. In her career she has taught, mentored, and befriended many.

Her professional gifts are enormous, but the gift that means the most to me after all these years is the gift of her friendship, and the couple friendship my wife and I share with her and Jennifer here in Guilford. We feel so blessed to live near them. They are our buddies, friends to whom we turn in sorrow and in joy. Their home is an oasis of delight, comfort, and ease. We have dinner together. We enjoy sharing the same convictions and prejudices. We know we are there for one another. And in this current time of Joan's illness, we have the privilege of precious conversations, glances, touches. It is a time to savor Joan's bright spirit, her marvelous humor, her fresh ideas about books and human events, the sheer fun of being around her.

I salute you, dearest Joan, and thank God we are among those whom you call friend.

CHAPTER 6

Over the Years with Joan
Ted Loder

J oan Hemenway came to the First United Methodist Church of
Germantown in Philadelphia a year or so after I did. I came as
the young co-minister, she as an even younger woman who
gathered with a group of prospective new members at my house
one Sunday afternoon. As the group was leaving, I made some
statement with which Joan dared to let me know she firmly dis-
agreed. She stayed on several minutes to explain her position and
invited me to re-examine mine. It was a healthy antidote to a mis-
guided presumption of an immoderate pastor. Fortunately, Joan decided to join the church in spite of my miscue, and that exchange
was just the first of continuous corrective dialogues between us as
well as the beginning of a close and treasured friendship that has
spanned over forty years. More pastors could use such a personal
antidote to their pretensions. Those for whom Joan has been a colleague, clinical supervisor, teacher, or friend surely have experienced that gift and are as grateful for it as I am.

Consistently I found that wherever she is, Joan is an unmistak-
able presence. She has an edge. She is keenly intelligent and articulate. She is loyal but not blindly so. She is shy personally but
not intellectually or dialogically. She may suffer fools gladly, fortunately for many of us, but not for foolishness or dissembling or
careless thinking or sloppy conclusions. Hers is a tough love and
so a trustworthy one.

Yet Joan is a complicated person, hard to characterize. Any
profile of her will inevitably fall short of a full picture of this
amazing woman. With that caveat, I've come up with three descriptive phrases in my brief effort to present key attributes of Joan
as I experienced her through the years: 1) processing integrity; 2)

empathetic realism; 3) relational particularity.

The first attribute, Joan's processing integrity, has been a necessity in her life. By processing I mean a primary dynamic psychic/spiritual activity which distinguishes a person's identity. Such processing takes the courage, persistence, breadth of vision, hope, and honesty typical of Joan. By integrity I mean the effort to integrate the parts and phases of one's life into a more complete whole, an increasingly healthy condition. Processing integrity, then, touches on the theological issues of faith, grace, and salvation, which is frequently defined as a state of wholeness or restoration of the broken pieces of one's life. And like faith, grace, and salvation, processing integrity is ongoing. I believe this ongoing effort is an essential attribute of Joan's life and work.

In any case, it is what I saw Joan constantly engaged in doing for herself and for others. She struggled with the wounds and deprivations of her childhood and early adulthood, perhaps particularly those from her father who, after her mother's death, essentially disowned her. She went through a private wrestling with her sexual orientation until middle age. She had so many gifts that it was a struggle to find a professional focus or outlet for them. In her younger years she endured the typical oppression of women. In the years after she moved to New York City she could not find a church community to which she could commit and in which she might feel accepted and respected. Her continual processing integrity defined her. It was her core identity and direction in everything she did and in her working through all her relationships, as I will elaborate on later.

When I first knew Joan, she was on the staff of *Youth* magazine, the United Church of Christ publication which was unquestionably the best, most thoughtful, and theologically clarifying periodical for young people in the country. She wrote brilliant, illuminating articles, did wonderful interviews, helped to edit, and could have become the editor of the magazine. But she decided it wasn't her calling in spite of the mutually respectful relationship she had with the editor for whom she worked.

As a lay person in the church, she helped me and the whole congregation negotiate a turbulent breakdown in a staff relationship.

She was one of a small group that began Covenant House, a medical mission to a poverty area in the Germantown section of Philadelphia where she lived with Jennifer Allcock, M.D. Joan and Jennifer became close friends but had to go their separate ways for many reasons, one of them being the realization that being the part-time, informal social worker of the project was not Joan's calling.

Joan's processing integrity was part of each of those experiences as she tried to bring together the pieces of her life in a meaningful direction. It also gave her a diversity of experiences and exposure to a wide variety of people that deepened her self-awareness as well as her experiential understanding of human beings and their struggles.

Her processing took her off to Union Theological Seminary, at first as an experiment, a testing of her spiritual longings. It turned out to be a seminal experience, and Joan got her M.Div. and went on to train in clinical pastoral education. At the same time she was one of the leaders of the Women's Group of First United Methodist Church of Germantown (FUMCG) that advocated for feminist issues and theology in the church and community. That was another processing integrity effort for Joan.

That experience prompted her to begin the procedure for ordination in the United Methodist Church. FUMCOG rejoiced to recommend her. But being ordained in a church which Joan was not at all sure would fully accept and confirm her for the woman she was made it a risky venture. Even in the years after her ordination Joan had a rather tentative relationship with the United Methodist Church, though she responsibly met her obligations to it, partly out of love and loyalty, partly because her ordination was critical to her vocation as a CPE Supervisor. It was hard for her to negotiate some of the discriminatory positions and practices of the United Methodist Church, but she managed with the support of a visionary bishop and many clergy who knew and respected her. So the processing went on.

After a short period as a highly respected associate pastor at FUMCOG, during which she also served as a hospital chaplain at the Hospital of the University of Pennsylvania and helped me through a difficult run-up to a divorce, Joan decided she had found her calling in CPE. She served first in Philadelphia as a chaplain and pastoral counselor, then as chaplain and CPE supervisor at New York City's Sloan Kettering, then in Hartford, Connecticut, and finally Bridgeport, Connecticut. She has emerged as a leader, teacher, and sought after CPE supervisor, speaker, and pastoral counselor. She has published many articles as well as the critically acclaimed, *Inside the Circle*, on the crucial importance of process groups in CPE. In November 2005 Joan was proud to be elected President of the Association for Clinical Pastoral Education.

Joan's processing integrity has generated significant progress toward more wholeness and restoration of the broken pieces and relationships of Joan's life. Before moving on, some integrating steps in her processing should be described.

The first is the restoration of family of origin ties through Joan's investment and delight in her two nieces, the daughters of her sister. Joan has been an integral part of the nieces' lives since infancy and in that way she has reworked and deepened her relationship with her sister and stood with her sister through a difficult marriage and divorce. Primarily through Joan's processing integration a newer, healthier experience of family has resulted for Joan and the family. The processing is ongoing and family differences are enriching rather than threatening.

The second step, also ongoing, is the fulfillment of the relationship between Joan and her beloved partner, Jennifer Allcock. This relationship had been difficult due to the social sickness that disallowed expression of a love and commitment that did not match social norms and therefore needed to be hidden. To go through the years of hiding involved courage, pain, and trust. The fulfillment of Joan and Jennifer's personal relationship has also contributed to the healing of social brokenness and led to a broader inclusion in the processing.

The third piece in the processing of integrity was Joan's turning in her ordination orders in protest of the United Methodist Church trial of Beth Stroud for her homosexuality that resulted in the rescinding of Beth's ordination as a clergy person. Beth had been a member of FUMCOG during her college years and served as an associate minister before and during her trial. A result of her processing integrity, Joan's protest has been liberating for herself and for the church. And Joan's processing integrity goes on in her struggle with her debilitating illness and its prognosis. That struggle is an inspiration to the processing integrity for all who know and love her.

The second attribute I want to present in this article is Joan's empathetic realism. This empathetic realism follows from her processing integrity and is actually a function of it. Joan has the capacity to empathize with all sorts and conditions of people in the various struggles of their lives. That capacity enables her to establish a bond of trust with them and to understand them viscerally as well as intellectually. It also helps to keep relationships more symmetrical than hierarchical, whether with friends, students, or other professionals.

Her capacity for realism also builds trust. Realism dispels the fog of sentimentality that often reduces empathy to mere sympathy and encourages self-pity and/or an attitude of victimization in the parties involved. Sentimentality renders empathy impotent to impel change and growth in a person, situation, or relationship. To effect such change requires the realism of honest assessment, recognition, and a willingness to work toward the desired change or more healthy condition.

Joan is an empathetic realist. She worked at recognizing and accepting her responsibility for whatever deprivations and issues she was confronting in her own life. The emotion which characterized true empathy arose from the pain of those deprivations and issues, but was not a cheap sentiment poured over them. Honest emotion was fuel for her processing integrity. She refused to see herself as a victim and did not accept either internal or external conditions as intractable, only difficult.

Joan was never afflicted with the sort of idealistic perfectionism that subverts efforts to change one's life and situation. She was constantly about trying to change, continually moving toward better possibilities. Much of what I related in the processing integrity section of this article exemplifies that about her, so it is unnecessary to reiterate them at this point.

It is also true that Joan's empathetic realism shaped her personal theology and her relationship to the church. Her religious stance is rooted basically in the relevance of religion to the present struggles of human beings. I think she came to believe that God was in "the between" of people. Precisely because God's kingdom is in the midst of us God is discerned in our relationships and not in abstract suppositions.

That conviction energized her faith and drive to find more wholeness in herself and her relationships with others, both within the church and outside of it. Or, perhaps it is more accurate to say that her faith enabled her to walk with one foot in the church and one foot out. Social and cultural expressions of church theology mattered more to her than liturgical and doctrinal expressions. For Joan, the latter could not justify any form of oppression, exclusion, discrimination, injustice, or violence. She not only empathized with those who experienced the consequences of such a theology, but she supported and joined active, realistic protest and advocated remedial policies for herself and others.

The other dimension of Joan's empathetic realism is obvious in her vocational choice of counseling and CPE. Empathy and realism are key aspects of effective therapy with clients of any and all descriptions. That's what made Joan such an excellent counselor, chaplain (especially in a hospital setting where realism, however gently offered, is essential to patients and families facing and dealing with trauma), CPE supervisor, and teacher.

I will share one of many possible personal examples of Joan's empathetic realism in a relational context. When Joan was on the FUMCOG staff there were two disturbing crises for me and the church. One was a staff conflict which escalated into a full blown battle and threatened to split the congregation. The other, which also became a public squabble three years later, was the inception of my bitter divorce from my first wife of 22 years. In both instances Joan empathized with me and the painful difficulties I was experiencing, but she also helped me find realistic options to try to resolve and heal the breaches. She was not the only counselor to me or to the church in these chaotic episodes, but she was a very important one. Empathetic realism characterized her ministry at

FUMCOG. During that time she became and continues to be a role model for women in the church and, I venture to say, for many clergy, CPE students, and therapists. I am one who is grateful for his gift from her.

Finally, the third attribute of Joan I want to present is her relational particularity. Perhaps this is too contrived a term for a relatively simple quality, but what I mean is that she individualizes each of her relationships. That may be harder to do than it seems. Of course, there is a degree of general categorization of people in her relationships, but it is minimal. She tries not to assign people to categories but rather tries to respond to them as particular individuals. She tries not to reduce complex realities or persons into simplistic codes—clients with particular diagnoses, a typical male, a classic female, straight people, gay people, married, single or divorced people—and then assume that those codes refer to similar problems and that responses can be effectively and efficiently pre-packaged. That may be a convenient and common methodology but it is a distorting and dehumanizing one. Such expedient objectification of persons was not Joan's way. Her relational particularity is also part of her processing integrity, so I will be brief about this attribute and trust that it is evident to those who know Joan and in what I have said about her.

Joan has struggled all her life to be a subject and resisted all attempts to make her an object. She has insisted that others respect that about her. She establishes and keeps boundaries with people and respects those of others. She maintains a core of privacy and resists uninvited incursions into that privacy. This was one way she acknowledged the particularity of relationships. She is also aware that particularity is an unavoidable aspect of the loneliness of being a human being. I have no data to confirm my supposition that the emphasis on affirming herself and others as subjects made relational particularity an underlying influence on her counseling, teaching, and work as a CPE supervisor. But I would surmise that for her the purpose of counseling was to heal persons not by some pre-determined outcome according to categories of mental health but to help them find, claim, exercise, and be subjects in the relational particularity of their lives.

Indeed, Joan's sense of herself and others as subjects kept her from making premature decisions about her vocation and prevented her from becoming locked into any relational situation which diminished her own particularity or that of others. An example is her advocacy of feminism and feminist theology. The goal was not to shift women from one object category to another but to liberate women to be the particular subjects they are and to trust and use their particular gifts. For women relational particularity involves establishing or recognizing inherent boundaries, accepting limits, acknowledging and trusting their core of privacy as human, female and mortal, and so grounding themselves in their particularity to be able to resist selling out to external pressures of conformity and the marketing of themselves as products.

When Joan was a FUMCOG staff colleague she was the only woman for most of her tenure. She insisted that we respect her relational particularity and her being a subject and not classified as minister, or associate, or woman, or feminist, or pastoral counselor. In turn, she responded to staff persons who were very different as subjects, and she dealt with each of us with relational particularity. She helped confirm me as a subject, not a member of some class such as a clergy, and she encouraged me to respond to every situation with relational particularity. I suspect she has helped others in similar ways over the years.

One last thought. Joan and I had many lengthy theological discussions. Many of them were in the direction of confirming God as the "Thou" to which our "I" is addressed, as well as is the "us" of the Lord's Prayer. We came "to see through a glass darkly" that the heart of faith, prayer, worship, awe, morality, of even life itself, is, as Jesus revealed, in our addressing God as a subject in relational particularity. "I" to "Thou" as Buber put it. In my last conversation with Joan, we touched again on that view, but at that moment, she didn't have the energy to pursue it. As I sat looking at her, I realized that perhaps not consciously, or with certainty, that was what Joan has been about in the entirety of her life. It is to that "Thou" I commend Joan with profound love and gratitude.

CHAPTER 7

Holding on While Letting Go...
Audun M. Ulland

Abstract

This contribution reflects on the impact Rev. Dr. Joan E. Hemenway had as a CPE supervisor on my chaplaincy and her skills in group process had on my work as a group analyst. I also address her impact as a friend. I illustrate how her methods and theories in the CPE Open Agenda groups in 1999, which were based on Wilfrid Bion's (1961) theory of basic assumptions and developed in her book *Inside the Circle* (1996), correspond with the latest current psychoanalytic contribution of Anthony Bateman and Peter Fonagy (2006), defined as the Mentalization-Based Therapy.

The title of this chapter is not my own, but Joan's title from her booklet of reflections in times of grave illness (Hemenway, 2004; See Chapter 4 in this volume). I have borrowed her words because they so precisely describe my own feelings ever since I received the sad news about her grave illness. As I write this I realize how difficult it is to reflect on "while letting go." Actually I am not sure if I am ready for that step yet. That is the context of this writing. In a couple of days I am flying to Guilford for three days to hold on to Joan before I can let go on my own, most probably without her. I am not only writing this to honour my most important supervisor, but also to honour one of my best friends.

Before I proceed let me introduce myself. My name is Audun Magne Ulland. I am an ordained Lutheran minister and a licensed group analyst. I have been a chaplain since 1993. I first heard of

Joan Hemenway in 1998. After five years as a chaplain in a psychiatric hospital I had come to what Yvonne Agazarian (2001) describes as a "fork in the road." I needed a deeper theological understanding and a stronger identity as a chaplain, and I applied for my first Clinical Pastoral Education program in the United States.

I asked one of Norway's leading CPE supervisors, Reverend Kirsti Mosvold for advice. She looked down the list of summer programs, stopped at one name, looked at me and said; "Audun, it has to be Joan Hemenway! The goddess of CPE! I just know she will be the best one for you! But hurry up; send your application soon, her programs fill up quickly." I called "the goddess" the following day. She sounded surprisingly normal and practical over the phone. She said my request to have most of my training in psychiatric units could be arranged as could a place to stay at the dorm. But most important, she said, was that the long written application and $100.00 fee should be sent to her very soon. She told me these last requirements in a kind but firm way, and I had no doubt that if CPE was going to happen the next step was mine.

Eight months later Dr. Joan Hemenway was my supervisor. My first morning at Bridgeport Hospital she welcomed me with a hug, gave me compliments about my Scandinavian appearance, and said she was happy to have a student who made it all the way from Norway. Again I was surprised how normal, human, and vivid this goddess was. Maybe she understood that this tense Norwegian student had to ease up a little bit before he was ready to sit down and get inside the circle.

CPE with Joan is "start working" from moment one. We had not come all the way to Bridgeport to relax, but to learn by practicing chaplaincy. With authority, inspiration, and progression she moved us through the first week. We got the message: morning report starts at 8:00, not 8:03. There was no doubt about who the captain was on this boat! The seven of us may have felt very secure about holding on to her this week, but she made it very clear "the Hemenway way," it was time to let go! Saturday needed an on-call chaplain! So the first week of introduction ended with a call for one of us to take the first on-call duty. I volunteered and got a beeper. My first on-call turned out to be a nightmare, and the beeper and I really never got along after it.

It did not take me long though before I loved CPE, or as Joan expressed it: "Audun, you eat CPE!" For years I had been looking and longing for a discipline that combined theology and psychology and finally I had found it.

At that time Joan used Wilfrid Bion's (1961) basic assumptions theory for her process groups. This was before her training with Yvonne Agazarian and Systems-Centered Therapy functional sub-group methods (Agazarian & Gantt, 2000). In the open agenda group Joan often made this observation: check out your assumptions, this is important! Most of the time, she said this somewhat playfully, as if encouraging us to play with reality. For me it became extremely important to check my assumptions about Joan, about my peers, about my church, and about my relationships with important others. Even though Bion groups are known for frustration and aggression, Joan was able to establish safety and a working culture in the group that made it secure enough to check my assumptions and to play! Oh, what a breakthrough that was! And what a release to discover how many of the assumptions had a place only in my head and not in the outer world. Through this method I found enough confidence to share material with my peers from the "dark side of the human life," stories and feelings that I had never shared with others before. Joan did not say much in these groups, but as an active listener she filled the room. In this way she became an important role model for my later work as a group analyst.

Actually I was reminded of Joan's group process work last week when I attended a workshop in London with the psychoanalysts Anthony Bateman and Peter Fonagy about Mentalization-Based Therapy and Attachment Theory, one of the latest "hot" theories and methods in group treatment of personality disorders. I found it very interesting how they described non-mentalizing processes as the inner stance that never checks out the assumptions of the other, and how mentalizing processes first become mentalizing when the assumptions of the other are checked out and then reflected on (Bateman & Fonagy, 2006). I mention this to give an example how updated, skilled, and advanced Joan's knowledge of different theories about group processes is, and how well she integrates theory in her performance as a group conductor!

Writing this contribution to the festschrift has given me an opportunity to go through the weekly reflection reports I wrote as a CPE student. In many ways this is my 11th reflection report, 7 years after I wrote my tenth. When reflecting today on what Joan has meant to me as a supervisor, this comes to my mind: CONNECTION through REFLECTION. The outcome of my CPE was an increased connection with God, with others, with myself (including the lighter and the darker sides of myself), with the chaplain inside me, and last but not least, with Joan as a friend. It is impossible to outline which connection was most important because each has felt extremely important and in many ways they connect to each other.

In CPE one of my struggles was whether or not I could be a good enough chaplain. I was confused about my theology and chaplaincy. I was angry and hurt with my own church. Joan urged me to reflect on these issues and that was hard work.

In Mentalization-Based Therapy, the therapist tries to keep the thinking process going by encouraging the individual to see the Other as an intentional being, with her or his own intentions, motives, thoughts, and emotions. In situations when overwhelmed with emotions, in order to keep the Self protected, the tendency is to create a "psychic equivalence," and the individual claims that what is true "out there" is equivalent to what is true "in here." In Mentalization-Based Therapy, the individual is encouraged to check out his or her assumption about the Other. In doing so the person realizes that what is frequently claimed as a categorical statement or truth about the Other is just an assumption that needs to be reflected on. When the individual starts to reflect on the other perspectives the therapist or the other group members suggest, the mentalizing capacity increases and the Other becomes an Intentional being.

Although the CPE context of supervisor and student is different from the therapeutic context of therapist and patient, I would be surprised if I am the only student Joan supervised who developed an increased mentalizing capacity due to her methods and her focus on checking out my assumptions about the Other. In CPE training situations often occur that are emotionally stressful and difficult. Under these circumstances our ability to reflect is put under pressure. Joan continually invited us to check out our assumptions in order to recapture the reflective mode.

I think Joan's goal and hope for us was that through reflection we would make a better, more solid connection with the different parts of our life. Individual supervision and the open agenda group (plus Joan's remarkable marks on the left side of the reflection report) were one long psychological process that made it possible to accept and to connect to myself in new ways. Freed from my scary fantasies about others, especially my church, I could walk into new rooms, surprised to find the doors open, not closed. I came to Bridgeport confused and grey; I left Bridgeport proud and blooming! This method is what Bateman and Fonagy recognize as the core in Mentalization-Based group therapy!

Today I recognize that reconciliation also took place in this process. Swedish theologian and psychotherapist Göran Bergström claims, "The Reconciliation can first take place when we start speaking honest..." (Bergström, 2000). To illustrate this he uses the examples of Cain and Job, and he challenges chaplains and therapists to use these stories in work with clients who are deeply hurt. Bergström underlines the reason that Cain never came to reconciliation with God had to do with Cain's inner stance. His eyes and ears were closed for any honest dialogue God tried to have with him. Cain was too hurt. The only thing Cain was able to focus on was the fruit of the ground, the symbol of the offering God had ignored and the symbol of the offence.

Job, on the other hand, never stopped his honest dialogue with God. With great intensity he kept asking God what he had done and why he had to suffer. Through honest speaking, reconciliation took place between God and Job. Job found his way back to the good father he once had confidence in and was able to recapture the relationship with God, "his father." For me to start CPE grey and confused and leave CPE proud and blooming, meant that I had to move from the position of Cain to that of Job.

I mentioned earlier how my CPE experience with Joan turned into an experience of being increasingly connected. When Joan found out I was coming to Guilford to see her, she immediately invited those involved with this festschrift to a gathering in her and Jennifer's home—"Just so you can meet and get to know each other...." Even in the midst of grave illness Joan continues to help humans to connect!

I will close this contribution the same way I closed my final evaluation of my relationship to Joan at Bridgeport Hospital back in 1999:

> "Father, the son said, I've sinned against God and against you. I am no longer fit to be called your son." But the father called his servants. "Hurry"! He said. "Bring the best robe and put it on him. Put a ring on his finger and shoes on his feet. Then go and get the prize calf and kill it, and let us celebrate with a feast.... We had to celebrate and rejoice, because this brothers of yours was dead and had come to life; he was lost and has been found" (Luke 15).

In my church I often felt like the prodigal son. As he must have felt confused whether or not his father would accept him, I have felt confused whether or not the church would accept me. Thank you, Joan, for not only being my supervisor, but also for being my minister: a minister who so deeply reflected God's grace, God's love, and God's care; who put the best robe on me and said "Let us celebrate, the table is ready"!

I needed to meet you Rev. Joan Hemenway at this time of my life. I needed your holding and containing, the blessing, acceptance, and encouragement from you as a clergy about my own ministry. To trust has never been easy for me. I have been afraid of being harmed and hurt by trusting the wrong person. I managed, though, to trust you. It was easier to trust you than to distrust you. Because you always pointed out and underlined for me that the best robe and a ring was offered to me, and the table set. I have heard the underlying tone in your work with me: "Welcome Home, Audun, to yourself and to your chaplaincy."

Your ministry as well as your knowledge of psychology and theology, along with your gift of sharing that knowledge, has been an inspiration. Through didactics skill training and verbatims, this CPE turned out to become so much more than I hoped for; an experience and a journey for me that will go on. I have eaten CPE with huge bites, it tastes good, and I am still hungry for more. I think CPE at some level will be a part of my future life! This start has been so fulfilling, it has been all I longed for. What more can I say? (Audun Ulland, Bridgeport Hospital, August 13, 1999)

Instead of our plan to celebrate the 2006 New Years Holiday in London, we will see each other in Guilford in a couple of days, Joan. For me that means an opportunity to still hold on to you. That is truly a gift and a blessing from God. I also hope it will make the "letting go" part easier. Or as one of my patient at the Psychiatric Unit in Bridgeport, diagnosed with paranoid schizophrenia, once wrote. "In my life I have seen people come and go. But it seems like when you go, you are always leaving something behind."

Oslo, Norway
October 2006

References

Agazarian, Y. (2001). *A systems-centered approach to inpatient group psychotherapy.* London: Jessica Kingsley Publishers.

Agazarian, Y. & Gantt, S. (2000). *Autobiography of a theory: Developing a theory of living human systems and its systems-centered practice.* London: Jessica Kingsley Publishers.

Bateman, A., Fonagy, P. (2006). *Mentalization-based treatment for borderline personality disorder.* Oxford: Oxford University Press.

Bion, W. (1961). *Experiences in Groups and Other Papers.* London: Tavistock Publications Ltd.

Bergström, G. (2000). Försoningen kan börja när man talar ärligt

(Reconciliation can first start, when we start speaking honest). *Norwegian Journal of Pastoral Care_*(Tidsskrift for sjelesorg)(3), 24-35.

Hemenway, J. (2004). *Holding on while letting go: Reflections in times of grave illness, revised edition.* Cleveland: Pilgrim Press.

Hemenway, J. (1996). *Inside the circle: A historical and practical inquiry concerning process groups in clinical pastoral education.* Decatur, GA: Journal of Pastoral Care Publications Inc.

PART TWO

Systems-Centered Training and CPE Supervision

CHAPTER 8

A Systems-Centered Approach
Yvonne M Agazarian

T his paper is dedicated to Joan E. Hemenway, for her understanding of a systems-centered approach, for her participation in it, and for her friendship. It is with sadness
that we recognize that her contributions to the field have come to
an end, and we share the existential grief of losing someone we
cannot bear to lose.

Introduction

The theory of living human systems defines a hierarchy of isomorphic systems that are energy-organizing, goal-directed, and self-
correcting. The first application of this theory was in the field of
psychotherapy (Agazarian, 1997). However, thanks to isomorphy
(systems in a defined hierarchy are similar in structure and function), the principles of application apply to all living human systems, and the current focus is as much on organizations in the
private and public sectors as it is in clinical settings (Gantt &
Agazarian, 2005). The systems-centered approach is a theory driven
system, and the methods and techniques are derived from the opera-
tional definitions of the constructs. Thus each intervention tests
both the validity of the theory and the reliability of its practice.

Developing Systems-Centered Practice

The first time the theory was tested in practice was with forty
people, who came from different groups that I had led in Austin,

Boston, New York, and Philadelphia. We gathered in Newark in 1991 to explore the impact of this novel theoretical approach on the dynamics of groups. This experiment continued annually, and by 1995 the systems-centered orientation was formalized as Systems-Centered Therapy (SCT). Through this process, the Systems-Centered Training and Research Institute emerged, and our first conference was held in 1997.

All the early experimental methods of putting theory into practice were tried out in the context of training groups, where the members gave feedback on what did and did not work. Although some of my innovations seemed to fly in the face of my own training (both in psychodynamics and group dynamics), they turned out to introduce useful methods to both the theory and the practice of Systems-Centered Therapy.

Context

In clinical work, thinking "systems" appeared to significantly reduce the tendency to personalize all experience and to understand that it was the personalized view of childhood that engendered painful disappointment and resentment. The systems-centered perspective views childhood in the context of a family system. Family is seen as a system of inter-locking systems, each of which contributes to keeping the family stable. It is the family system, not the person, which elicits family roles. Thus, it can be argued that system dynamics have more influence on who and how one can be than do person dynamics, and that this is as true in adult life as in childhood.

Viewing the past through the lens of systems also brings into awareness that the sometimes painful role relationships, forged in compromise, were the best that two humans could do to make a relationship. Recognizing the benefits as well as the costs of early role systems can permanently change the recall of childhood events and the adult experience of the present. When the pleasure and love, as well as the pain, anger, and hatred, are experienced, the split between good and bad is undone. In systems language, crossing the boundary between the person system (a world of one) to the system context of relationships (a world of two, three, or many) is a developmental step towards the awareness that even though we can not have the relationships we want in our fantasy, we can have the relationship we can make in our reality.

In organizations, thinking about the various contexts as systems, e.g. a meeting, a briefing session with the boss, or a negotiation with another department, reduces the tendency to take system dynamics personally. Frustration is inevitable in the work place, and frustrations easily arouse irritability and the impulse to take our frustrations out on others, particularly those in authority. Thinking systems adds an objective dimension to frustrating situations. The impulse to act out the hurt and blameful feelings is more easily contained when one has a bird's eye view of events. Seeing from a system's perspective, personalized energy is more likely to be freed so that it can be directed towards the goals of work (Agazarian & Philibossian, 1998).

Boundary Permeability

An essential aspect of applying systems thinking is managing the appropriate permeability of boundaries within and between systems. All systems open their boundaries to clear information and close their boundaries to noise, defined by Shannon and Weaver (1964) as ambiguities, contradictions and redundancies. As Shannon and Weaver demonstrated, there is an inverse relationship between noise in the communication channel and the probability that the information contained in the channel will transfer. The challenge for SCT was to develop methods to reduce 'noise' in communication so that more information is available to solve the problems that lie between the system and its goals.

SCT is both deeply grateful, and deeply indebted to Kurt Lewin (1957) for his concept of the force field, which is the basic orientation in all SCT methods for change. The force field identifies the driving and retraining forces that hold a system in equilibrium. Thus every force field gives an active picture of where a system 'is' along its path to its goal in that moment in time. There are two ways of influencing how a system moves towards its goal. One is to increase the driving forces; the other is to reduce the restraining forces. Lewin pointed out that movement towards the goal is more easily obtained by reducing the restraining forces (so that drive energy is released) than it is by increasing the driving forces (a method which requires additional energy to overcome the restraints). Reducing restraining forces that the system is ready to weaken is a core concept in SCT.

Deliberately reducing the ambiguities, redundancies, and contradictions in communication so that information can be exchanged within and between systems is an example of putting this concept into practice. SCT calls the methods for so doing "the hierarchy of defense modification," in which the restraining forces to system development, inherent to each phase of development, are deliberately reduced (Agazarian, 1997). Each restraining force that is reduced releases the drive which moves the system along its developmental path.

In practice, for example, reducing social or politically correct behavior releases the potential for authentic and spontaneous responses. Reducing anxiety provoking thoughts, like negative predictions about reality, increases the potential to explore and test reality. Reducing the straightjacket of tension that constricts access to information in the physical experiences of the body increases the potential for integrating both cognitive and sensory information. (One of the goals of SCT is to make the boundary appropriately permeable between comprehensive and apprehensive experience.) Reducing the restraining forces to development increases the potential for developmental information to cross the boundaries between and within systems thus increasing the flow of energy and information. Miller, in his introduction to *Living Systems* (1978) equates energy and information. Accepting this equation, SCT claims that the amount of energy available to a system will be determined by the discrimination and integration of information that has crossed its boundaries. Information, then, is energy without which systems cannot survive. Fundamental to this process is the organization of information. Organizing information is a process which depends on the ability to discriminate and integrate both similarities and differences.

Discriminating and Integrating Information

The developmental process of all living beings, including human beings, relies on the process of coming together around similarities and separating around differences. A theory of living human systems assumes that systems develop by discriminating differences in the apparently similar and similarities in the apparently different, as well as by integrating the information. Observing group life from this perspective makes it clear that this is exactly how people behave: coming together when there is sufficient similarity, splitting away when the differences are too different.

Integration of differences into the whole is a great challenge. Difficulties in integrating differences leads to the formation of a series of separated group systems, which have one communication pattern within them and another communication pattern between them. This in turn gives rise to the many different versions of 'them and us' around race, gender, age, class, etc. Scapegoating is often the outcome of this process. These realities challenged SCT to discover methods that increase the potential for tolerating and integrating differences instead of splitting around them.

Functional Subgrouping

The SCT conflict resolution technique of functional subgrouping encourages groups to discriminate and integrates differences instead of scapegoating them. Functional subgroups manage differences by requiring members of group systems to come together around their similarities instead of separating around their differences. This introduces a different kind of communication pattern into the system. In SCT members are required to say "anybody else" as soon as they have finished saying what they want to say.

Saying "anybody else" calls for a "join and build on" response on the part of other members and discourages the more familiar "yes...but" response.

Members who have a difference are asked to hold back until the first subgroup has become established and has done the work of exploring their point of view. This allows the subgroup to develop a supportive communication pattern that encourages discovery. As the first subgroup continues to explore, small differences naturally arise and become integrated. The greater the emergence and integration of difference within the subgroup, the greater the development of the capacity to discriminate and integrate.

When the energy within the first subgroup comes to rest, space is made for the work of the subgroup that held a difference. The work of this second subgroup repeats the process. The final step occurs when the similarities between the two 'different' subgroups are perceived and integration takes place in the system-as-a-whole.

The method of functional subgrouping has had a significant impact on both clinical and organizational interventions. Functional subgrouping develops a climate that enables the exploration of issues rather than avoidance or enactment. In clinical work, this enables exploration of underlying dynamics in a climate of containment and support rather than angst. In organizations, the emphasis on enquiry into all sides of every question weakens the drive to flight/fight and increases the drive to work (Gantt & Agazarian, 2005).

Phases of System Development

SCT takes for granted that there are predictable, observable phases of system development that follow a specific sequence that can be identified and described. Among the many theorists who have defined phases of development, SCT owes its greatest debt to Bennis and Shepard (1957). They identified three phases of development: authority, intimacy, and work. SCT has not only identified the force fields in these phases and their subphases, but has developed specific methods to reduce the restraining forces in each. It became apparent that when phase issues are explored in subgroups instead of enacted, certain specific, predictable developmental events are common to all systems no longer occurred. For example, the emergence of the identified patient and scapegoat roles does not occur when both sides of the conflict these roles represent are explored in subgroups. In the case of the identified patient, the drive to give care and seek care is discovered as common to all. In the case of scapegoating, there is insight into the human drive to externalize reactions to difference.

A significant advantage of identifying each phase and subphase by the constellation of driving and restraining forces is that it makes it possible to diagnose the phase in which a system is working (whether the system is a dyad, small group, large or larger group, or even an individual). When the phase is identified, it becomes possible for the SCT leader to choose the SCT methods or techniques specific to the phase that will enable the work. Keeping the phase context for work in mind is important to the SCT orientation.

For example, in all organizational or clinical groups there is a common pattern that SCT calls "leapfrogging" that frequently occurs when the group is close to flight. Leapfrogging jumps from the past into the future and over the present ("It didn't work before so it won't work now."). When the group is asked how the present is different from the past, the group is directed to gather present data and in the process the implied negative predictions about the future are undone.

This next example introduces implications that may be important clinically. Depression and despair frequently surface together. When this occurs, SCT clinicians make a judgment about the phase of system development in order to make interventions that will be supported by the context. Thus, in the fight phase, subgroups are encouraged to explore how the depressive reaction is the consequence of turning frustration and rage back on the self instead of recognizing the impulse to retaliate. In this earlier phase, the system is not yet prepared to work with despair.

Thus work with despair is delayed until the system is in the intimacy phase, where the foundation for exploring the dynamics of separation and individuation has already been laid. Exploring despair dynamics of loneliness, alienation, and bitterness in a subgroup of members who share these feelings makes it possible to experience them but also to experience feeling contained and understood. It is unlikely that in the earlier phases of development the group would have been able to provide a subgroup. Exploring the dynamics of despair without a subgroup is likely to repeat and reinforce the experience rather than change it.

All SCT work is done in functional subgrouping. Subgrouping leads to a supportive, containing climate that encourages exploration rather than an enactment of the common tendency to blame and scapegoat. The emphasis is on choosing which side of every conflict to explore first, without defensive explaining or psychologizing. Although SCT methods require leaders to shift from active listening to active intervention, psychodynamic insights continue to emerge from the preconscious and from the understanding of transference.

Perhaps a significant contribution is that the systems-centered approach can speed up the initial phases of therapy. Anxiety is reduced more quickly, as is depression and maladaptive roles. In other words, the authority phase in system development is managed with less anxiety and more mastery, including the work of modifying the negative transference. In the intimacy phase, subgrouping containment fosters the work related to maladaptive roles and early attachment issues with less angst and more integration. In the work phase, where the SCT methods are familiar and almost automatic, the group can orient itself to subgroup around whatever restraining forces emerge on the path to the goals.

Conclusion

The systems-centered approach offers a method in which differences are discriminated and integrated and the appropriate permeability of boundaries is addressed. SCT applies not only to the world of therapy and organizations but to all living human systems. Functional subgrouping, which is perhaps SCT's major contribution, is not only a conflict resolution technique, but also the fundamental method that distinguishes SCT and non-SCT groups.

References

Agazarian, Y. (2007). *Selected papers*. London: Karnac Books.

Agazarian, Y. (1997). *Systems-centered therapy for groups.* Guilford, New York: Karnac Books.

Agazarian, Y. & Gantt, S. (2003). Phases of group development: Systems-centered hypotheses and their implications for research and practice. *Group dynamics: Theory, Research and Practice*, 7(3), 238-252.

Agazarian, Y. & Gantt, S. (2000). *Autobiography of a theory*. London: Jessica Kingsley.

Agazarian, Y. & Philibossian, B. (1998). A theory of living human systems as an approach to leadership of the future with examples of how it works. In E. Klein, F. Gabelnick, & P. Herr (Eds.), *The psychodynamics of leadership* (pp.127-160). Madison, CT: Psychosocial Press.

Bennis, W. G., & Shepard, H. A. (1957). A theory of group development. *Human Relations, 9(*4), 415-437.

Gantt, S. & Agazarian, Y.M. (Eds.). (2005). *SCT in action, applying the systems-centered approach in organization.* London: Karnac Books.

Lewin, K. (1951). *Field theory in social science.* New York: Harper & Row.

Miller, J. (1978). *Living systems*. New York: McGraw-Hill.

Shannon, C. E., & Weaver, W. (1964). *The mathematical theory of communication.* Illinois: University of Illinois Press.

CHAPTER 9

The Clinical Pastoral Circle: Using Systems-Centered
Methods to Develop a Clinical Pastoral Team
Susan P. Gantt

C linical Pastoral Education has a long tradition of placing an emphasis on experiential learning. Within this tradition Joan Hemenway's classic text, *Inside the Circle* (1996), has been central in developing the group process component of the CPE. Joan's impact on the Clinical Pastoral Education process with this book is greater than many make in a lifetime, yet she did not stop there. Instead, she did what few accomplished leaders do. Relatively late in her career she began to explore a new approach to group work, the systems-centered approach, to see what it might hold for Clinical Pastoral Education. This led to her more recent contribution, "Opening Up the Circle," published in *SCT in Action* (Hemenway, 2005a) and reprinted with small modifications in the *Journal of Pastoral Care and Counseling* (Hemenway, 2005b). In "Opening Up the Circle" Joan addresses some of the challenges process groups in Clinical Pastoral Education face and re-thinks these challenges from a systems-centered perspective.

Joan's far-sightedness and willingness to venture beyond what she knew led her to Systems-Centered Training (SCT) developed by Yvonne Agazarian and to apply SCT theory and methods to Clinical Pastoral Education. Joan, who was strong on synthesizing, was drawn to the integrative aspect of SCT. As she put it: "On a theoretical level Agazarian is making an ambitious attempt to integrate general systems theory (von Bertalanffy), psychoanalytic tradition (Bion), field theory (Lewin), communication theory (Korsybski & Watzlawick), and developmental psychology (Erikson)" (Hemenway, 1996, p. 194). Furthermore, Joan recognized the usefulness of systems-centered methods for opening boundaries to difference, a value dear to Clinical Pastoral Education (Hemenway, 2005a, 2005b) and one that SCT has developed practical methods to address. She also intuited the usefulness of a group model that not only reduces pathologizing, but also lowers the tendency to personalize one's own responses or the responses of others (personalizing is often the bane of experiential education). She also understood the usefulness of applying the systems-centered model of role, goal, and context and being clear that the primary goal of a process group in CPE is educational. In sum, part of Joan's legacy was to suggest and identify ways that SCT "...can make a substantial contribution to CPE group process work" (Hemenway, 2005a, p. 82).

I offer this brief article in tribute to Joan's leadership in bringing SCT into Clinical Pastoral Education. I will describe an application of systems-centered methods in the organizational context of developing a CPE center.

Brief Introduction to the Theory of Living Human Systems

Interestingly, Joan's use of the metaphor of the circle to represent the CPE process group is near and dear to the heart of SCT where we often draw a circle to represent a system, with the line of the circle representing the boundary that contains system energy so it can be organized toward a goal. Yet SCT never works with a single circle. Instead SCT thinks of systems in sets of threes and draws a system as a set of three concentric circles. For example, Joan's circle refers to the process groups within Clinical Pastoral Education. From a systems-centered view, the circle representing the process groups in CPE exists within the circle of the CPE training program, which is in the circle of a clinical pastoral center (Figure 1). All three are interdependent systems with one existing in the context of another and being the context for the third. SCT calls this a hierarchy of systems (Agazarian, 1997)

Figure 1. A systems hierarchy defines a nested set of three systems: the middle system exists in the context of the system above it, and is the context for the system below it.

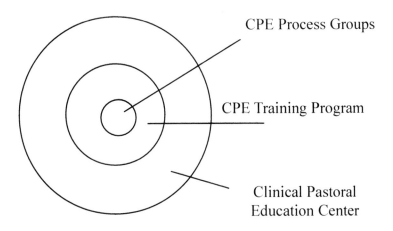

CPE Process Groups

CPE Training Program

Clinical Pastoral Education Center

Thus in a systems-centered perspective, Joan's circle is always seen as a part of a hierarchy of circles. The idea of hierarchy emphasizes that a system is never in isolation but is always in a systems context and illustrates this as a nested set of three circles.

SCT then defines the set of three circles in a defined hierarchy as isomorphic systems (Agazarian, 1997). Building on von Bertalanffy (1969), SCT defines isomorphy as similarity in structure and function at all system levels. Structure is defined by boundaries, and function is defined by the process of discriminating and integrating energy/information. With isomorphic systems, learning something about the structure and function of one system informs about the others in the system hierarchy. So with the CPE hierarchy described above, learning about the structure and function of the CPE program will lead to understanding the similarities in the structure and function of the process group as well as the CPE center.

Overview

This article describes a systems-centered consultation with a CPE center that contracted with me to work with them in team development. This synopsis illustrates some of the systems-centered methods used in any organizational context and discusses how these systems-centered methods were used to address some of the particular issues that clinical pastoral education centers face. This article expands from Joan's focus on applying the systems-centered methods to CPE and its supervisory process by bringing in an illustration of using the systems-centered approach in an organizational context.

How the Consultation Started

The newly appointed director of the clinical pastoral center contacted me to consult with the staff. One of the members, Kathy (pseudonyms are used throughout this paper), had been complaining about the new director's behavior. Kathy had accused the new director of inappropriately communicating her frustration and anger to Kathy. The director agreed that she had lost her temper with Kathy and contacted Human Resources for help with the staff. The human resources department met with the staff. Subsequently, the director, with the endorsement of the staff, hired me to work with them as a consultant. Importantly, this all happened a few months after the new director had been appointed to her role, an appointment met with mixed feelings by the clinical pastoral staff. The previous, recently retired director had been very popular. The staff was suspicious of the new director and resentful of her appointment.

Introducing the Team to Systems Thinking

I began the work by introducing the idea that the *system* they had developed had more to do with how they were able to work together than anything else. Thus, being able to work together more effectively (a team goal) would require changing the behavior and communications they used that maintained that system. This idea, that change requires changing the *system* rather than particular *people*, is essential in a systems-centered approach.

I also discussed with the team the inevitability of mixed feelings whenever there is a change in leadership. The reality is that all living human systems try to "keep in" the "old" and the familiar, and "keep out" the "new" and different. This reality contrasted with the task of finding out how to relate to and support their new leader. I emphasized that the energy of "keeping out" or resisting the change had more to do with how living human systems function to ensure stability than with the particular people per se. In both of these communications, I was training the team to think "systems" and not just people. For example, learning to see their resistance to the change in leadership as a common system dynamic in any change began to lay the foundation for not taking their feelings about the change or the leader only personally.

Our next step was to establish an effective communication pattern, i.e. one in which information could be exchanged and would support exploration of their particular challenges in adapting to their new director. To this end, I introduced them to the systems-centered method of functional subgrouping, a communication tool for integrating differences and resolving conflicts. We then used functional subgrouping to help the team integrate and consolidate around important changes, especially the "difference" of a new director and the necessary differences in learning to work with her.

Functional Subgrouping

Systems-Centered Theory puts forth the idea that the essential function of any living human system is to survive, develop, and transform through the process of discriminating and integrating differences, differences in the apparently similar and similarities in

113

the apparently different (Agazarian, 1997). Functional subgrouping puts this theory into practice: members are first taught to say "anyone else?" once they have made a contribution so that others who see it similarly can join and build on the idea or experience they introduced.

For example:

> Sam: I am interested in seeing how Tanya (the new director) will be as a director. I know her in other ways but not as a director.
>
> Consultant: Ask "anyone else?" so the group knows you are done and can then build on what you have contributed.
>
> Sam: Anyone else?
>
> Judy: I am curious about that too and a little excited. Anyone else?
>
> Dick: I am both excited and anxious.
>
> Consultant: And then say, "anyone else?"
>
> Dick: Anyone else?
>
> Sandra: I'm a little apprehensive too; hard to know how it will go, (pause), oh, anyone else?

Often, as groups are learning this process, someone then comes in and says, "Yes, that is a good idea, but...." The emphasis on the "but" signals a difference. When this happens, the member and the group are taught to hold the difference until all the information that is similar to the first idea (or subgroup) has come into the work group. For example, continuing with the above:

> Jonathon: Yes, it is an unknown, but I am more concerned

about Steve's leaving than I am about Tanya taking over.

Consultant: You have introduced a difference, Jonathon, and a very important one for the team to discuss, and it is almost certain that others will have the same concerns. So hold onto that one. Once we have finished talking over the curiosities and apprehensions you can then start the discussion of exploring these concerns. Who else has the curiosity and the apprehensions?

Over time, members with a difference learn to ask, "Is the group ready for a difference?" When the group is ready, the "difference" is then introduced and followed by the question "anyone else?" so that all those who relate to and resonate with the difference and have information can contribute their part to the group's understanding of the issues.

Within each subgroup, as members explore with those who share their view, they discover "just tolerable differences." In turn, the other subgroup explores their side, by building on similarities and creating a climate where differences are more easily tolerated within the similarities. At some point, integration occurs between the two subgroups as members discover their similarities with those in the "different" subgroup. At this point, the group-as-a-whole has developed from simpler to more complex, and the differences can be used as resources rather than used as ammunition for fighting (Agazarian, 1997).

For example, as the first subgroup explored their curiosities, apprehensions, and anxieties they began to recognize differences. Some were anxious from their negative predictions and speculations about the future, and others were apprehensive from the uncertainty the team was facing. In turn, the second subgroup explored their concerns about Steve's leaving. This subgroup began to identify that some concerns came from speculations about the impact that not having Steve would have, and others recognized their discomfort with the uncertainty. At some point, members began to recognize the similarities across the differences, discovering that in both subgroups there were those who noted the pull to speculate, as well as the inevitable challenge of living with the uncertainty at the edge of the unknown.

Introducing functional subgrouping was an essential part of this early work that helped develop the consulting system. This choice was very deliberate in that SCT emphasizes the importance of a team learning how to communicate so that all differences are legitimized as information for the team to use. This enables the team to work in a way that integrates differences as an ongoing part of its work. The idea of learning to use their differences as resources made sense to the team as they recognized how easily they could have ended up split between the pull to Steve on one hand and the anxiety over change on the other, and with their reactivity to each other's differences becoming the focus. Instead, they ended up recognizing that the human pull to speculate moved them away from learning to live with the uncertainty of change. They were then able to shift their speculations into important reality questions that helped clarify the current reality. Those that had been "speculators" developed a pathway for testing reality and collecting data, and those tuned into "uncertainty" were able to mobilize their curiosity and help the team recognize and support each other around the inevitable apprehension in a time of change. Shifting away from the human tendency to react to difference and toward building a way to use differences as resources was easily compatible with clinical pastoral values. The team quickly understood the value of functional subgrouping and learned to use this systems-centered tool whenever different points of view emerged.

The developmental challenge was to build a functional communication system that potentiated the team's development. The reality context was the work of integrating a new director. This early work to establish the norm of functional subgrouping supported both goals. This norm of using functional subgrouping to explore differences built a foundation that served the team well early in the work and later. For example, as the team developed and began working with the issues related to authority and to fight/flight, the ability to explore the two sides of an issue lowered the pull to fighting and helped the team surface and explore all of the perspectives.

Establishing functional subgrouping early with the team was also important for Kathy, the member who had voiced the early dissatisfactions. Kathy had previously been the sole voice for differences or criticism of the new director. This old pattern had left Kathy and the new director holding the "fight energy" for the whole system. From a systems-centered perspective, Kathy had been in a role that contained the defiance and authority issue for the team, a role the team implicitly supported their passive behavior of watching or "checking out" rather than contributing. Using functional subgrouping changed this old pattern and the team members learned to bring in their own dissatisfactions and explore them as information for the system. Kathy was no longer left holding this difference alone.

Before describing more of the consultation, it is important to introduce the phases of system development as the systems-centered change strategies used with work groups always link to the system phases framework.

The Phases of System Development

As mentioned earlier, SCT begins with the premise that the living human system has more to do with how people in the system relate and work than the people per se. To this end, SCT diagnoses the phase of a system's development by identifying the individual behaviors and communications as outputs reflective of the system phase and system conditions.

In beginning a consultation with a work group, the systems-centered consultant builds a consulting system containing the consultant and the team that can support the team's development. SCT uses the phase of system development as a map for both guiding the development of the consultation system and for diagnosing and then guiding a change process within the team. The consultant then tracks both the developing consultation system consisting of the team and the consultant, as well as the system of the team in its work context.

Building on Bennis and Shepard (1956), SCT has identified

three major phases of system development: authority, collaboration, and integration. Each phase has identifiable challenges essential in system development. The challenge in the authority phase is to learn to give and take authority; in the collaboration phase, to learn to use differential resources collaboratively; in the integration phase, to learn to use one's knowledge in role, goal, and context.

Borrowing from Lewin's (1951) force field model, SCT has operationally defined each phase of development as a force field of driving and restraining forces that represent the quasi-stationary equilibrium or balance of the system in each phase of development (Agazarian, 1994; Agazarian & Gantt, 2003; Gantt & Agazarian, 2007). Driving forces move a system toward its goals, and restraining forces compete with the goals. Change strategies are then developed to weaken the restraining forces that compete with development, freeing the driving forces to move the system forward along its developmental path.

Influencing work groups in their developmental process is especially important in that SCT has hypothesized (Gantt & Agazarian, 2007) and Wheelan (2005) has demonstrated that a work group's phase of development correlates with its degree of productivity and efficiency. In Wheelan's research, there is a positive correlation between productivity in work groups and greater phase development, and a negative correlation between productivity and less phase development.

Developing a systems-centered consultation system always begins at the beginning: developing the system of the team and consultant working together toward the goal of the consultation. Inevitably, this requires weakening the restraining forces of flight and developing a communication system that can communicate.

The initial work with this team focused on weakening the flight communications or the flight subphase restraining forces, which shifts the system out of stereotyped social communications into functional communications (see Figure 2).

Figure 2. The systems-centered® approach to development in work groups: A force field depicting the driving and restraining forces in each of the phases of system development.

Phase of Development	DRIVING FORCES ➡	RESTRAINING FORCES ⬅
Authority Phase *Flight Subphase*	**Developmental Goal: Create reality-testing culture** ➜ Forming functional subgroups, asking "Anyone else?" ➜ Exploring ➜ Specificity, bottom line ➜ Data, reality-testing ➜	⬅ **Implicit Goal: Don't rock the boat, play it safe** ⬅ Maintaining social status communication, personalizing, stereotyped subgrouping ⬅ Explaining ⬅ Vagueness, redundancy ⬅ Speculations
Fight Subphase	**Developmental Goal: Explore differences in context of** ➜ **the work focus** Subgrouping around differences ➜ Recognizing and acknowledging frustrations ➜ Collecting data about hesitations ➜ Making alternative proposals ➜	⬅ **Implicit Goal: Do it my way, repel invading differences** ⬅ "Yes, but" communications ⬅ Complaining or blaming oneself, personalizing frustration ⬅ Blaming others, reacting to differences or withdrawing ⬅ Discharging in righteous outrage, indignation, sarcasm

Role Locks with Peers Subphase	**Developmental Goal: Develop functional work →** **role relationships with peers** Clarifying work role relationships with peers → Descriptive language →	**←Implicit Goal: Manage issues of dominance and control** ← Creating one-up/down relationships ←Personalizing language that induces role locks
Role Locks with Leader Subphase	**Developmental Goal: Make a working relationship →** **with one's leader** **and discover one's own** **authority** Clarifying differential role responsibilities → Learning to work with the leader one has → Giving and taking authority → Bring in what one knows & negotiate with leader →	**← Implicit Goal: Sabotage authority, avoid responsibility, maintain status quo** ← Complying or defying leader instead of task focus ← Making a case against the leader or organization ← Blaming the leader, overtly or covertly ← Denying one's own authority, or one's own competence
Collaboration Phase	**Developmental Goal: Use differential resources of members while working in an interdependent team** Contribute to positive work climate while exploring → differences in the apparently similar Exploring similarities in the apparently different and work → out a functional collaboration Take up team role →	**← Implicit Goal: Personal style at the expense of teamwork** ← Focus on friendship at expense of work, avoid differences to preserve affiliation ← Denial of similarities and l insistence on working alone ← Go it alone or resist autonomy

Integration Phase	Developmental Goal: Work in role, goal and ➜ context with common sense & emotional intelligence	⬅ Implicit Goal: Self-focus at expense of system-focus, knowledge at the expense of common sense or context
	Working in role and contributing to the goal & climate of ➜ the context	⬅ Blurring roles, ignoring goals & context, or only orienting to self-centered goals
	Using emotional and intellectual intelligence ➜	⬅ Avoiding reality, resist intuition or reasoning
	Common sense reality-testing ➜	⬅ Losing common sense
	Maintaining a sense of humor ➜	⬅ Losing perspective, personalizing
	Seeing the bigger picture ➜	⬅ Self-focused at expense of context
	Using emotional knowledge in decision-making ➜	⬅ Decisions without heart leading to ill-formed implementation
	Using the spirit of the law ➜	⬅ Legalistic, letter of the law

From Gantt and Agazarian (2007). Systems-Centered® is a registered trademark of Yvonne Agazarian and the Systems-Centered Training and Research Institute, Inc., a non-profit organization.

Role, Goal, and Context

In addition to introducing functional subgrouping, the early work with the clinical pastoral team focused on clarifying the various contexts throughout the health care system in which team members were involved. This began by identifying the various subsystems that contained clinical pastoral services within them. We worked by drawing circles to represent all the relevant subsystems in which clinical pastoral services existed. For example, we drew one circle for geriatric services and another for oncology. Not surprisingly, drawing a circle for each system context that contained pastoral care services filled a large board. By creating the visual picture, we could all see the complexity of their system.

Once each context was named, the team identified the goal of each context and the role or roles that clinical pastoral services had in each specific context. The identification of roles in each system context was a very important piece of work for the team. Identifying the roles enabled the team to begin the essential work of separating role and person and seeing the role as linked to the context and goal. The person's job is to contribute energy to the system via their specific role in the context. Introducing this task early on was very important in that we also used this process for the team to identify its strengths. This task provided an easier context for changing the communication norms than the presenting issue of a disgruntled, suspicious team. Much later in the work, the team developed a similar picture of the various contexts to help the team diagnose a problem in terms of whether it was primarily a problem related to a single context or to communications across the boundary between contexts or subsystems. It was also used later to clarify the lines of authority and accountability between system contexts.

Establishing the role, goal, and contexts also enabled the team members to appreciate the challenges they all had in changing roles with each other as they changed context. For example, in the context of the CPE supervisors' meeting, the member in the role of CPE coordinator had the authority, responsibility, and accountability for student evaluations. In another meeting context, this same member was in a peer role with members that she had authority over in the CPE context. Learning to recognize the role shifts necessary in changing contexts facilitated their work together in each context and enabled the team to learn to support the authority roles in each context, irrespective of who was in the role.

In this process of identifying the array of contexts, each with its own goal, and the pastoral care roles within each context, the team practiced functional subgrouping and learned to build on each other's contributions, thus learning to explore similarities and differences and developing a good climate for working together. It also provided a context in which the consultant worked with the team to lower the restraining force of "noise" in their communications as described below.

Taking Noise Out of "Talk"

Functional subgrouping enables a system to organize information in a way that makes it more likely that differences can be integrated as energy and information for the system, instead of settling for the human tendency to react to and exclude differences. Reaction to differences often puts "noise" into a communication process. "Noise" is like static on the telephone line, the more static, the harder it is to hear the other person. Noise in a communication system competes with the goal of communication, which is the transfer of information.

SCT works with the idea that boundaries open to information and close to noise, and that the capacity for successful communication increases to the extent that the system filters noise out of its communications. SCT builds on the work of Shannon and Weaver (1964) who identified two sources of noise in communication: ambiguity and redundancy. In their theory of communication, Shannon and Weaver demonstrated that the degree of information transfer is inversely proportionate to the degree of noise in a communication. Simon and Agazarian (1967, 2000) identified contradiction (e.g., "yes, but") as a third source of noise in communication.

Part of the early work in the flight subphase is weakening the restraining forces of noise in communications in order to build an effective communication system in which information can be exchanged (see Figure 2). Introducing functional subgrouping manages the noise of the contradictory "yes, but" communication and enables a work group to legitimize the exploration of both perspectives. Asking a member to be more specific weakens the noise of ambiguity. Encouraging the "bottom line" when someone is talking on and on weakens redundant explanations that close boundaries as listeners quit listening to communications that are redundant.

Highlights of the Team's Work
Through the Phases of System Development

The early work was largely related to the authority phase where the goal is to learn to give and take authority. This begins by first establishing a reality-testing culture, and then learning to work with the reality of frustration and use the energy in the frustration and anger for work. This lays the foundation for learning to shift from personalized roles to functional work roles and to make a functional, supportive relationship with one's leader.

In this situation, the goal in the early flight subphase work was to weaken the restraining forces in flight (Agazarian, 1997; Gantt & Agazarian, 2007) and develop a reality-testing system that would enable the team to take up the reality challenges of working with a new director. Team members learned to modify their communication patterns. They learned:

- To move from vagueness in their communications to specificity and to ask each other to be more specific
- To shift from overly redundant explanations to the bottom line
- To refrain from "yes...but" and make room for the difference in a different subgroup
- To undo "mind reads" of each other and to establish reality-testing, for example, saying, "My mind read is that you are frustrated with this idea. Is that true?"
- To shift from complaints to active proposals, for example, changing a communication from "We never make up our mind on things." to "My proposal is we make a decision today on this one."
- To undo "leapfrog" thinking where negative predictions about the future are made by remembering the failures in the past and leapfrogging from the past to the future without clarifying the reality of the present.

Most significantly, over time the team moved away from a norm of passive compliance with the director in the meetings while gossiping and complaining outside the meetings, to active team membership in the meetings. It was particularly useful for the team to learn how to build their team actively and to contribute as a member or "citizen" of the team by weakening the restraining forces of passivity, compliance, and complaining behaviors that contributed to the team being different from the team they wanted.

As the team developed their skill in weakening the restraining forces typical of the flight phase, they shifted into the fight phase. It then became especially important for the team to recognize and legitimize the inevitable frustration that comes from working as part of a team and the concomitant differences team members bring. This led to the team's learning to use the energy of frustration to influence the work of the team. For example, in one meeting Donna and Kathy were able to recognize their frustration with the slowness of the work in the meeting and were able to see how they could help the team work more efficiently and stay on task.

This work built the foundation for the next phase, the phase of roles and role locks. Working with roles enabled the team to undo the roles various team members had taken for the team like the "complainer" or "checking out" and instead to reclaim the authority issues that Kathy's defiant, rebellious role had contained for the team. This set the framework for beginning to recognize the ongoing challenges related to the issues of giving and taking authority. Recognizing the inevitability of the authority issue enabled the team to shift from blaming the director to seeing their responsibility for the director they helped create. The membership responsibility was learning to work with the director they had rather than the one they wanted her to be. This enabled the team to shift from passivity, complaining, and criticizing her leadership or waiting for her to be different, to learning to work with and support her. Over time, the team strengthened their working relationship with the director and came to value and appreciate her contributions and particular resources in developing the department. Equally important, the team learned to recognize, compensate for, and work with their director's liabilities. For example, one of the director's liabilities was taking on more than she could do. Instead of going along compliantly when the director volunteered for tasks that were not specific to her role, team members learned to speak up to address this and to take on the tasks themselves.

In the work with roles and role locks, the team understood how they had passively supported Kathy taking on the role of challenging or complaining about the director, and they recognized how their passivity kept them from learning about their own challenges and responsibilities for working with their leader. Team members also developed their capacity to take an active member role and understood that not taking one's member role or citizenship in the team made it easier for all to fall into the personalized roles that hijack the work context. For example, taking either a "complaining" role or a "passive" role not only sabotaged taking one's team member role but also simultaneously created a complaining climate where frustrations increased and individuals went into personalized roles in response. The shift from complaining to proposing moves one from person to member, using the resources one has as a person to actively take citizenship in developing the team and working with the leader.

Perhaps most important, the team developed beyond their early stereotype of "being personal" in a way that maintained "niceness" but actually interfered with taking up their work roles or citizenship in the team. The team began to work to discriminate the personalizing that interferes with work when personal feelings are brought into one's member role in supporting the goal of the work group. For example, in one meeting, several members recognized that personalizing their frustrations led them to withdraw and go into passivity. Instead, the "frustrated" subgroup was able to bring in their frustrations and see how the information contained within their frustration was relevant for the team and its current task. As the team worked through its authority phase and relinquished the idea that being close was the goal, the team actually developed enormous satisfaction and felt closer as they learned to collaborate in their work roles supporting the goals of CPE. This marked a further development in the team, as they shifted into the collaboration phase where they were able to work explicitly with the tension between affiliation and work.

The major work in the collaboration phase is to manage the

personal roles of either the pull to affiliation and friendship at the expense of the work or the tendency to do it one's own way and go it alone that interferes with the team or collaborative role functioning (Gantt & Agazarian, 2007). This team's first work with collaboration phase issues deepened their understanding of the challenges of changing roles as the context changed from friendship to work, specifically by separating from the friendship roles when in the work group context. For example, several members recognized that they held back from bringing in a different point of view when their "friend" was advocating for a particular decision. This led to understanding that "friend" was not a relevant role in the work context and not a functional role in the decision-making process in the meeting. In fact, the "friend" role when out of context interfered with taking one's "member" role in context where the work included contributing one's views in service of a thorough exploration to support the decision-making. "Friend" might be a relevant role once again at lunch following the meeting but was not the role that supported the goal of the meeting context. As team members learned increasingly to make these role transitions, more and more differences emerged in the discussion and were integrated in the team meetings. This enabled the team to make decisions with greater complexity and depth of understanding, and with much less personalizing.

The second major aspect of the collaboration phase work was the ongoing work of recognizing the "do it my own way" role and its the impact on the team. The team identified how this role avoided the realities of accountability and undermined the team functioning. The team also understood how they had implicitly supported this role by going along with it and not holding each other accountable to use team membership behaviors, while simultaneously complaining and gossiping about members who "did it their own way." Though this role reflected the personal work style preferences of many team members, the team was able to see that at times this would need to be modified in order to build the working system of the team and the collaborative roles.

In the integration phase the major work is the ongoing task of moving from person to member to use what one knows in one's role, goal, and context. A useful example of this occurred when this team was working on its strategic plan:

> The team was working hard on this over several sessions. During one meeting several members became notably quiet. Eventually, one member spoke up, announced that she was bored, and then asked if she had a subgroup. Two other members joined, and as they explored their boredom together they discovered that they were reacting to the tediousness of the work and withdrawing in frustration. As they continued to talk this over, they recognized the team had lost its original passion for its plan and was getting mired in the details without any heart in it. Once this subgroup understood this, they recognized that their challenge was to keep the team's passion and vision alive, a goal whole-heartedly supported by the team.

The team understood in greater and greater depth the citizenship challenges of bringing what one knows into one's role to support the goal of the context. In this work, the team was also able to recognize the relevance of acknowledging frustration so that the team could assess whether the frustration was an inevitable by-product of the work or reflective of a system solution that put unnecessary stress on its members.

New Members, Recycling through the Phases of System Development, and the Authority Issue with the Consultant

During the last year as we were beginning to see what work needed to be finished before discontinuing the consultation, two events occurred that had a strong influence on the team's phase and functioning. First, a large number of new members were added to the staff. From a systems view, this always introduces a challenge. Systems function to survive, as well as to develop, and when "survival of the familiar" is threatened, the system works to keep the "old" intact. This often results in finding creative ways of keeping new members out, while the new members often resist their task of learning the existing group norms. This team was no exception to this typical dynamic. In addition, and predictably, this influx of members triggered the team through a revisiting of earlier phases of development. Such a revisiting is often very useful in that aspects of the development that were not fully worked initially can be addressed more thoroughly with greater resolution made in each of the phases.

In this same time period, a second significant event occurred which involved a crisis with a student and supervisor. Helen, the supervisor, had often taken an "outsider" role since joining the team two years earlier. This had been supported implicitly by the team for some time, though just prior to the crisis, the team had already begun addressing the problems in supporting this implicit role. The crisis occurred as the team was also re-working the fight subphase conflicts so that the scapegoating energy was strongly aroused and readily available to target Helen.

In my consulting role, I required the team to look at the system first to see how the problem was a product of the system, rather than scapegoating Helen as the problem. Shifting to the system level did in fact contain the scapegoating, and not surprisingly drew the frustration and anger toward me in my consultant role instead. This proved useful in that over several months the team's anger with me enabled the team to take on a deeper exploration and understanding of the authority issue. In this process, the team recognized a dichotomy that had not been fully resolved between their pastoral value for people and the systems view that I continued to introduce. The passion that maintained this split was fueled by scapegoating energy and the belief that getting rid of the perceived threat would maintain their identity. It is exactly this kind of belief—where differences are seen as threatening survival and the leader is the perceived threat— that is prevalent when the authority issue is active.

The team then acted out the authority issue by making a decision to end the consultation without consulting the consultant! The defiance was no longer contained in passive acting out. The defiant subgroup had found its voice. Unfortunately, ending the consultation without recognizing and understanding the authority issues that fueled the precipitous decision would undercut the team's learning to take their authority rather than rebel. This was particularly important as several team members were taking on new leadership roles in the program, making the issues of giving and taking authority especially salient.

A final meeting with me as consultant was arranged to bring closure to the consultation process. The meeting started with a strong pull to end with polite appreciation, without real ownership of the team's defiance or of the authority issue in spite of my best efforts to call attention to these. Ending in this way would have sabotaged the consultation. I continued to challenge the team, emphasizing that the kind of ending they did with me would have a big impact on what they would be able to do on their own. A senior member spoke up to support my leadership on this and was supported by the team. This was significant in that the team was then able both to take effective leadership via this member and to cooperate with my leadership to make a very significant closure. In doing so, the team was able to recognize the personalized roles reactive to authority that various members took that were supported by the team and that kept these team members resentful, passive, and acting out. By the end of this session the team was able to realize and integrate both their appreciation of my leadership and their hatred of the strength with which I took authority. The team and the director discussed that the ongoing challenge was for the team to continue to weaken the personalized roles they used when the authority issue was active. A number of members identified the specific personalized roles they would need to weaken and understood how these roles actually prevented them from actively supporting leadership and leader roles. The team voiced their challenge and eagerness to try doing this on their own, to take their own authority to influence and develop the system they wanted, and to support leadership in their leader and each other, rather than passively or actively defying the leader and sabotaging leadership throughout the team.

In addition, the director recognized that the force of the authority issue would now fall fully on her role without the role of the consultant to contain some of it. The director identified her apprehensiveness about this and her challenge to contain the authority issue whenever it was aroused until the team could take back whatever the authority issue contained for them. This was clear to the director and the team, as all could see that in the closing session the team was doing just that with me: they were learning their strength to take authority in their member and leader roles with the team and each other.

Summary of the SCT Hypotheses Illustrated in this Case Example

In describing this systems-centered consultation, this paper presents aspects of the theory of living human systems and its systems-centered practice (Agazarian, 1997) with an organizational workgroup (Gantt & Agazarian, 2005/2006). This case example illustrates how key tenets of the theory of living human systems and its SCT methods can be applied with workgroups. The SCT hypotheses presented in this discussion are summarized below:

- The system has more to do with how the people in it function than the people per se.
- Changing the communications and behaviors that maintain the system changes the system.
- Functional subgrouping shifts communication patterns in a way that the impact of reactivity to differences on a system is lowered and the differences can be more easily integrated as resources.
- Identifying the phase of system development defines the developmental context for change.
- Change strategies linked to the phase of system development will increase the likelihood of change and lower the stress in a change process.
- Operationally defining each phase of system development as a force field of driving and restraining forces enables a sequence for introducing change strategies that link to the phase of system development.
- The force field of the phases of system development provides a map for guiding change strategies by weakening restraining forces rather than by increasing drive.

- Change is more easily achieved by weakening restraining forces than by increasing drive.
- Building the consulting system builds the context for consulting to the team.
- Clarification of role, goal, and context increases the resources for taking one's role in context and lowers the pull to take oneself just personally.
- Learning to shift one's role as the goal and context change lowers personalizing.
- Taking "noise out of talk" increases the likelihood of successful communication and information being available for development and work.

Thus, this case discussion of a work team in an organizational context illustrates some of the essential SCT methods and hypotheses that are used to influence and foster the development of living human systems in work contexts.

Building Teams in Clinical Pastoral Education

Though one case example can not be generalized to all situations, several issues in this systems-centered consultation may be useful for understanding the particular challenges that clinical pastoral centers face in their development.

The first relates to the challenge for clinical pastoral educators in integrating their value for the person with the challenge of shifting from person to member and taking citizenship in one's team. Orienting a team towards one's personal feelings without awareness of role, goal, and context often leads to emotionality at the expense of emotional intelligence (Gantt & Agazarian, 2004).

In this area CPE faces a challenge similar to many human service agencies: how to use process for the sake of developing a task-oriented system and accomplishing its task, not for the sake of process itself or emotionality.

From a systems-centered perspective the challenge is how to build human systems that not only develop and do the work that they were designed to do, but also simultaneously develop the people that contribute the energy, including the emotional energy or knowledge, that develops the system. This is the heart of systems-centered emotional intelligence (Gantt & Agazarian, 2004). The "bored" members example described earlier illustrates this well. If being bored had been personalized by the member herself, she would likely withdraw and eventually become a marginalized member. If her being bored was taken personally by the team, either a fight would ensue or the team would work hard to see how to "fix" her so she was not bored. Instead, translating one's personal reactions into information for the context strengthens the development potential for the system and simultaneously weakens the tendency that many experiential education programs unwittingly evoke of personal exploration at the expense of the role, goal, and context. Joan Hemenway (2005b) referenced this herself in her discussion of how the lack of role and goal clarity impacts the functioning of the CPE process group. Thinking isomorphy, it then makes sense that issues of role clarity and role confusion may be relevant in clinical pastoral programs at all system levels: the clinical pastoral center, the CPE program, and the process group.

This same issue has certainly been a developmental process in our organization, Systems-Centered Training and Research Institute, which relies heavily on experiential education. It has taken some years to understand that an essential step in the education process is explicit training in how to translate the increased personal knowledge gained from experiential exploration into the system context and contribute it in one's member roles to support the goal of the context. Gaining personal knowledge in experiential exploration is often so gratifying that the motivation is low for making the shift from gaining or sharing personal knowledge to using the knowledge in context. Yet it is moving into context that enables teams to lower the tendency to self-absorption, where we take ourselves or each other just personally. This move is essential to being able to do one's work, meet one's goals, and develop one's team. The challenge then becomes how to bring in one's personal energy, including emotional energy, in a way that it supports the goal of the context or, put another way, how to bring one's person into role in context (Gantt, 2005).

Second, for this team, clarifying the roles and contexts led to surfacing the implicit power hierarchy related to the differences in roles between clinical supervisors and staff chaplains. This enabled the team to undo the stereotyped hierarchy and clarify the functional hierarchy and division in roles. This undid an implicit embedded authority issue that may have relevance for other clinical pastoral centers.

Finally, dealing with the issues related to giving and taking authority was central in this consultation. At a general level, this was not surprising since most organizations either flourish or flounder based on how well authority issues are managed. More specifically, this team worked hard to clarify and understand the authority and responsibility vested in the director's role and the ways in which they supported or undermined her authority. The director learned to be clearer and more explicit as to when she was delegating her authority to the team for decision-making versus asking the team to advise her but retaining her authority for the decision. Many of the team members recognized that they operated with high autonomy in their roles most of the time and were resentful when external authority intervened. They learned to separate their personal reactions to authority from their responsibility as a team member to support the director, and to make sure that information they held as a difference was integrated as information for the team. It is also possible that the humanistic values CPE holds dear make it harder to confront the inevitable authority challenges in relating to the realities of hierarchy. In fact, this may be similar to the confusion to which Joan alludes in *Inside the Circle* (1996) when she talks of the dual influence of the humanistic and psychoanalytic influences in the history of CPE.

In concluding, I offer this paper about how a systems-centered approach can be used in a team development process as an appreciation of Joan Hemenway's voice, which represented the willingness and capacity in CPE to be open to differences and to embrace them and explore them.

Author's Note: Much appreciation to Bettie Banks for her feedback and editorial suggestions on this paper and to the excellent editing provided by the editors of this festschrift.

References

Agazarian, Y.M. (1994). The phases of development and the systems-centered group. In M. Pines & V. Schermer (Eds.), *Ring of fire: Primitive object relations and affect in group psychotherapy.* London: Routledge, Chapman & Hall.

Agazarian, Y.M. (1997). *Systems-centered therapy for groups.* New York: Guilford Press. (Re-printed in paperback (2004). London: Karnac Books).

Agazarian, Y.M. & Gantt, S.P. (2003). Phases of group development: Systems-centered hypotheses and their implications for research and practice. *Group Dynamics: Theory, Research and Practice, 7*(3), 238-252.

Bennis, W.G. & Shepard, H.A. (1956). A theory of group development. *Human Relations, 9*(4), 415-437.

Bertalanffy, L. von (1969). *General systems* (rev. ed.). New York: George Braziller.

Gantt, S.P. (2005). Functional role-taking in organizations and work groups. *Group Psychologist (APA Division 49 newsletter), 15*(5), 15.

Gantt, S.P. & Agazarian, Y.M. (2004). Systems-centered emotional intelligence: Beyond individual systems to organizational systems. *Organizational Analysis, 12*(2), 147-169.

Gantt, S.P. & Agazarian, Y.M. (Eds.). (2005/2006). *SCT in action: Applying the systems-centered approach in organizations.* Lincoln, NE: iUniverse. Reprint (2006). London: Karnac Books.

Gantt, S.P. & Agazarian, Y.M. (2007). Phases of system development in organizationalworkgroups: The systems-centered approach for intervening in context. *Organisational & Social Dynamics, 7*(2), 253-291.

Hemenway, J.E. (1996). *Inside the circle: A historical and practical inquiry concerning process groups in clinical and pastoral education.* Decatur, GA: JPCP Publications.

Hemenway, J.E. (2005a). Opening up the circle: Next steps in group work for clinical pastoral educators. In S.P. Gantt & Y.M. Agazarian (Eds.), *SCT in action: Applying the systems-centered approach in organizations* (pp. 81-97). Lincoln, NE: iUniverse. Reprint (2006).London: Karnac Books.

Hemenway, J.E. (2005b). Opening up the circle: Next steps in process group work in clinical pastoral education (CPE). *The Journal of Pastoral Care & Counseling, 59*(4), 323-334.

Lewin, K. (1951). *Field theory in social science.* New York: Harper & Row.

Shannon, C.E. & Weaver, W. (1964). *The mathematical theory of communication.* Urbana, Ill: University of Illinois Press.

Simon, A. & Agazarian, Y.M. (1967). *S.A.V.I.: Sequential analysis of verbal interaction.* Philadelphia: Research for Better Schools.

Simon, A. & Agazarian, Y.M. (2000). The system for analyzing verbal interaction. In A. Beck & C. Lewis (Eds.), *The process of group psychotherapy: Systems for analyzing change.* Washington, D.C.: American Psychological Association.

Wheelan, S. (2005). *Group processes: A developmental perspective* (2nd ed.). Needham Heights, MA: Allyn & Bacon: The Simon & Schuster Education Group.

CHAPTER 10

Functional Subgrouping in CPE: A Case Study
Angelika A. Zollfrank

A t the end of one of my clinical presentations during supervisory training at Yale-New Haven Hospital I remember turning to Joan, my training supervisor at the time, and saying: "The individual group member is finite and dies. The circle itself is infinite. It continues to evolve as other members take up the voice of the one that left." Then and now my grief about the loss of her life is touched with gratitude for Joan's unique life and for life itself.

Many of Joan Hemenway's convictions have become important to my supervisory practice. For example, "All anyone ever needs is a holding environment." In CPE it is particularly the small process group that offers such a holding environment and system. In each CPE small process group I seek to legitimize all of my students' experiences as human. Another one of Joan's convictions was that every useful and goal-oriented practice must be based in an intellectually sound theory. "It is so satisfying to see a theory at work," Joan commented at the end of a Systems-Centered Training (SCT) group workshop. I shared this satisfaction with Joan, and my theory papers for certification in ACPE were an early attempt to integrate SCT concepts into my theoretical understandings of supervision (Zollfrank, 2005, pp. 156-186). Beginning in 2003, and as a direct result of Joan's teachings, I have been involved SCT on a beginning and intermediate level with the goal of applying and integrating SCT into my CPE supervisory practice.

Introduction

CPE promotes emotional and spiritual awareness with the goal of developing a spiritual care giver's ability to relate empathically to patients, families, and staff in the complex multi-religious environment of a hospital. To be spiritual means to grow in connection with all of human life and life itself. Spiritual care giving is the ability to legitimize, empathize, and respond to any human emotional and spiritual experience; using this definition, spiritual care giving can be offered by all persons. Professionally trained chaplains offer theological expertise as well as spiritual and emotional care giving skills.

The goal of spiritual care is to establish spiritual care relationships and to build a spiritual care giving system. Such a system allows for the exploration of emotional and spiritual experiences and resources. Another goal is to work toward resolution of emotional conflicts and spiritual struggles. In order to be effective as spiritual care givers, CPE students need to learn to access their common sense. Common sense in the context of SCT is understood as depending "on the connection between reality, thought, and emotion" (Agazarian, 1997, p. 123). In the language of ACPE standards and objectives, CPE focuses on the functional use of students' resources: emotional, cognitive, cultural, biographical, spiritual, and theological. CPE students explore how to create emotional and spiritual connections that matter, and learn to throw their whole heart into the spiritual care giver role.

This article hypothesizes that functional subgrouping is beneficial in accessing and developing a CPE student's ability to use emotional and spiritual resources towards the goal of providing effective spiritual care. It builds on Yvonne Agazarian's (1992; 1997) work in developing SCT and Joan Hemenway's (2005) application of SCT to CPE.

First, I will define the three fundamental SCT concepts of systems hierarchy, isomorphy, and role and apply them to the context of a CPE program. After stating the goals for CPE small process group work I will introduce functional subgrouping as a method in working toward these goals. In a next step I will introduce a CPE group and describe the tools used to study the effect of functional subgrouping in this group. Then, the outcomes of a questionnaire, as well as material from the students' theological reflection papers are discussed. Further reflection includes insights on the pastoral role and the dynamics of care taking and care giving. Finally, re-calling a group sculpture offers insights relative to the supervisory role. Based on these findings I draw conclusions relative to the use of functional subgrouping in CPE.

Systems-Centered Concepts in CPE

CPE emphasizes the study of the living human document as the foundation of spiritual care and pastoral education. SCT adds as the primary focus the study of living human systems. SCT tech-niques and methods are theory-driven, building on a theory of liv-ing human systems (Agazarian, 1997). This offers a relatively novel approach to supervising CPE groups. Living human systems are defined as a "hierarchy of isomorphic systems that are energy-organizing, goal-directed, and self-correcting" (Gantt & Agazarian, 2005, p. 3). Systems hierarchy is defined as a "set of three subsys-tems." This can be diagrammed as three concentric circles, with the middle system existing in the context of the larger system and being the context for the smaller system" (Ladden, Gantt, Rude & Agazarian, 2007, p.2). Comparable to nesting containers, the CPE group can be viewed as the middle system surrounded by the con-text of the larger chaplaincy department, while the CPE group also creates the context for the individual CPE student.

Another set of three systems would be the CPE intern in the role of spiritual care giver. This role can be conceptualized as a subsys-tem. The pastoral role is then viewed as the context for the many as-pects of the person system with its resources: emotional, cognitive, cultural, biographical, spiritual, and theological. Both the person system and the subsystem of the pastoral role exist in the context of the CPE program. Similarly, in the CPE small process group (SPG) students take up the role of learners and group members. The mem-ber role in SPG is also conceptualized as a subsystem. Each group member is fed by the energy and information of the person system and exists in the context of the subgroup. Members work towards the goals of small process group, which is nested in the context of the CPE program.

The SCT concept of isomorphy assumes that changes on one system level will effect change on other system levels, since systems in a defined hierarchy are similar in structure and function (Gantt & Agazarian, 2005, p. 11). Changes and growing complexities in the subgroup will therefore influence similar changes and complexities in the system below and the system above. For example, growing complexities on the subgroup level have a look-alike in the person system of the individual student, as well as in the CPE group-as-a-whole. In as far as CPE is an educational experience, it aims to influence and bring about change according to the objectives of CPE. "SCT hypothesizes that intervening to the middle system is the point of greatest influence on all three subsystems, as the middle system has contiguous boundaries with both other systems" (Laden, Gantt, Rude, Agazarian, 2007, p. 3). Thus, according to SCT theory, it is functional subgrouping, here examined in small process group work, which holds most promise as an educational method in working towards the stated goals. The goals of small process group are aligned with the goals of CPE.

The Goals of CPE Small Process Group

Building on the work of Hemenway and Agazarian (Hemenway, 1996; Agazarian 1997; Gantt & Agazarian, 2005) I propose the following goals for small process group (SPG) work in CPE:

1. To train participants in the skill of functional subgrouping to enhance their ability to take up a functional member role
2. To increase the student's awareness of and access to cognitive and emotional experience as a source of information and a resource to the group
3. To develop in students a beginning understanding of roles,

group dynamics, stages of group development, and dynamics of leadership.

While I share these goals with students, they remain abstract until experiential knowing and developing insight makes them come to life. As the leader of the SPG group I intervene in ways that are designed to assist students to:

- make space for a wider range and depth of emotions
- express emotions in the here-and-now
- explore and make use of their emotional experiences
- explore similarities and differences
- give and receive feedback about specific behavior
- reflect on role behaviors and experiment with taking different roles
- begin to differentiate between taking things "just personally" and contributing to the work of the group as a member
- learn to participate and observe at the same time
- explore dynamics relative to their own and others' authority
- apply experiential learning in the group to their pastoral role.

Working towards these goals and using the behaviors mentioned is an unfamiliar and complex task for most students. All the better then if one does not have to do this work alone.

Functional Subgrouping: Why Bother?

"All groups naturally come together around similarities and separate on differences" (Agazarian, 1997, p. 41). In each new CPE group members tend to gravitate towards each other based on stereotypes, like religious affiliation, divinity school enrollment, age, gender, race, ethnicity, etc. Usually in these groups, members split around differences. Once differences are experienced as too different and create too much conflict to be integrated, the information they contain cannot be utilized as a resource for the group (Agazarian, 1997, p. 41). This is the reason for systems-centered CPE group work to focus first on building a system rather than working out differences interpersonally. This allows for any human experience to come into the group in such a way that it can be utilized in the service of the educational goals. The differences experienced by students are best managed by functional subgrouping. Using this method, both sides of an issue can be explored. "Functional subgrouping is thus a conflict resolution method that contains [differences] in separate subgroups until the [difference or] conflict can be discriminated and integrated in the group-as-a-whole" (Gantt & Hopper, 2008, p. 101).

I introduce subgrouping in the first session of SPG by saying, "As we are sitting in the circle now, please give voice to what matters most to you at the moment. And when you are finished, say 'Anybody else?' That does two things: we know when you are done talking and the group is required to join you. When you join, add something to what was said already. Or if you have a difference, please, hold it until the group signals that it is ready for it" (Agazarian, 2007, p. 3). Since this way of communicating may feel unfamiliar, it is useful to allow for an experience of subgrouping prior to the first group session. The SCT exercise of "push, wave, and row" is a playful way students learn subgrouping and being deliberate about their communication (Agazarian, 1997, p. 55).

The use of functional subgrouping is a productive alternative to "getting stuck in the 'hot seat' dynamic," which so often leads to groups creating an identified patient or a scapegoat dynamic (Hemenway, 2005, p. 84). With deepening exploration of difference in the experience of similarity, or similarity in the seemingly different, more information and energy comes into the group without the information without rejection, judgment, or caretaking. Functional subgrouping allows CPE students to make space for these human experiences and to explore new territory within themselves. Functional subgrouping ensures an educational focus, builds a supportive enough environment for the individual student and learner, and offers opportunities to explore the dynamics of caretaking often prevalent in first unit CPE students. The skills learned from functional subgrouping, for example non-judgmental empathy, working along in attunement, and tolerating all kinds of human experiences are crucial for the pastoral development of our students.

One CPE Group: A Case Study

During an eleven week summer CPE unit at Massachusetts General Hospital, I supervised a group of five students using SCT techniques and methods. The educational component of the program included verbatim seminars, didactic presentations, Experience of Faith Seminars, and Chaplaincy Grand Rounds. The students also met twice weekly for one and a half hours in small process group. Additionally, each student met with me weekly for individual supervision. In the clinical component of the program the student group provided crisis ministry and spiritual care interventions. Each student was responsible for providing spiritual care to patients, families, and staff on one Intensive Care Unit and one or two intermediate care units. Clinical assignments ranged from oncology and cardiology to medical and transplant units. Students also rotated the responsibility for crisis ministry during 24-hour on-call periods in collaboration with staff chaplains.

There were five students in this unit, three women and two men. All were Caucasian. Their religious affiliations were Lutheran, Presbyterian, Unitarian Universalist, and United Church of Christ. It was a first unit of CPE for all of the students, and it was also part of their theological training requirements for their respective religious groups. They came from three different seminaries and ranged in age from late twenties to early forties.

In addition to encountering the stark clinical realities of a major academic medical center, in this particular group four out of five students experienced an unusual extent of suffering and crisis in their personal lives: a parent of one participant was terminally ill and was hospitalized several times during this unit. The sibling of another member was serving in the military overseas and sustained injuries. The seriously ill child of a third student had an emergency hospitalization. A parent of a fourth student was chronically ill with a degenerative neurological disease. The hospital setting brought these realities and the related fear and distress to the forefront. In addition, during this unit the spouse of a peer in another local CPE group had a major accident, was hospitalized in our institution, and died a week later. All of these events had a profound impact on the life of this CPE group.

I had planned in advance of this unit to collect data related to the use of functional subgrouping. The data was designed to help me examine several specific questions. Would SCT concepts and methods indeed turn out to be useful to this group of students? Would the use of SCT help them to access and use emotional and spiritual resources towards the goal of providing effective spiritual care? Would I be able to use my skill and understanding to build a strong enough holding environment and system? Would this experimental project of using SCT become an additional burden with little benefit?

Data Collection

In order to examine these questions I collected several types of data. First, I used three brief surveys: the SCT Subgrouping Questionnaire (O'Neill et al., 1997), the Learning Evaluation Form (Piper, Connolly, & Salvendy, 1984) and a Group Climate Questionnaire (MacKenzie, 1983). These instruments respectively assessed: a) students' ability to observe functional subgrouping while using the technique; b) the effect of functional subgrouping on the group's climate; and c) the relationship between functional subgrouping and self-reported professional effectiveness. The Subgroup Questionnaire and the Learning Evaluation Form were filled out after each of the unit's sixteen SPG sessions. The Group Climate Questionnaire was completed after four sessions: the fourth, ninth, fourteenth, and sixteenth session. Students also had an opportunity to write down some adjectives that came to mind to describe the experience of functional subgrouping after each session. To simplify the analysis I will focus on one question from each of the three questionnaires:

1. *How often did you feel subgrouping occurred in today's group?* This question is part of the SCT Subgrouping Questionnaire and was asked after each group session. The questions ask students to focus their observation of the group-as-whole and its progress, rather than focusing on individual membership behavior. Ratings were given on a five point scale, 1 = not at all and 5 = a great deal.

2. *As a result of participating in Group, I believe that I have learned things that will increase the effectiveness of my professional work.* This question is part of the Learning Evaluation Form, which was completed after each session. The question explored the applicability of experiential learning in SPG to the pastoral role. Responses were recorded in a six point scale: 0 = no learning; 1 = slight; 2 = minor; 3 = moderate; 4 = considerable; to 5 = extreme learning.

3. *Did members have a sense that what was happening was important and was there a sense of participation?* This is one of several questions on the Group Climate Questionnaire, which was completed after the fourth, ninth, fourteenth, and sixteenth session. Again, responses were recorded in a six point scale; 0 = not at all; 1 = a little bit; 2 = somewhat; 3 = moderately; 4 = quite a bit;, 5 = a great deal; and 6 = extremely.

Additionally, at the end of this unit students were asked to write an experience of faith paper, which invited them to reflect theologically on their experiences and learning in SPG.

My analysis was based on the average score for the group for the selected group session. In general, the students' scores for the session were similar, so their average is a useful measure of overall group response. My focus was on the sessions with particularly high (session four and nine) or low ratings (session twelve and thirteen), assuming that those sessions marked key points in the life of this group. (For sessions twelve and thirteen responses to the third question are missing). Additionally, I included the ratings of the fourteenth and sixteenth sessions. Quotes from students' faith papers on the experience of SPG provide additional perspectives.

Findings

Subgrouping was introduced in our first group meeting and was continually encouraged throughout the unit. In response to the first question (How often did you feel subgrouping occurred in to-day's group?), it is clear that for all the sessions the students' average rating for subgrouping was moderately high. Functional subgrouping appeared to happen relatively consistently. In the beginning of this study and over the course of the first four sessions (two weeks), an increase in the average ratings of functional sub-grouping was evident (see Figure 1). In response to the question from the Learning Evaluation Form whether participation in SPG led to learning that would increase professional effectiveness, three members rated <u>considerable</u>, and two members rated <u>moderate</u>. This equals an average group rating of 3.6. Members felt that what was happening had <u>quite a bit</u> of importance and there was a moderately strong participation.

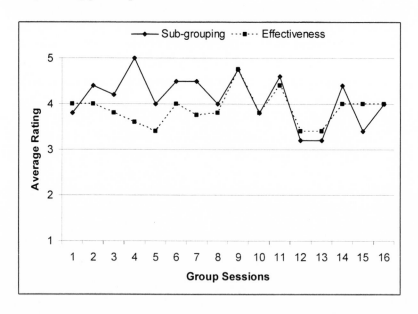

Figure 1. Ratings of Functional Sub-Grouping and Professional Effectiveness

Subsequent to session four (week three) and over the remainder of the program, for the group-as-a-whole there was a slight trend towards feeling less functional subgrouping happened. In the ninth session, at the unit's midpoint, the group's rating of subgrouping was surprisingly high at 4.75. One student was absent during this session due to a family emergency. In terms of the session leading to learning that increased professional effectiveness, students also rated 4.75, between extreme and considerable. What was happening had a great deal, even extreme importance and there was a high sense of participation in this session as shown by members' average rating of 5.25 (on a 0-6 scale).

Sessions twelve and thirteen took place during a difficult week in the life of this group. On top of the previously mentioned stressors, the group sustained a 'close hit' when the spouse of a peer in nearby CPE group died at our institution subsequent to an accident. For the students (and for me) this event felt overwhelming, tragic, and sad. Over the course of the week my students provided support to the grieving peer and family. As role boundaries became difficult to manage, I clarified that I would relieve the student assigned to this particular unit and take on the role of chaplain to the grieving family. I invited my students to offer support as friends and peers as they felt appropriate, honoring prior relationships. As I remember the SPG sessions during this time, I recall the palpable shock, numbness, and sadness as group members struggled to find words for their experience. The events of that week changed functional subgrouping negatively as documented by the group's questionnaire ratings. The average rating is notably less than 4, reflecting the group's and my struggle to facilitate the group's ability to comfort itself. The group process felt disjointed. Not surprisingly, they rated the affect of participation in group on professional effectiveness between moderate and considerable (3.4).

The third to last session was rated at a relative high average of 4.4 relative to functional subgrouping. Students felt that group participation increased their professional effectiveness considerably. And, with the exception of one group member all students felt that the group's work was extremely important (5.6).

In the last SPG session, ratings on whether functional sub-grouping occurred averaged 4.0. The SPG earning was felt to increase professional effectiveness <u>considerably</u> (4). The group also felt that events in the session had <u>extreme</u> or a <u>great deal</u> of importance and group members participated a <u>great deal</u> (5.6).

Reflections and Interpretations

The data suggest that functional subgrouping has a potentially important role in CPE. This new method of communicating was described by interns as "challenging and rewarding." A peak of appreciation—and possibly compliance—was documented in the fourth session with its unanimous highest rating. Written comments on the session included adjectives like "positive," "upbeat," "hopeful," "invigorating," "aware," "supported," and "open." Clearly, this group was highly motivated to do its best to experiment with a new skill.

Overall, during the first portion of the unit, the interns' responses suggested an increasing learning and use of functional subgrouping. Additionally, students appear to have found their learning in SPG personally enriching and professionally valuable. While we as CPE supervisors hope that this is true for students in any CPE group, the following quotation specifically focused on functional subgrouping. In the theological reflection about participating in small process group one student wrote:

> Sharing emotions and being asked to join has helped me see that my emotions are not unusual or strange. This emotional resonance has made it possible for me to treat emotions as gifts to be shared, explored, and utilized in my care giving rather than as negative feelings to be feared and suppressed. Asking 'Anyone else?' has enabled me to experience the transforming power of joining and being joined. There is something so liberating, so exhilarating, so empowering about not being and feeling alone. Having my emotional pain held by a group has helped me see and feel the presence of something larger than myself.

I have come to see, a sacred connection, which is the web of life and love that I understand to be God.

How did their experiences in the group relate to the interns taking up their pastoral role as members of the multidisciplinary team and as spiritual care givers with patients and families? In application of the SCT principle of isomorphy, I expected a relationship between the students' growing ability to bring their personal energy into the member role in SPG and their increased ability to take up wholeheartedly the pastoral role. This seems partially true. Students were not immediately able to make a connection between their learning in SPG and their functioning as chaplains. However, the overall data shows an increasing congruence between ratings of functional subgrouping, the importance of participation, and increased professional effectiveness. This suggests that the students grew in their ability to appreciate and reflect on the connection between SPG and their pastoral work.

One student reflected: "Without question, one of the most challenging and rewarding experiences of CPE has been participating in small process group. From feeling confused and uncertain as to what small process group was to needing that space to be joined and held, my experience with small process group has been a journey with deep theological and vocational significance."

By the ninth session, the group had moved beyond initial anxiety and compliance. Members were able to bring what mattered most to them using functional subgrouping to access deeper emotions. They also began to understand experientially what it meant to shift from the person system (taking things 'just personally' and thinking one is the only one feeling a particular way) to the member role (engaging in deeper resonance and exploration). I recall a turning point in this session when a member who had just been going along with subgrouping joined wholeheartedly. This person got teary as she expressed resonance with two of her peers. The subgroup subsequently explored worries about illness and death, acceptance of uncertainty, and sadness in the face of life's fragility and finitude. The subgroup's exploration was moving and freed up energy for all members. The students recorded that it was important to use, and to participate, in the group. One member commented at the end of this session that sharing felt "safe, liberating, and refreshing." Another member commented that the session was "energizing, productive, cohesive, helpful, and enthusiastic."

Around the middle of the unit with multiple crisis situations and one member missing due to a family emergency, it was difficult for the group to explore openly frustration, irritation, and anger (which I have often seen at the midpoint of the program). Instead, there was a pull to caretaking: first in exploration of the impulse to take care of and "fix things" for the missing member; then, in the pull to give pastoral care to each other. Functional subgrouping required all members to join in exploration of what was happening for each of them. While this was seemingly met with some resistance, use of functional subgrouping also kept the absent member from becoming the 'identified patient.' Additionally, group members used subgrouping effectively to join each other in a way that made for connection, care, and comfort. The session marked a shift from a more avoidant stance of sympathy to more authentic and deeper attunement in the midst of the impact of real life events.

In isomorphy with the group's development, the data of the ninth session also demonstrated that the students were gaining clarity about the implications of functional subgrouping for their pastoral practice. Ratings relative to subgrouping paralleled ratings relative to learning in the group increasing professional effectiveness. Resonating and working along silently in the group offered a model for empathizing and staying with a wider variety and depth of feelings in pastoral care. The interns' pastoral connections became more meaningful, more intensive and extensive. One student reflected, "...the single greatest theological argument in favor of small process group is that it allows you to love other people more genuinely. It forces people to find that common ground and to support them in their feelings, to be in the same boat with someone else as Jesus was with humanity. In that manner of speaking, the incarnation itself is the ultimate 'join'...God had to 'join' humans." And one might add, students in CPE learn to join humanity and make their theology come true in their pastoral care.

Another group member commented on the importance of SPG for the practice of pastoral care and expressed appreciation for the support in his personal development:

The goals of Small Process Group are as follows: to explore my own emotions thereby increasing my self-awareness and helping to utilize my reactions to my emotions, to investigate my resonances to other people's emotions so that I can improve my pastoral care practice, to develop skill in working with groups and group dynamics. Thus defined, the goals of Small Process Group have strong roots within the Christian tradition. This might not initially appear to be the case. The Christian tradition has been virtually constructed off of emotional repression, the opposite of emotional health.... Jesus stands out as someone who would support Small Process Group and its goals. Jesus only began his ministry after forty days of intense self-reflection in the Judean wilderness.... During his ministry Jesus does not repress his emotions but uses them to further his ministry in effective ways.

The data about sessions twelve and thirteen seem to reflect the impact of the tragic death of the spouse of a peer in another CPE center. Noticeably less functional subgrouping happened in these sessions. Yet, interestingly, participation in and importance of the session was rated high. It was important to be together but it was difficult to find words for the experiences of this traumatic week. Generally, in order to engage in functional subgrouping, one needs to stay in touch with oneself and the group at the same time. This is not an easy task, and the unusual intensity of this crisis made it particularly difficult to engage the newly learned skills of functional subgrouping. The students understandably struggled to get in touch with, organize, and direct their energy into the member role or pastoral role. My learning was that when we are personally affected in such a way that we cannot cross from person system to role, it is functional to attend to "just us personally." The main task for the group was to comfort itself, and my task was to facilitate this process.

It would have been interesting to invite the group's reflection and subgrouping around the barriers experienced in these two sessions. Was the method of functional subgrouping creating the difficulty? Or did the overload of crisis and death leave the group speechless, no matter what the method? One student stated, "I found Small Process Group to be an interesting, supportive group, but also a bit stressful. Although I was inspired by how powerful it felt to be joined by others when I related my emotions surrounding my experience, I also sometimes felt a bit confined by the unusual format of the group. Sometimes my concern about the correct protocol of the exercise constrained me from what I really wanted to share."

The accumulation and the timing of crisis events in this CPE unit did not leave enough time to process and digest their impact prior to the end of the unit. Interestingly, the students did not mention the experience of the death of their peer's spouse in their final evaluations. In the last three sessions, with the end of the unit looming, the group had several tasks: to process as best as they could the events, to consolidate CPE learning, and to say good-bye. The group worked hard and well as they experienced "shared vulnerability, resonance, and affirmation." In session fourteen group members expressed feeling "supported," "energized," "successful," and "productive" as they explored irritation and anger, belonging and separation. Finally, in the last SPG, feelings of "sorrow" "nostalgia," "appreciation," and "closure" were prevalent. And appropriately, group members seem to have said good-bye to their role as chaplains in our institution and to their role as members of the CPE group.

These findings illustrate that functional subgrouping in SPG provides a context for exploring the concept of role as bridge concept between the person system and any functional role in a particular context. According to SCT theory pastoral authority as well as authority as a group member can be conceptualized as the ability to take up a functional role, i.e. to use one's emotional energy and to contribute behaviors that serve the specific goal of a particular context. This particular CPE group struggled at times to be in role enough not to be flooded by their personal emotions. Other times they functioned in role, but found it difficult to 'show up' emotionally. In parallel, my role was to keep the educational and professional focus of the CPE program while also bringing my whole heart to the task. In a CPE unit, so challenged by crisis, we all learned to know more about, and to act less on, the pull to create identified patients and the pull to the reciprocal caretaking role. Pastoral Role: Caretaking or Caregiving?

Many people choosing the helping professions and ministry as careers have experienced caregiving deficits and lack of attunement in early life. This can be a strong motivation, yet also a liability when one takes care of others instead of exploring the experiences that arise in one self. This particular CPE summer unit offered lots of opportunities to identify inner impulses and emotional experiences that are in the category of caretaking. For example, to act on the basis of one's cognitive map of what others' needs are or should be; to take on limitless responsibility for the imagined needs of others; to be misattuned to the other and to self; to manage a need that is in oneself by taking care of the perceived needs of others, effectively ignoring one's own need; to fix in others what calls for attention in oneself; to defend against a human experience that appears to be too different to ever be one's own.

The context of the SPG and the method of functional subgrouping proved effective in exploring these issues. For example, when one student shared a current personally painful experience, a caretaking response was elicited in others. Rather than encouraging caretaking behaviors, like questioning or expressions of sympathy, the students were invited to join authentically with an emotionally similar enough experience. This led to subgroup exploration of the existential experiences of uncertainty, human finitude, experiences of pain or sadness, and others. Meanwhile another subgroup explored the impulse to take care of, to do away with, or fix these experiences in one self and others. The group-as-a-whole held the difference. Students recognized the application to pastoral care: if we work along and join others silently in pastoral care, we take steps beyond the patient/helper dynamic, which dominates our healthcare system. And we can give and take the invitation to be human together.

The ingredients of a caregiving (vs. caretaking) pastoral role are to be aware of the experiences in the moment and to work towards an empathic relationship; to stay with others and actively find resonance; to create a space in which the naming of all kinds of experiences is legitimate; to be sensitive to and in touch with the energy that is contained in any emotional or spiritual experience; to create relationships in which giving and receiving is the same and energy is exchanged freely. In sum, the traditional main learning in CPE, not to impose an agenda on patients, is greatly supported and effectively promoted by functional subgrouping.

Small Process Group Member Role and Pastoral Role

Based on the data collected in this unit of CPE, it is useful to take a closer look at the similarities and differences between the skill of functional subgrouping in one's member role in small process group and the skill of resonating with others in one's pastoral role. The similarities are establishing trusting and empathically attuned relationships and working along emotionally, while also observing the system. Additionally, it is useful in pastoral care to be aware that there is usually another side, another subgroup relative to any issue. A significant difference between the member role in SPG and the pastoral role is that the chaplain does not share or add to what a patient is expressing. Rather the chaplain works along silently and gets in touch with similarities in his or her experience in order to listen and respond with head and heart. Overall, the evidence from this group suggests that functional subgrouping in SPG trained these students to do this more effectively.

Additionally, functional subgrouping allowed the students to gain insight in the pastoral role. In the pastoral role what one authentically wants to say is most useful when it connects with what is called for in any given moment. In CPE we value specific life experience, unique personality, and even charisma. However, what is important in the pastoral role is the pastoral caregiver's ability to check whether his or her unique contribution comes alongside and subgroups functionally with the members of the pastoral caregiving system. The pastoral caregiving system may consist of the patient and the chaplain, the family and the pastoral care giver, the religious leader and the congregation, or the multidisciplinary team, which includes the pastoral perspective. This means that one's unique voice and experience belong to the system and the community. It comes most to life and is most connected when it serves the system's goals. Put in theological terms, SPG is a space in which to experience the transcendence of the self and the sacredness of living, developing, and transforming community. These challenges were very much alive in this CPE group as members attempted to live their values and to operationalize their theology. While this is a learning issue prevalent in many CPE groups, it also reflects a general human challenge: the challenge to reduce the discrepancy between one's convictions and the reality of one's ability to live these beliefs and values.

One student playfully reflected: "What would happen, if we began our worship with 'I have sinned, anyone else'?" Another student formulated:

"The group fits quite neatly into my theology.... We are asked to make connections, which is what I see as holy in this world. We are asked to build a web by joining others so that they are not alone, which is what I see as the presence of God in community, and, in part, the role of the church. We are asked to be fully present, which is another important aspect of my faith. Theologically, I love small process group. Experientially, I really struggled to figure out how to share my full self...so much of what I was feeling seemed deeply tied to the past and to the future and anchored outside of the group. It's taken all summer for me to be able to throw that anchor into the center of the group. Over the summer we created and then strengthened our web of connections and were all held by that web as we experienced deep sadness, confusion, anxiety, frustration, anger, and even silliness. With each 'join' the web grew stronger, as did the realization that if we fell, it would catch us."

Supervisory Role

Throughout the unit, I wondered how the group experienced me in my role. During one session, the group had the task to sculpt and embody the dynamics of their group, including the supervisor. The goal was to help students gain awareness of the group's dynamics and any roles they assigned to each other. Another goal was to make visible what was often invisible in regular small process group sessions.

The result was a playful sequence of a group sculpture: students held their hands in a praying gesture in front of their chest. Each of them seemed to be on his or her individual search for connection, using the praying hands like the needle of a compass. Meanwhile they had me positioned in the middle of the group, with the instruction to turn slowly in a circle, my praying hands pointing towards the group members. Soon each of them adjusted their 'compass needle' to the 'magnetic field'. The group created a circle with an energy field in the middle. Then, they embodied the practice of functional subgrouping by briefly touching each other with the tips of their praying hands, picking up the 'magnetic' resonance from each others' 'compass needles'. They had fun staying in connection and creating new connections with one another. The dynamic sequence of the sculpture ended with each group member turning from the center to face away from the group. Now they picked up the resonance beyond the group, symbolizing their pastoral care practice. As they prepared to become 'compasses' in other communities, they learned by resonating with each other and also by resonating with my role as a leader.

Throughout the unit, I shared some of the students' challenges. In the midst of the group's palpable pain and sorrow, I felt at times overwhelmed by the intensity of these weeks. There were days when it was difficult to negotiate my different roles: pastor, educator, chaplain, administrator, group leader, and colleague. Reflection on role, goal, and context was helpful. I also worked along with the group's struggle to keep going, to stay grounded, and to trust the value of our work together. With my students I shared the sense of hope as we all kept showing up, literally and metaphorically. Together we celebrated the many accomplishments of the unit: work well done and real growth was nurturing to all of us. But most importantly, none of the students ultimately felt alone in the process of this unit. I am grateful and moved that this group allowed me to be their compass in turbulent waters.

One student wrote, "In many ways, churches are like small

process group. Church members bring a host of emotions, which often get pushed aside or swept under the carpet, making resonance and joining difficult. As a spiritual leader, I want to be a catalyst for joining, for encouraging the community to listen, to share, and to join. If I can do that, then my parishioners will have the opportunity to experience something sacred and holy as they go about the work of building beloved community." I believe this student's application of SPG to a future context of a church also reflects the experience of my leadership and the group's work.

Conclusion and Future Research

Based on the evidence from this unit of CPE, I would argue that there is consistent indication that functional subgrouping does indeed benefit student learning and development in CPE. The data points to the role of functional subgrouping in increasing professional effectiveness in the pastoral role. From a research perspective what I have presented here is preliminary data. While the survey questions showed changes and improvements, they are also self-reported. While the results of this limited case study support the use of Systems-Centered Training in CPE, the number of students was small and the evidence only comes from one CPE group. Also, it is possible that the outcomes that resulted were the result of other elements of the CPE experience and not just the use of SCT techniques and methods. Finally, my skill and experience as leader trained in SCT is still developing. (For more information on training in SCT see: http://www.sct-institute.org).

Despite these limitations, the findings suggest that functional subgrouping trained these students to observe the group as a whole while participating in its development; to develop a deeper capacity to resonate and empathize with others; to empathize and explore experiences in the moment rather than to act on the impulse to 'fix' things; and to become more able to take up their role as member in the group and as chaplain on the clinical units. The students learned to take responsibility and ownership in the process of building a system that allowed for exploration of all kinds of emotional and spiritual experiences. Clearly, the students found functional sub-grouping personally valuable and professionally useful. They gained appreciation of groups, counteracting the widespread tendency in ministry to be(come) a lone ranger. They learned to reach inside themselves to find similarities rather than to defend against differences. The students also used SPG effectively to experience their growing ability to put their conceptual understandings in theology into practice in a community.

I am unaware of other investigations that have gathered evidence that allows us to test our supervisory theories and help us to improve our supervisory practice in order to better accomplish the goals of supervision and the goals of CPE. The results of this case study engender more curiosity as to the use and integration of SCT in CPE. Future studies of functional subgrouping should include objective ways of examining how CPE supervisory practice, particularly supervision of the CPE small group process, affects students' pastoral functioning. It would be interesting to compare the learning of a CPE group using the SCT method of functional subgrouping with a group whose SPG experience was based on a different group theory and different methods. A larger sample of student groups over time might also warrant additional insights. Future research could also examine how students' learning in SPG does or does not apply to effective functioning in their pastoral role. Finally, it would be interesting to apply SCT to a yearlong CPE program to include observations on the phases of group development and their possible impact on pastoral functioning and development in ministry.

We have much to learn about how supervisory practices influence students' learning and professional functioning. Systems-Centered Training, with its emphasis on functional subgrouping and on research, provides one very promising approach to this exciting work.

References

Agazarian, Y. (1997). *Systems-centered therapy*. New York, London: Guilford.

Agazarian, Y. (2007). *Systems-centered core skills*. Good Enough Press.

Gantt, S., & Agazarian, Y. (Eds.). (2005). *SCT in action*. New York, Lincoln, Shanghai: iPublisher.

Gantt, S., & Hopper, E. (2008). Two perspectives on trauma in a training group: The systems-centered approach and the theory of incohesion: Part I. *Group Analysis, 41*(1), 98-112.

Hemenway, J. (2005). Opening up the circle: Next steps in group work for clinical pastoral educators; In Gantt, S., & Agazarian, Y. (Eds.), *Systems-Centered Training in Action* (pp. 81-97). New York, Lincoln, Shanghai: iPublisher.

Ladden, L., Gantt, S., Rude, S., & Agazarian, Y. (2007). Systems-centered therapy: A protocol for treating generalized anxiety disorder. *Journal for Contemporary Psychotherapy, 37*(2).

MacKenzie, K.R. (1983). The clinical application of a group climate measure. In R. R. Dies & K. R. MacKenzie (Eds.), *Advances in group psychotherapy: Integrating research and practice* (pp. 159-170) New York: International Universities Press.

O'Neill, R.M., Agazarian, Y. M., Ladden, L., & Carter, F. (1997). *SCT Subgrouping Scale*. SUNY Upstate Medical University, Syracuse, N.Y.: Unpublished manuscript.

Piper, W.E., Connolly, J.L., & Salvendy, J.T. (1984). Variables related to reported learning in brief experiential groups held at professional meetings. *Group*, (8), 43-51.

Zollfrank, A. A. (2005). ACPE theory paper, the work of care. *Journal of Supervision and Training in Ministry*, (25), 156-186.

CHAPTER 11

Systems Oriented Training and the Goals of CPE
Peg Lewis

Introduction

The goal of this article is to describe the ways in which the theory and methods of Systems-Centered Training can contribute to the educational objectives of Clinical Pastoral Education. In particular I have used systems oriented theory and techniques with Level I units of seminarians and of health care professionals in the clinical setting of an acute care hospital. During the interview process, prospective students agreed to participate in a CPE unit based in systems oriented theory and methods. In particular they were alerted that the peer group seminar components would have the goals of learning how to be members of a working group and learning to see interactions from a systems perspective. In addition, I discussed how systems-centered theory applied to the three goals of CPE (Pastoral Competence, Pastoral Formation and Pastoral Reflection).

Systems Oriented Theory

Systems-Centered Training and Research (SCTRI) posits a theory of living systems: "A theory of living systems defines a hierarchy of isomorphic systems that are energy-organizing, goal-directed and self-correcting" (Agazarian, 1997, p. 18). Systems-Centered Training (SCT) has a structured sequence of interventions for groups that are intended to facilitate the work toward the primary group goals of survival, development, and transformation. As the group's development is facilitated the explicit goals or tasks of group can also be more fully achieved. This systems oriented methodology is consistently subject to action research, both immediately within the group ("Do you feel more here, less here or the same?") and longer term within more formal research protocols.

An essential construct of Systems-Centered theory is that of hierarchy—the understanding that each system is nested within a larger system and contains a smaller system (Agazarian, 1997, pp. 21-22). Within a systems oriented group there are persons (with lots of their own identity components) who become group members when they bring their energy and curiosity to create or join a subgroup which is one of the components of the group as a whole. The member system is nested within the subgroup which is nested within the training group as a whole. The construct of hierarchy can be applied at a variety of levels. The CPE students become participants in the different component groups(sub-groups) of the unit of CPE which is nested within the hospital's Department of Religious Ministries.

Another essential concept is that of isomorphy—that the dynamics of change and growth in any one of the components of the hierarchy will affect all the other components (Agazarian, 1997, pp. 23-24). The most effective site for creating change is the subgroup since it contains the possibility of affecting all the members contained within it as well as the group as a whole (Gantt & Agazarian, 2005, pp. 6-7). Similarly, awareness and behavioral changes achieved in members of subgroups can also affect the awareness and behaviors of individual persons as they engage and relate in other contexts.

Systems oriented thinking places great emphasis on being clear about the goals of the particular context so that one can also be observant of which behaviors or functions contribute to achieving the goals and which create barriers or inhibit the goals being achieved.

Systems Oriented Thinking Applied to Level I CPE

As I apply systems oriented thinking to a summer CPE unit or to a CPE for Health Care Professionals unit, I want to be clear about the overall goals of the training unit organized within the categories of pastoral competence, pastoral reflection, and pastoral formation, as well as the goals of each program component (pastoral care/verbatim seminars, small process group seminars, didactics, and individual supervision). Further, I want to make those goals explicit in each session so that we can see what contributes to and what inhibits our learning in each context. It should be noted that the two types of CPE programs are also nested within different institutional contexts which also have different goals, and hence shape the goals of each CPE program differently.

An 11 week summer CPE unit at Yale-New Haven Hospital (YNHH) is usually comprised of seminarians, often but not always from several different seminaries. In addition to the students' learning goals, the goals of the summer CPE program are shaped by the theological educational goals of the seminaries and by the ministry preparation goals of various judicatories as well as by the spiritual care expectations of the hospital. The extended unit of CPE for health care professionals is comprised of YNHH staff members plus representatives from the wider health care and/or religious community. The goals of this program are shaped by the institution's patient care and spiritual care expectations. The health care professionals in the program are not preparing for professional ministry but are seeking to integrate the spiritual dimension into their particular clinical practice; thus this program's goals are also shaped by the professional expectations and allegiances represented in the group, as well as by the participants' individual learning goals.

For the purposes of this article I want to address the larger goals of a unit of CPE and describe how some of the systems oriented training methods contribute to achieving those goals. The most basic method which we use as normative throughout all program components is that of functional subgrouping (Agazarian, 1997, pp. 24-26). In the CPE group, functional subgrouping is applied as students are encouraged to participate in group discussion by joining on similarities rather than separating around differences. As one member voices an observation or experience, other members listen carefully to see if they have a similar-enough observation or experience to join the subgroup (or exploration team) initiated by the first speaker. Those members who cannot identify a similar-enough resonance are asked to wait to speak unit the first group reaches a pause in its exploration. Then another subgroup, with a different experience can be introduced and another aspect explored. All members' voices, all subgroup explorations, as they contribute to the goal of the particular program component, are considered important to the work of the group.

Pastoral Competence

In the context of an urban hospital, a key component of pastoral competence is the ability to provide spiritual companionship, comfort, and care to patients and families from a variety of faith traditions and cultures. A significant first step is learning to listen and accompany persons suffering from illness, trauma, transition, and loss with an open heart and empathetic spirit. Learning to join authentically with another in a functional subgroup creates and enlarges the capacity to find the emotional resonance to meet and steadfastly companion another. Learning to listen to another subgroup work with a different experience while still staying connected to one's own primary experience exercises the observing self (Agazarian, 1997, p. 34) so that one is neither absorbed by nor closed to the experience of the other.

Pastoral care and verbatim seminars, with the overall contextual goal of developing pastoral competence, begin with the presenter articulating her or his particular learning goal(s) for this verbatim. After the introduction and dialogue are read, participants are invited to identify places of resonance with the content of the verbatim and to offer feedback relative to the student's particular learning goals and questions. The subsequent discussion takes place within the norms of functional subgrouping, emphasizing that the student presenting is also presenting on behalf of a learning group which has similar contextual goals. Thus students are encouraged not to take things 'just personally.' The focus is also on observed behavior, with interpretations open to the research of looking back to the specific data (words spoken, body language reported) within the verbatim.

For summer unit students especially, looking to join with the dilemma of choice represented in many verbatims frees them from needing to perform and be right since there is a subgroup of members who are exploring pastoral response choices. Two students in a summer group were more than 10 years younger than the other members, and they both expressed their relief that these pastoral care seminars did not become occasions of advice giving but helped them explore shared pastoral experience and pastoral response options with peers.

A program component new to me is the Experience of Faith seminar. This seminar has been a staple of CPE for health care professionals because the participants have usually had less theological training than the seminarians in the summer units. However, they have proven so effective, used in conjunction with systems oriented subgrouping and communications techniques, that I now include them in all my Level I programming. For the experience of faith seminar, students are asked to write a few pages about their experiences of the holy, of suffering, of hope, of community, etc. They are then asked to talk or read about their experience in the seminar. Again other group members are invited to respond by discovering what part of their own affective and/or spiritual experience is similar and to join the experience of the initial speaker. Especially when there are differences (in SCT terms 'stereotypic differences' of culture, race, faith tradition), the practice is that of finding the essential human experiences that connect us as a way to integrate without negating our differences. We are intentional about trying to hear each other's particular experience set within different cultural contexts and social conditions without excluding that experience because it is too different or 'other.'

One CPE Health Care Professionals unit was comprised of folks from a variety of cultural and faith backgrounds: Hispanic, both Pentecostal and Roman Catholic; African American Holiness, and Anglo, both Roman Catholic and Methodist. Although they were very different, they all found ways to connect with some portion of the others' experiences. Each experience of faith seminar brought members closer as they shared from deep and tender places. These were sometimes emotional sessions, as people remembered encounters with the Holy and experiences of suffering and hope. As members shared these deeply personal, emotionally charged experiences, the group as a whole was able to contain and hold each other with generosity, compassion, and the relief of a shared humanity. While we don't engage differences directly in this context, differences become apparent as the next student shares her or his experience of faith, and the rest of the group seeks to find other places of resonance with this new speaker's experience.

Pastoral Formation

In a CPE summer unit of seminarians, forming pastoral identity involves learning which aspects of oneself are useful to bring to the many components of the pastoral role. In a summer CPE program pastoral identity is the primary organizing identity that incorporates many sub-roles: pastoral care giver, worship leader, colleague among them. As health care professionals participate in CPE, their primary organizing identities continue to be that of nurse, social worker, physician assistant, etc. Goals relating to pastoral formation in a CPE-HCP unit address how to integrate spiritual care 'sub-roles' (spiritual supporter, prayer partner, family comforter) within the other primary professional identity. Both program contexts require educational methods that develop the capacity to notice differences in context and role and to act in accordance with changing goals. Systems oriented thinking is very attentive to our roles within specific contexts and their particular goals (Gantt & Agazarian, 2005, p. 8). Learning to be a group member, experiencing—and observing—the process of bringing that aspect of one's personal energy and information to contribute to the goals of each program component and to the different roles required of the many different contexts of the educational and clinical settings, develop the capacity to observe and to function within the different aspects of pastoral identity.

Another Systems-Centered Training method applied across the elements of the CPE program is the practice of stating the context and the goal(s) of each session and clarifying the functional roles for each subsection. For instance, in small process group a stated goal might be "to experience and learn about group membership via functional subgrouping." In addition to the important structural boundaries of the group in time and space, the small process group has three sub-sections: an introductory teaching section of 15 minutes, an experiential section of 60 minutes, and a concluding evaluation section of 15 minutes. Each subsection has a different goal and the students' functional roles are therefore different as well. In the initial teaching component participants enact their more familiar student roles of listening and questioning intellectually; in the experiential section students explore being group members in the here and now, intentionally accessing their affective as well as cognitive ways of knowing; in the concluding section, they are encouraged to step outside of their experience to become observers and researchers, looking back to notice what contributed to or detracted from the stated goal of the experiential session.

In any small process group, then, the participants are invited to bring aspects of themselves into at least three different roles (more if they join more than one subgroup) and to notice their internal as well as external shifts in role, goal, and context. Throughout the day students are similarly invited to notice how they bring different aspects of themselves in different roles as the contexts shift, from ER trauma bay to family lounge, from staff meeting to peer group, from colleague lunch to dinner at home. This sharpened awareness contributes to our discussions of how they bring aspects of themselves—their own complex identities—to the functional roles of ministry. They also are encouraged to notice what helps and what gets in the way as they try to take up functional roles and to be curious about how they might be importing something from the past which may or may not be useful now (Agazarian, 2006 work in progress).

One of the challenges of small process group is to help members get into the here and now, since that is where we can make some choices about how we experience and respond to the present environment. One systems oriented intervention, the distraction exercise (Agazarian, 1997, pp. 73-79), helps students distinguish between the facts and the feelings of a distraction (worrying about a previous patient encounter, pre-occupation with something that happened at home) that pulls their energy away from the present context. Once they have named the facts and then the feelings associated with those facts, they are invited to bring one or more of those feelings into the group. In a recent summer group this exercise helped the students share bits of their present stories from different contexts, to identify the specific emotional energy associated with each story, and to bring that emotional energy into the present context. Once all members were able to be present with their emotional energy, they would often begin the work of subgrouping around the feelings active in the here and now. One student was able to name the facts and identify the feelings of a very distressing contact with his elderly parents and to bring the considerable energy of his grief and sense of loss into the group. Other members were connected, not with the specific facts of his experience, but with the feelings he brought forward. In this instance, the whole group found ways to join in the deeper exploration of grief and longing.

Pastoral Reflection

Another essential component of systems oriented education is enlarging the capacity of group members to observe from multiple perspectives and to widen their range of choices (Agazarian, 1997, pp. 34-36), initially as group members and reciprocally (isomorphically) as person systems, that is persons who have learned and are learning a variety of roles or organized ways of interacting in the many contexts we find ourselves. As persons we have learned ways of looking at our experience, acquired mental maps and ways of responding to our contexts, and have learned various roles that have helped us to cope and survive in the past. Those maps and those roles can be automatically invoked, especially in situations of stress, yet they may or may not apply to the present reality. Many

of the systems oriented methods for group leadership involve helping members in the context of the group—i.e. not working alone—
to get new perspectives about their maps and roles and to notice if
they are useful in the present context. As students learn to become
observers of their previously learned and adaptive roles and
whether or not they function within the context of the group, they
can make choices about whether to continue the thoughts, feelings,
and behaviors identified with that role. Thus they acquire some
freedom of choice and an opportunity to explore something different within the present context (Agazarian, 2006 work in progress).

Pointing out opportunities of choice is an important function of
group leadership, known in SCT parlance as identifying 'forks in
the road' (Gantt & Agazarian, 2005, p. 21), including choosing to
work with the leader as a member on behalf of the group; choosing
which side of a difference or conflict to work on first, choosing
whether to explore aspects of the origins of an old role, or to explore the present experience that the old role serves to defend
against. One challenge for the leader is to help identify the fork
which could move the member and the group in its discoveries of
present reality (Agazarian, 1997, p. 92). A challenge for the leader
is to identify a choice point and then to respect and support which-
ever choice the member selects.

An early step in subgrouping is to develop an observing self
sufficient to notice the resonance with a variety of subgroups, and
to then to decide which to join and when (Agazarian, 1997, Chapter 2). Working in a subgroup assists one in having an experience
with emotional content while staying connected to other members
and observing oneself in the context of the subgroup without being
'had by,' i.e. encapsulated or isolated in, the experience. The leader
can then work with group members to discriminate between
thoughts and feelings, between responses in the here and now versus responses shaped by the past or predictions of the future. This
subgroup supported skill development helps students feel safe
enough to explore their own experiences and to learn at their own
pace. One of the functions of the group leader is to teach and guide
the members through a sequence of skills that enable them as a
group—and eventually also in their person systems—to contain

and explore increasingly intense experiences and conflicts (Agazarian, 1997, pp. 92-96).

I have been deeply touched by what gets shared and explored, especially in the subgrouping experiences of small process group and the experience of faith seminars. Students gain confidence in their ability to hold, and be held with, their feelings. They realize that their experiences of inadequacy and shame are not unique but deeply human. And as they connect with each other with compassion they begin to extend compassion and forgiveness to themselves. In my supervisory experience, CPE student groups I have guided by systems oriented leadership have worked more deeply and affectionately with each other toward the objectives of CPE than groups where my supervision was not guided by SCT theory and methods.

In Conclusion

While my hope is to teach group membership skills that can be transferred to a variety of settings, it is also true that many of the groups in which we find ourselves function quite differently from systems oriented and guided ones. As a result I have come to see individual supervision primarily as consultation or coaching around problems identified by the students themselves. In systems oriented work, a consultation begins with a focus on the internal point of conflict within the person seeking consultation, since in reality any action toward change resides in the agency of that person. My individual supervision has become a consultation with the student that has a particular format: I begin with an invitation for the student to share a success in terms of progress toward a learning goal and I enjoy that success with the student. I then invite the student to share an area of challenge or problem relative to his or her learning goals and/or CPE learning objectives. We then try to explore the problem by accessing the student's affective as well as cognitive awareness, so that when possible solutions have been identified, the student's energy is freed up to pursue change. At the end of the session, the student is invited to summarize what he or she has discovered and to evaluate the effectiveness of the consultation.

Similarly at the end of each seminar, the group is invited to share their surprises and learnings, their satisfactions and dissatisfactions (Agazarian, 1997, p. 72) and to identify what contributed to and what distracted from their learning. In subsequent sessions we try to continue those elements that contribute and to change those that distract, so that we, as a group, are consistently engaged in evaluation and development. As we evaluate the behaviors that facilitated or inhibited the work of the group toward the explicit goals (in systems-centered parlance develop a force field of driving and restraining forces toward the goal)(Agazarian, 1997, p.30, pp. 125-129), we are also engaged in research and encouraged to distinguish between interpretations and the description of observable behavior. The force field diagram in the Table below is a composite of student evaluations at the end of our small process group seminars. It identifies behaviors that contributed (left column) and that restrained (right column) our work toward the goal of learning and exploring group membership. In the next unit of CPE that I supervise our final written evaluations will also be structured to reflect this model of evaluation toward the learning objectives of CPE and of the effectiveness, or not, of systems oriented group work toward those goals.

I have found, and have learned to address with each new CPE group, that they, as members of a learning group and as participants in their clinical settings, are the key elements of the CPE curriculum and that we are all teachers and learners together. Student evaluations to date have supported the effectiveness of the systems oriented methodology and have pointed to the ways that I can better structure and guide the learning experience. I am grateful to their contributions to our learning.

Force Fields from Small Process Groups: Summer 2006

Driving Forces	Restraining Forces
• Joining on shared • laughter • Being joined when asking 'anyone else' • Conscious choice to join on 'similar-enough' • To speak (think a bit out loud) to get to the feeling • Using metaphor/image to get at the feeling • Sharing a common image as a frame of reference • Sharing a snippet of a story as context • Speaking and adding one's voice • Feeling the energy of anger • Someone introducing the desire to retaliate • Freedom of choice • Conscious choice to stay with the tenderness- on a new edge • Eye contact • Noticing physical behavior rather than just interpreting it • Trusting the balance of the other subgroup's voices	• Inconsistent leader functioning (leader teaching during experiential part) • Trying to hold a subgroup topic alone • Too much talking–too much data from outside group; long story as explanation • Holding a subgroup component in silence (resonating but not joining) • Frustration when leave off exploring • Desire to be in all the subgroups • Frustration of having to choose • Distraction of physical restraints (need to pee or sleep) • Fear of taking risk and therefore silencing oneself • Exiting the present • Wanting to problem-solve • Wanting to think rather than feel • Too much eye contact • Getting flooded with feelings • Self-critique and blame • Silent subgroups that

<ul><li>Enjoying joining on similarities, then appreciating the differences</li><li>Distraction exercise helped to bring in feeling</li><li>Really noticing present experience</li><li>Awareness of move to old role</li><li>Identifying pull to care-taking roles</li><li>More invested, more real, 'deeper' emotion when exploring with words</li></ul>	<ul><li>don't get to say what they're holding</li><li>Worry about negative responses when not joined</li><li>Difficulty finding words for feelings, embodied experience</li></ul>

References

Agazarian, Y. (1997). *Systems-centered therapy for groups.* New York: Guilford Press.

Agazarian, Y. (2006). *Centering out of roles.* Unpublished.

Gantt, S., & Agazarian, Y. (Eds.). (2005). *SCT in action.* New York, Lincoln, Shanghai: iPublisher.

CHAPTER 12

Finding Life in Personal Storytelling
Catherine F. Garlid

C linical Pastoral Education educates students in the art and practice of pastoral ministry. CPE is grounded in the premise that effective ministry requires the self-awareness that makes possible a caring response to another, most often a person in crisis or social isolation. The most important tool in pastoral care is the very person of the caregiver. I mean this not only to refer to the "use of self," but even more basically in the sense of the physical person who just shows up in the first place. Students discover that it is not primarily the tool kit, i.e. the prayer book or the scriptures that they may carry in their pockets, nor their eloquence in offering extemporaneous prayer, nor their knowledge of the other's background or diagnosis that brings comfort and reassurance to those in their care. Rather it is first and foremost their non-anxious physical, emotional, and spiritual presence that makes the difference. They are challenged to develop knowledge of their strengths and weaknesses and to integrate their life experience in order to use themselves fully and effectively on behalf of the other. A primary tool for developing this self-awareness is reflection on their personal histories, beginning in the CPE interview and application, and continuing in a variety of ways throughout the CPE process.

In her article "Opening up the Circle," Joan Hemenway took the next of what she considered "baby steps" in applying systems oriented group work to group process work in CPE (Hemenway, 2005, see Chapter Three in this volume). One of those steps is expressed in the question, "Is there life after personal storytelling?" This question grew out of her observation that CPE's historic one-on-one focus on the individual and his or her personal history allowed that person to rehearse rigid relational roles and well defended narratives explaining the status quo and what was already known, instead of promoting exploration and growth. This paper will first examine difficulties related to personal storytelling in the educational setting, then re-examine the role of personal storytelling in CPE, including qualities of personal storytelling that promote growth and learning, and finally consider contexts within the CPE experience in which personal storytelling may serve to further its educational goals. In so doing the paper will shift the question from "Is there life *after* personal storytelling?" to "Is there life *in* personal storytelling?"

Difficulties Related to Personal Storytelling in the Educational Setting

In addition to new knowledge introduced in Systems-Centered Theory and practice (Agazarian, 1997, pp. 142 -149), research in neuroscience sheds light on the difficulties raised by the question, "Is there life after personal storytelling?" Research on memory and brain function points to distortions of reality that are inevitably part of personal storytelling (Siegel & Hartzell, 2000, pp. 51-52). As adults we like to think of ourselves as cultivating a deepening relationship to objective reality. Our perceptions of reality, however, are shaped by the way our brains have developed and functioned throughout our lives.

Information is stored in our memories in complex ways. Researchers across disciplines who study memory distinguish between implicit and explicit memory. In *Parenting from the Inside Out* (which might also be titled "supervising or pastoring from the inside out"), Siegel and Hartzell (2000) explain that implicit memory is memory that exists without recollection, beginning with pre-verbal emotional and physical experiences, and storing behaviors learned through repetition. Explicit memory is memory associated with the recollection of events incorporating what would be considered a sense of self interacting with the environment (pp. 22-25).

Siegel and Hartzell (2000) refer to "mental models"—cognitive maps formed out of implicit memory that serve as "a kind of fun-nel through which information is filtered." These mental models represent inflexible cognitive constructs that may seem very real, operate outside of our conscious awareness and shape the way we relate to ourselves, the world, and future possibilities (pp. 51-52). What this means is that personal storytelling may simply involve repeating often painful stories that have only partial relationship to reality. As Yvonne Agazarian writes, "Cognitive defenses involve the imagination in telling stories that simplify experiences and make them understandable." The storyteller is able to avoid "mixed feelings about the *real* frustrations and satisfactions of past life" and hold onto old externalized hurts and disappointments (Agazarian, 1997, p. 147, emphasis added).

Personal Storytelling in CPE

The scientific research and systems-centered theory referenced above challenge widely held assumptions within the CPE commu-nity. The question, "Is there life after personal storytelling?" strikes at the core of a dearly held tradition in the pastoral care movement. Studying the "living human document" with the focus on the indi-vidual is a practice that we understand to be formative for students and healing for the persons in their care. In an article published in 2000 Joan named as one of the six foundational elements of CPE the focus on the individual person. "His or her feelings, sense of self-worth, direction in life, family history, and relationship to God, are areas of constant valuing and exploration" (Hemenway, 2000, p. 61). Personal storytelling is a vehicle for this valuing and exploration, enabling individuals within their wider social contexts to find meaning, purpose, and engagement with matters of faith and the world around them.

Our valuing of personal storytelling was further highlighted for me during a didactic seminar for my students given by CPE super-visor Ray Cooley on "spiritual life review with medically chal-lenged elders." Over his 20 years at the Masonic Geriatric Health Care Center in Wallingford, CT, Cooley developed a program for recording and archiving interviews conducted by CPE students with residents of the facility. His rationale for doing so was to balance the overwhelming experience of loss and self-diminishment that so often goes hand in hand with aging and institutionalization. Cooley (1999) writes that "listening to those stories and the meaning the elderly person finds in telling them validates that person's sense of integrity. Perhaps it is with people who listen with an interested ear that very ill older people find their deepest contentment" (p. 42).

Cooley's experience raises an equally valid question: Is there life without personal storytelling for persons such as these frail elders? And if personal storytelling is so vital for this community of elders, how better to train students for effective pastoral care than through the practice of personal storytelling and listening to stories with patients or residents and with their peers?

For the purposes of this paper "personal storytelling" that "has life" in CPE (and contributes to its educational goals) is best understood as the autobiographical narrative that contributes to a student's development of self-awareness, pastoral identity, and authentic relationship to the complex world in which he or she ministers. Whether or not narrative accounts correspond to historical fact, they have been shaped and "rehearsed," becoming critical to the person's self understanding and the meaning he or she ascribes to facts and experiences. Schacter (1996) writes, "Complex mixtures of personal knowledge that we retain about the past are woven together to form life stories and personal myths" (p. 93). Human beings have the brain capacity to weave together a coherent, integrated narrative that makes meaning and helps to heal unresolved pain or conflict. Schacter (1996) uses the phrase "narrative coherence" for "a story that makes sense of our lives in a deep, viscerally full way, beyond merely rationalization and minimization" (p. 309).

Narrative coherence is relevant to CPE in two ways. First, as process education and experiential learning, at its best CPE encourages the development of a living personal narrative that unfolds in the present. A process of self-discovery begins with the standard application to a CPE program that includes an autobiographical statement reflecting key persons and events that have shaped the applicant over time. As students enter the program they are invited to risk exploring new knowledge, both self-knowledge and knowledge about the clinical environment. Each pastoral encounter presents an opportunity for new learning as students listen to the personal stories of the persons in their care.

Second, as theological education CPE enables students in pastoral formation to shape an identity in relationship to stories of their faith, religious symbols, and spiritual practice. So, narrative coherence in a pastoral context is developed through the integration of personal history, a living faith, and spiritual practice. This goal of integration is articulated in the Outcomes of Level I CPE. The student is expected to "Identify and discuss major life events, relationships, and cultural contexts that influence personal identity as expressed in pastoral functioning" (ACPE Standards, 2005). Self-awareness is understood to enhance understanding of the human condition overall and to increase the student's capacity for empathy and compassion.

Indicators of Growth Associated with Personal Storytelling

Once again research in neuroscience is helpful in identifying indicators associated with personal storytelling that promote learning and growth. Researchers are exploring the fine workings of the brain and specifically what may be happening, first as one attunes to one's own intentions, and then as one attunes to the feelings and mental processes of another. Even more exciting is evidence suggesting that the adult mind may be capable of increasing its capacity for attunement, actually reshaping neural pathways and strengthening underdeveloped brain functions. The neuroscientist Steven Porges suggests that one's brain experiences a state of "neuroception," or the experience of safety when experiencing the attunement of another person to their experience (Siegel, 2007, p. 129). He describes what parts of the brain are responsible for the assessment of the relative safety of an interaction. Interpersonal receptivity is manifested audibly and visibly through bodily, facial, and vocal relaxation and alertness as the interaction is experienced as safe.

Of equal importance to observable interpersonal receptivity is the development of the "observing self," which involves the mind "attuning to its own state" (Siegel, 2007, p. 189). Reflective learning is a cornerstone of CPE. The "clinical model" involves an experiential practice of action and reflection. Students learn in a variety of settings through a variety of means. What they practice in action, they step back to reflect upon before setting out again to try new behaviors and methods in their pastoral care giving.

There is convergence between the neuroscientific research on reflective learning and attunement and systems oriented theory and practice. The system-centered method of functional subgrouping to achieve the development and transformation of living human systems teaches group members to find resonance around similarities and to discriminate and integrate difference in their experience of the here and now (Agazarian, 1997, pp. 43 –46). Once members have learned to subgroup the practice begins with "centering" in order to cross the boundary into a discrete time and place and to shift from one's individual personal role to the role of group member. The process of centering is an intentional and physical experience of bringing one's focus, awareness, and energy for working within the system into the here and now (Agazarian, 1997, p. 54). Centering in this way is familiar to persons who practice meditation or contemplative prayer. Both involve the process of what Siegel (2007) calls "self-observational awareness" (p. 27). The capacity to center and self-observe is necessary in order to have access to both apprehensive experience (related to feeling or affect) and comprehensive experience (related to knowing or cognition). This integration of head and heart is central to the practice of effective pastoral care.

Another indicator of learning and growth in the process of personal story telling is the active exploration of experience in the here and now. In systems-centered group work the distinction is made between explaining and exploring, or "elaborating on the known versus discovering the unknown" (Agazarian, 1997, p. 303). Explaining what is already known, or repeating stories based on a distorted view of reality, does not lead to new learning. A student's explanation might sound like this: "I have trouble listening to my patients because no one ever listened to me." Or, "I always think that I need to move on and see the next patient, so I have trouble hearing what this one is saying." For this student these explanations communicate an established and familiar way of understanding her relationship to her environment. To explore her experience in a group context in the present she would center herself, pay attention to her body and her feelings, make eye contact with other group members, and listen for a place of internal resonance. She might join the group exploring the same experiences she explained above in this way: "Yes, I too feel curious about what is going to happen in group today and a little bit wary like I do when I enter a new patient's room."

In summary, findings in brain research and systems-centered practice suggest that we might look for the following as qualities of personal storytelling that indicate growth: first, *affective presence*, that is, emotional availability—not the flooding of emotion—but the presence of affect. We look for a relaxed state of *alertness*. We look for the presence of *curiosity* for the *exploration* of what is emerging as new awareness, as opposed to the rehearsal of old ideas and explanations. We also look for indications of *centering*, to include posture, focus, and *energy* for work in the here and now. Finally, we look for *receptivity to attunement* with the individual or the group engaged with the storyteller through facial expression, voice quality, and other non-verbal cues.

Contexts for Personal Storytelling in CPE

So how much personal storytelling is actually beneficial in CPE and in what contexts? I suggest that more important than how much, is the matter of what the goal and the contexts are in CPE for the use of personal story telling as an educational method. Incorporating personal storytelling into the curriculum should contribute to the overall goal of CPE: the development of self-awareness, pastoral identity, and authentic relationship to the persons and systems in the complex world in which the student ministers. CPE is first and foremost education for ministry, not the purposeful facilitation of personal growth. The educational experience holds enormous potential for personal growth, but personal growth is not the primary goal. Therefore, personal storytelling is most useful in furthering the goals of CPE when it has direct application to development of pastoral identity and the art and skill of pastoral care giving. As examples of contexts in which personal storytelling moves students toward the overall goal of CPE, I will focus first on the process of getting acquainted within the peer group and, second on verbatim seminars. I will then explore the difficulties associated with small process group as a context for personal storytelling.

Orientation: During orientation students typically introduce themselves repeatedly to each other, to staff chaplains, to hospital administration, to staff in their clinical areas, and to members of the Professional Consultation Committee. This happens before they even begin to think about how to introduce themselves to patients. These early introductions may be mindless repetitions of data about their public selves. However, they can be used as opportunities to explore ways of experiencing themselves as newcomers in a variety of contexts each of which invites the sharing of somewhat different personal information.

In the course of orientation to many CPE programs students introduce themselves to each other through extensive personal storytelling and self-revelation with the assumption that the process furthers self-understanding, valuable interpersonal intimacy, and group cohesion. Difficulties associated with this practice include the fact that students invariably feel anxious or self-conscious and distracted at the start of a program and the fact that norms have not yet been established for interpersonal boundaries and communication within the group.

An alternative is to have students share brief vignettes that have relevance to the pastoral task, such as "a time you were in transition" or "a time you felt truly understood." Framing these vignettes as discrete pieces may lessen the likelihood of students telling "the same old story." The process also shifts the attention from one person to another at relatively brief intervals so that no one person experiences the phenomenon of being "on the hot seat." Students are encouraged to listen with curiosity to their own telling of their vignettes and to listen for resonance to each other's vignettes. I intersperse these vignettes with some of the more tedious but necessary elements of orientation. Students have opportunities to mirror this approach as they transition into their role of chaplain and learn to assess the needs of persons in their care. For example, after some time they might ask a particularly anxious patient, "Can you tell me about a time you were able to overcome your fear of being left alone?"

Verbatims: The writing of verbatims and their presentation in verbatim seminars is perhaps the context best suited for focused personal storytelling. A student's choice to write up particular clinical material has roots in both conscious and unconscious psychological processes. It is frequently very difficult for a student to articulate why he or she chose particular clinical material or what it is that he or she hopes to learn in the course of exploring the material. I have added to the summary section of the verbatim format a question that reads, "How does your personal history impact this pastoral encounter and your choice to explore it further?" This encourages a student to be curious and discover ways in which who he or she is as a person, including past experience, personal relationships, and cognitive maps shape pastoral attunement and effectiveness. In a verbatim seminar I invite the peer group into this process of exploration with the presenter.

Other professional disciplines use the verbatim as an educational tool. Unique to the use of the verbatim in CPE is the inclusion of theological reflection. Students are confronted with real life challenges to their theological assumptions and the teachings of their religious heritage and theological studies as they encounter pain and suffering among the persons they care for in the clinical setting. They frequently find that their cognitive and theological constructs are no longer adequate. At best theological reflection is a deeply creative process through which stories of faith are integrated with personal and pastoral experience.

The key word is *experience*. Most students coming into CPE are far more adept at intellectual inquiry than experiential inquiry. I continue to find it difficult to move students away from using theological reflection as a way to explain their theological assumptions, such as "God is always present with me when I visit a patient." Depending on the dynamics of the pastoral encounter, my goal might be to have them explore in the moment how it feels to be with a patient who feels God's absence and to reflect on the dynamics of that experience instead. Students engage the process of shaping a new personal narrative as they are able to enter into this unfamiliar territory. Essentially they are challenged to engage the parts of their brains that contribute to narrative coherence in relationship to the resources of their faith communities.

Small Process Group: The skepticism reflected in Joan's question "Is there life beyond personal storytelling?" is most relevant to the context of Small Process Group (SPG), an essential component of all CPE programs also known as Interpersonal Relations Group (IPR) or Open Agenda Group. Early in a unit of training students commonly react to the newness of SPG by feeling anxious and "at sea." They are faced with a group experience that is boundaried in time and space with the primary goal of paying attention to the development of the group experience itself. One way students reduce or manage the anxiety is to use the time to tell personal stories from the past in the name of getting better acquainted. Joan writes, "The group atmosphere appears to become increasingly intimate, cohesive, and 'covenanted' (bound) together...[but] when personal story time is concluded, the group is still confronted with trying to figure out its purpose" (Hemenway, 2005, p. 90).

Towards the end of her career, Joan's supervisory theory and practice were influenced by her exploration of systems-centered theory and methods and the vital contribution she felt they could make to the CPE community. *Inside the Circle* (1996) reflected her study of CPE's group theory and practice up to that time. Subsequently, she experimented with systems-centered methods in the small process groups she led in her role as training supervisor. In this context she interrupted and redirected our personal storytelling. Parallel to the use of focused personal storytelling in verbatim seminars described above, the use of personal storytelling she encouraged was related to the exploration of our clinical work with students or in our quest for narrative coherence in the autobiographical statement required for certification as CPE supervisors.

184

Small process group provides a laboratory setting in which students can practice the skills associated with the qualities of personal storytelling that I suggest indicate growth, not only toward narrative coherence, but also as evidenced in their ability to resonate with the experience of the persons in their care. Again, these qualities or skills include centering into a relaxed state of alertness, paying attention to affective experience, and exploring what is new and unfamiliar with curiosity.

Although I generally discourage such sharing, there may be instances in a small process group in which information from a personal narrative is important to the group even when the method of functional sub-grouping is the encouraged norm. For example, prior to SPG a male student presents a verbatim recording an emergency room call involving a SIDS death. In SPG he realizes how the experience has touched his deep sadness over the SIDS death of his baby daughter years before. He may not have expressed his feelings in the small process group before (other than perhaps his frustration with the process). The feelings he is now experiencing could be handled as a distraction keeping him from being fully present in the here and now, or they could be brought in as important information with the invitation to other members of the group to subgroup or find resonance around intense pastoral care encounters that touch upon their own pain. For example, I might ask, "Is there anyone else who has encountered a pastoral crisis that has touched upon a personal loss?" It is significant for group members in a beginning CPE group simply to experience resonance with one another's feelings as opposed to adhering to the accustomed social norms of chit chat, banter, argument, or other forms of avoidance of engagement.

Conclusion

The use of personal storytelling in CPE should be deliberate and should further the overall goal of education for ministry. Education for ministry includes the development of self-awareness, pastoral identity, and authentic relationship to the persons and systems in the complex world in which the student ministers. Where personal storytelling is used deliberately as an educational method, one would look for physical centering, affective presence, receptivity to attunement, alertness, curiosity, and energy for the exploration of new learning in the here and now. These observable qualities are skills that can be taught and reinforced in the context of the Small Process Group and carry over to both other parts of the curriculum and to the student's pastoral context. These skills contribute to the students' ability to tell their own stories as new stories and to help others do the same, leaving behind the old versions and cognitive maps that no longer fit reality.

Ray Cooley's sense of the crucial healing connection made through the process of life review with elders corresponds to Siegel's descriptions of the power of interpersonal attunement: "As we align our being with the being of another, as we transfer energy and information between each other to resonate, we create an attuned state at the heart of interpersonal integration" (Siegel, 2007, p. 317). CPE students develop self-awareness through such an experience of attunement as they experience the focused exploration of pieces of their own stories that have bearing upon their pastoral care and effectiveness. Their ability to attune and engage another person in the here and now may well correspond to what the pastoral care encounters students describe as "sacred space" or the "experience of standing on holy ground."

References

Agazarian, Y.M. (1997). *Systems-centered therapy for groups.* NY, London: The Guilford Press.

Cooley, R. (1999). Selected conference papers and proceedings: *The Reminiscence and Life Review Conference.* New York, N.Y.

Hemenway, J.E. (1996). *Inside the circle: A historical and practical inquiry concerning process groups in clinical pastoral education.* Decatur, GA: Journal of Pastoral Care Publications, Inc.

Hemenway, J.E. (2000). The shifting of the foundations: Ten questions concerning the future of pastoral supervision and the pastoral care movement. *Journal of Supervision and Training in Ministry, 20,* 59–68.

Hemenway, J.E. (2005). Opening up the circle. *Journal of Pastoral Care and Counseling, 59*(4), 323-334.

Schacter, D. (1996). *Searching for memory: The brain, the mind, and the past.* New York: Basic Books.

Siegel, D.J., & Hartzell, M. (2003) *Parenting from the inside out: How a deeper sense of self-understanding can help you raise children who thrive.* New York: J.P. Tarcher/Putnam.

Siegel, D.J. (2007). *The mindful brain: Reflection and attunement in the cultivation of well-being.* New York: W.W. Norton and Co.

CHAPTER 13

The Mentoring Relationship
in the Development of Clinical Pastoral Educators
A. Meigs Ross

Introduction

The role of the clinical pastoral educator (CPE supervisor) is complex and multilayered. It combines the functions of teacher, administrator, clinical supervisor, group leader, and occasionally pastor and counselor. The intricacies of the supervisor/student relationship and the complexity of the CPE supervisory tasks make the development of a clinical pastoral educator a time consuming and in depth process of education. The mentoring aspects within this complex role of clinical pastoral educators are varied, and change and expand as relationships with students change and expand over time. The education and training needed to become a clinical pastoral educator necessarily involves the development of a complex array of skills, and these skills and their attendant abilities are acquired largely through intricate intentional learning and mentoring relationships with peers, supervisors, and consultants.

Joan Hemenway, although she was never my supervisor, was an important mentor for me as I grew into the role of CPE supervisor. Joan served as my consultant for two years as I progressed from associate supervisor to final certification in ACPE. Once I was certified, our relationship changed when we were peers for five years in a System-Centered Theory (SCT) training group under the leadership of Yvonne Agazarian, the developer of SCT theory and practice.

During the years in which Joan served as my consultant, we learned together about the role of the mentor, and the limits, responsibilities, and growth that the mentoring relationship can provide for both mentor and student. Joan had gifts as a mentor that she exhibited time and again and which I was privileged to receive. She provided astute critique, which she gave with clarity and precision, and she provided a wealth of knowledge. She understood how to let go and let her students take their next steps independently, and most importantly she also knew how to love and be loved by her students. During our time as peers in our SCT training group, we learned together about how the formerly functional roles of the mentor-student relationship can be both adaptive and maladaptive as colleagues grow and continue to learn together. This shift from mentor-student to peers provided glimpses into the learning and growth that takes place as relationships are intentionally altered with changes in context and role. Through the sharing of two vignettes, one from my relationship with Joan and one of a relationship with one of my primary supervisory CPE supervisors, I hope to present some ideas about the development of the mentoring relationship system in the supervision of pastoral educators, and the simultaneous development of authority, autonomy, and creativity.

Mentoring within the adult learning relationship has been extensively studied in recent literature on adult development and education (Daloz, 1986; Daloz 1999; Clark, Harden, & Johnson, 1999). The role of the mentor is a powerful one. As Daloz (1999) writes, "If mentors didn't exist, we'd have to invent them.... They proceed from a place in us as deep as our dreams" (p. 17). The role of the mentor in the development of pastors and within clinical pastoral education has also begun to be explored as well. Haines (2001) examines the erotic and attraction dynamics in the mentor/supervisor relationship and provides a review of clergy mentors through a critical lens, noting both the benefits and challenges of such relationships.

This paper will explore the mentoring relationship, one aspect in the education of the clinical pastoral educator, from a developmental and systemic perspective. The mentor in CPE, whether he or she is a supervisor or a consultant, provides a relationship with the student that necessarily develops over time in a trajectory that allows for increasing reciprocity. The mentoring relationship is a system, which like all systems, has specific stages of development each of which contains different tasks, responsibilities, and characteristics (Agazarian, 1997). Systems-Centered Theory states, "Living human systems survive, develop and transform from simple to more complex through a developing ability to recognize differences and integrate them" (Agazarian, 2008, www.sct-institute.org). Looking at the supervisory relationship as a system, we look at the development of this particular relationship system as necessarily involving the discrimination and integration of new information and differences that lead to changed and developed interpersonal and intrapersonal systems. To illustrate this I will explore four specific developmental stages of the supervisory relationship: Dependency; Authority/Autonomy; Separation/Individuation; and Colleagueship.

The Mentoring Relationship System

I could list the unique qualities and gifts of my mentors during my CPE journey and describe what I learned in relationship with each one. However, it is not the wisdom of my mentors that has been most instrumental in my development. What has been transformational is the strength and uniqueness of my relationships with each one. Knowledge and skills training, an important part of the development of a clinical pastoral educator, are developed and integrated in the student when the mentor/supervisory relationship provides challenge and structure within a relationship of affection. ACPE respects age and wisdom; elders are honored, not with indulgence but with reverence. There is an underlying assumption that those who have gone before us are to be given respect and love, and that they are repositories of knowledge and affection. On occasion, this can lead to overvaluing the past and overlooking the faults and limitations of our mentors and thus stunt new growth and development. More often, however, the mentor's ability to give and receive provides a firm foundation for the development of the pastoral relationship in students.

Haines (2001) proposes that the mentor and protégé necessarily have a strong attachment to each other that fuels the relationship and propels both toward the goals. Students most value mentors who know both how to give and how to receive in a companionable learning system. In my development as a clinical pastoral educator the most valuable mentors have offered a learning relationship and provided me with increasingly complex educational opportunities. In this crucible, the level of anxiety and affection were balanced as my skills and abilities developed.

There are several pitfalls when the mentoring relationship is central to supervision. One is the danger of perpetuating mediocre standards, or remaining stuck in particular modes of thinking, as learning is passed down from one generation to another without being reflected upon, revised and updated (Gortner & Dreibelbis, 2007). The guild system is excellent on one level for passing on specific skills and keeping traditions alive, but it is less advantageous in preparing critical thinkers who can take up the tasks of ministry with autonomy and creativity. Another danger is over valuing certain benefits of the mentoring relationship and not allowing it to grow, develop, bend, reshape, and ultimately end. Because the mentoring relationship is more powerfully felt and observed from the viewpoint of the student, I've chosen to write from this point of view.

The concept of relationship is referenced so often as the central element in the mentoring relationship that it has lost its meaning and can be difficult to define, live out, or teach. Applying systems thinking to the mentoring relationship can open up the possibility of looking more closely at the relationship with a developmental lens that allows for more specificity about roles, developmental trajectories, and goals. With more specificity about these tasks there is a greater possibility for the development of the relationship and the learning environment that is the relationship.

Research about the complexities of attachment behaviors in adults is helpful when elucidating the relationship of the mentor/student. Heard and Lake (1997) describe the therapeutic relationship as a "companionable caregiving system" that includes both the one seeking care and the one giving care. The mentor/student relationship, while not a therapeutic system, is also a companionable caregiving system in which learning and growth take place. Heard and Lake (1997) outline five "instinctive goal-corrected behavioral systems" that are part of the helping relationship:

1. the system for caregiving which is wholly interpersonal
2. the interpersonal careseeking system
3. the intrapersonal system for self-defense
4. the exploratory system, manifest in the intrapersonal exploratory self and in the interpersonal interest-sharing self
5. the sexual system, which has both intra- and inter-personal components (pp. 67-116).

The mentor/student relationship is akin to a companionable caregiving system, and it is possible to observe all five aspects of the goal-corrected behavioral systems at play. The above behavioral systems provide a foundation for looking more clearly at the mentoring relationship and the development of the clinical pastoral educator. The mentoring relationship is a system in which the individuals and the relationship that they create, shapes and shifts in relation to the goals of the context and to the individual and relational goals as well.

For example, the mentoring system created by both the supervisory education student and mentor/supervisor includes the careseeking of the student and the caregiving of the mentor/supervisor. Each person impacts the other. The student and supervisor/mentor are also intrapersonal systems that are developed by the system, and the intrapersonal system of self-defense is activated some times. Students are dependent on the evaluation of their mentor/supervisor and this can activate their fears and defenses. Receiving critique, which puts the student in a vulnerable position, may unconsciously activate the defense system and lead to attacking or self-protecting defensive behavior. Knowledge and awareness of this aspect of any helping system allows both those giving and receiving critique to attune themselves to one another and to the agreed upon goals, so that information can best be exchanged and growth achieved. Lastly, the sexual system is activated in the attraction dynamics within a mentor/student relationship. This can provide energy to the system (Haines, 2001), and yet is a system that is not acted out explicitly within a healthy mentor/student relationship.

The interpersonal exploratory system is the most critical within a supervisory/mentoring relationship. Once this exploratory aspect of the careseeking/caregiving system is developed and anxiety is lowered by the building of a trustworthy system, both the student's and the mentor/supervisor's energy is available for exploring and learning.

Goal—Corrected Empathic Attunement

Una McCluskey (2005) built a bridge between the fields of adult attachment studies and System-Centered Theory (SCT) in her study of the professional caregiving relationship. Her extensive studies of professional counseling relationships include carefully filmed and analyzed sessions. These provide in depth results that clearly point to the important role of attunement in caregiving/careseeking relationships. McCluskey (2005) developed a concept of effective interaction between caregivers and careseekers that she calls "goal-corrected empathic attunement" (pp. 79-81). McCluskey's detailed definition of empathic attunement includes such indicators as focuses attention, modulates response, provides input, and facilitates exploration, all of which together, make up attunement in a caregiving relationship. "Attunement refers to rhythm and harmony between therapist and client so that each is responding to the other in such a way that the experience for the client intellectually and emotionally is deepened" (McCluskey, 2005, 145). In brief, when there is affect regulation and attunement between a client and therapist the client's and the therapist's anxiety is lowered, the client's affects are contained, the client's exploratory drive is engaged, and both client and therapist experience relief. This language is more technical than what clinical pastoral education students are familiar with; it is, however, helpful language in assessing the effectiveness of the mentor/student relationship. If we see the mentor/student relationship as a system of caregiving/careseeking, which is dependent for its effectiveness on attunement and development, then we must also look for the balance of anxiety and the growth of engagement leading to a greater ability to explore and learn.

Dependency

In the initial stage of any mentoring relationship both members are observing and testing new means of relating, and in so doing are creating spoken and unspoken rules, norms and learning alliances, and building the system of learning and the attuned alliance. The responsibility for the development of the relationship is at once firmly centered in the mentor and in the student. The mentor is expected to make an assessment of the student's needs, learning styles, and abilities, and within prescribed limits and expectations, to adjust to provide for these. Ultimately, however, the student makes the most adaptations as he or she adapts to the styles of a new mentor/supervisor. The student is the one being assessed, has the most need, and is in the position of lesser authority. The person with less authority in any relationship is the one who, like it or not, does the most observing, adapting, and changing in order for the relationship to be fruitful. I remind myself of this as I begin any new supervisory relationship with a new student. I must be aware of adapting to my student's learning needs and be observant of the fact that my student will be working diligently to adapt to my style as well.

This earliest phase can be thought of as the dependency stage (Agazarian, 1997; Wheelan, 2004). Its tasks are building the caregiving/careseeking system, building "trust, through tested expectations" (Agazarian, 1997), personal communication, and the development of an alliance that is strong and flexible enough to bear the tasks of testing authority that will follow.

Authority and Autonomy

Following the dependency stage of the mentor/supervisory student relationship is the student's work of developing authority and autonomy of thought and function. Initially, the student must work under authority to adapt to the expectations of the student role and learn about the expectations of the context in which that role will be lived and the expectations of the supervisory authority. The necessary dependency of the early supervisory relationship is stretched and eventually broken as the student develops skills and internal authority and moves toward independence. The stretching of the dependency relationship between mentor and student may be like that of an adolescent testing parental authority and through periods of relational stress, developing an independent identity. In adolescent development it is not the experience of conflict but the ability to resolve the conflict successfully, that is central to the development of autonomy and self-initiating authority (Longres, 2000; Arnett, 2004).

The candidacy, or middle stage of my own development as a CPE supervisor, mimicked the changes and challenges of adolescence in respect to the development of autonomy and authority. On one hand I was expected to supervise independently; on the other hand I was expected to remain under supervision, carefully attending to the structures of the educational environment and the expectations of my own supervisor. This was largely an excellent learning environment; I was given increased opportunities to function autonomously and to develop authority appropriate to my level of development and certification. There were, of course, internal shifts to be made along the way as I made the external shifts in behavior. This movement toward autonomous functioning was not always a clear trajectory. I remember quite well one evening when I acted out my frustrations within my then supervisory/mentor relationship. The resulting growth that I was able to attain from this outburst was a testament to the strength of a strong, flexible attuned mentoring relationship.

It is hard to go through adolescence twice, but adolescence is exactly what being a supervisory candidate felt like. One particular moment stands out as a time of transition. I had worked carefully with a fellow student to plan a training event for my peers. The event went off as scheduled, but the learning format we had chosen was not the best for the type of learning in which we were engaged. Our supervisors were naturally frustrated and during a community meeting let us know that they would be taking responsibility for planning in the future and would provide different, better learning activities. From my vantage point now, this makes perfect sense. From my role as a supervisory student that particular decision triggered outrage. I was careful not to express the full extent my outrage in the meeting, but instead saved up all the energy for my supervisor who got an earful for having challenged and curtailed my nascent authority and autonomy.

I didn't fear the consequences of my outburst; I was too blinded by my own indignation and letting off steam felt good! My mentor/supervisor was taken back but didn't flinch. She contained her own feelings and heard my emotions in full force, and without encouraging or trying to moderate them, she engaged them affectively. These actions helped to diffuse the outrage and provided an experience that could be explored more fully in the next supervisory session. I felt foolish about my outburst, but my mentor's ability to take up her authority, set structure, and then provide an attuned and contained learning environment turned an outburst into a learning event. I began to see that underneath the outrage were fear, anger, and even sadness at not being at the level of development to which I aspired.

The most difficult work was not exploring the authority issues but applying to my work of supervision my new found insights about my strengths and weaknesses in taking up my authority and working under authority. I had experienced my mentor containing her anger in order to help create the exploratory system for my learning. It was now my task to do the same with my own students: to see their authority dynamics as opportunities for them to learn while I contained, explored internally, and remained engaged with them. I also had to explore my relationships to others' authority in order to move forward in the certification process. Only when a student is able to take up his or her own authority as a clinical pastoral educator while also accepting the authority of the certification commission, can he or she move successfully toward certification.

Separation and Individuation

Joan and I once made an impulsive decision in front of a group of our SCT training peers and volunteered to give a joint presentation to the class. Neither of us gave the decision much thought until six months later when the time for the presentation was looming. As the time approached, we had each done our homework and prepared the material with care, but we had not thought about how we might work together in developing and presenting the material. The presentation was titled "Roles in the Phases of Group Development—the Transitional Phase between Flight and Fight: Managing Depression and Mis/Attunement in the Helper/Helpee Roles"—quite a mouthful!

The first step in our work together was to share our notes. In that simple action, the theme of transition in our presentation was highlighted in the transition happening in our relationship. When each of us received the other's suggestions, the suggestions were printed in red. That was all it took—red letters on our computer screens—to trigger both of us into familiar maladaptive roles. I went into the role of a younger pupil—"Why in the world can't she accept my scholarship, see that I'm now a peer and no longer her junior in this endeavor?" Joan went into her perfectionist role, "Uh oh, I want this presentation to be perfect, and I must take charge and see that perfection is achieved or else it will be a total failure!" Both of us also went into action—my anxiety came out in feelings of annoyance and Joan's in feelings of hopelessness. The mis/attunement created by feedback in red ink was absolutely indicative of the stage of development that we were studying and the stage of development of our working relationship.

We were each holding one side of a familiar dynamic pattern. We had moved from working as mentor/mentee to working together as peers, and the transition triggered familiar patterns in both of us. This, however, is exactly the work of the mentor/mentee relationship—to move toward a colleague relationship with increased reciprocity. The growth is dependent, however, on both members working through interpersonal and intrapersonal dynamics independently and together as a working system. I cannot claim that

Joan and I worked through this dilemma to perfection or that either of us was able to shed our maladaptive roles, but I can state with certainty that I learned much from the discussions that ensued and from Joan's great willingness to share herself and become more transparent to me, her protégé turned colleague. Together we were both able to name and explore our emotions and the maladaptive roles that we had entered into. Joan was able to claim her fear of failure, and I was able to claim my fear of success. As a mentor/student system we moved toward peership as she became increasingly vulnerable and I allowed myself to become increasingly independent and my own creativity to flourish.

I see the work in this stage as the work of separating and individuating. Joan and I moved through some of the work of authority and autonomy in our consultant relationship. The next step in our working together was to develop the intimacy of colleagueship and this involved working through issues of separation and individuation. It was quite enjoyable for a time to see Joan as the expert, to work with her critique but stay in a relationship that kept a mentor/protégé distance. By putting ourselves into a peer working relationship we each opened ourselves to sharing more of our foibles and insecurities. This prompted some anger and jockeying for new positions, but with reflection and working together also provided the opportunity for each of us to separate, individuate, and develop new knowledge about ourselves that each of us could take to our own work. I won't presume to name Joan's learning. I, however, was prompted to face my own insecurities to see how I like to bask in the skills of a senior mentor and pretend that perfection exists, and how I can find that same basking to be confining and annoying. My task was to examine the cost of keeping myself in the junior role and to risk moving toward professional intimacy through differentiating and taking up the newer more appropriate roles of friend and colleague.

I needed to look at the costs of continuing to be an admiring follower and the gains of separating, of giving up the glow of basking in Joan's reflection and stepping out and applying what I had learned in our relationship to my own work. This was a liberating, creative process that Joan was most willing and able to support.

Our mentoring relationship provided some of energy that helped to ignite the exploratory drive in my own supervisory work and compelled me to look for new methods and theories to support my supervisory practice. One of Joan's huge contributions to my growth, for which I will be eternally grateful, is System-Centered Theory (SCT). It was in the SCT training context that Joan shared the most of herself as she subgrouped and explored alongside her former students and encouraged us as we moved beyond her in this learning process.

Colleagueship

The work of moving from a mentoring relationship to a colleague relationship is the work of the later stage of the mentor/student relationship. In order to teach well, to help students take up their full authority and take on colleagueship, a mentor/supervisor must not only risk being thrown from the pedestal but must allow students to see the clay feet and to put on the mantel. This delicate process is generated out of the relationship itself. Beyond this work of encouraging our students' authority is the work of encouraging students' creativity. This begins most fully once the work of separation and individuation has begun. Working through authority issues with a supervisory student can be challenging and requires a great deal of containment on the part of the mentor. Working through the process of separation and individuation takes even more courage. It involves helping students to move beyond their mentor and develop themselves in areas about which the mentor knows little. It also involves preparing them to take up leadership creatively and with energy. The work at this stage involves helping students to claim what they know and to see limitations to what the mentor has provided for them. This can be a fearful, painful process for both mentor and student. It involves giving up the dream of perfection and embracing the hope that comes with the unknown and living on the edge of the new.

In the two years or so before Joan died, she spoke often about sharing what she had learned and about encouraging the leadership of those who would take the next steps in building and changing CPE for the next generations. We laughed together about how often it seemed we fought the same battles over and over as we strived to move forward as a profession and organization. It was my great joy to learn with and from Joan. Her ability to claim her own strengths and to share her own vulnerabilities in our learning relationship has helped me to do the same. I'm indebted to her and to all of my CPE mentors; their ability to contain, to model, to teach, and to love continues to guide me. It is my great joy to continue to be surrounded by the relational learning community that is ACPE and, with my colleagues, to build on the work of my many CPE mentors.

References

Agazarian, Y.M. (1997). *System-centered therapy for groups.* New York: Guilford.

Arnett, J. J. (2004). *Emerging adulthood, the winding road from the late teens through the twenties.* New York: Oxford University Press.

Clark, R. A., Harden, S. L., & Johnson, W. B. (2000). Mentor relationships in clinical psychology doctoral training: Results of a national survey. *Teaching of Psychology, 27*(4), 262-268.

Daloz, L.A. (1986). *Effective teaching and mentoring.* San Francisco: Jossey-Bass.

Daloz, L. A. (1999). *Mentor, guiding the journey of adult learners.* San Francisco: Jossey-Bass.

Gortner, D.T. & Dreibelbis, J. (2007). Mentoring clergy for effective leadership. *Journal of Supervision and Training in Ministry, 27,* 62-82.

Haines, D. (2001). Desire, intimacy and attraction: The erotic nature of CPE supervision. *Journal of Supervision and Training in Ministry, 21,* 46-65.

Heard, D. & Lake, B. (1997). *The challenge of attachment for caregiving.* London: Routledge.

Longres, J.F. (2000). *Human behavior in the social environment* (3rd ed.) Australia & US: Thomson, Brooks/Cole.

McCluskey, U. (2005). *To be met as a person: The dynamics of attachment in professional encounters.* London: Karnac.

Wheelan, S. (2004). *Group process, A developmental perspective.* New York: Allyn & Bacon.

PART THREE

Reflections on Supervision

CHAPTER 14

The Chaplain's Specialty: Relational Wisdom
John Patton

The last time I saw Joan Hemenway was at the 2006 meeting of the Association of Professional Chaplains in Atlanta. This paper is adapted from the Dicks-Boisen memorial lecture delivered at that meeting. I offer it as another way to remember Joan Hemenway, a colleague, friend, and chaplain extraordinary, one who well represented the heritage of Boisen and Dicks. Joan, like Russell Dicks, was a person who could see the potential depth in ordinary conversation—taking seriously and learning from what was said when chaplain and patient communicate to each other in an ordinary visit on an ordinary day. Like Anton Boisen Joan was one who could recognize the dimension of depth and mystery in a person's life, the patient's loneliness and his search for meaning. Joan Hemenway was a chaplain who embodied both these kinds of relational wisdom.

Wisdom is commonly understood as the ability to make sound choices and good decisions. It is not something a person is born with. It comes from living, from making mistakes and learning from them. A person who has wisdom is one who can maintain a larger view of the situation to be addressed without losing sight of the particularity and the intricacies of interrelationships within that situation. Wisdom involves an assumption that human situations are almost always complex, defying quick solution. Relationships between persons and things are constantly changing. Wisdom recognizes that there is a messiness and disorder in life that must be dealt with.

I have recently come to a new appreciation of the books of the Bible known as the wisdom literature—Proverbs, Job, and Ecclesiastes. At first glance these books seem less inspiring than other books of the Bible because there is less talk about God and more language that is not specifically religious. Similarly the chaplain is often involved with the same kind of practical concerns. In somewhat different ways the wisdom literature offers insight for the kind of personal and pastoral wisdom that a chaplain needs. Wisdom in Proverbs, for example, has a threefold dimension. It offers a way of seeing reality, a way of conducting oneself, and a way of relating to the order of life provided by God. The Biblical wisdom literature is not narrowly confessional but affirms with many spiritual traditions that creation is good and that the good life in a material sense is not in essential conflict with the good life in the moral sense. It is concerned with the creation of a good life in the family, in the local community, and in the larger society.

The chaplain's wisdom, like that of the wisdom books, does not argue for or try to prove the presence of God. It simply assumes that a relationship with God or a dimension of spirituality is a part of a person's life whether God or the practice of religion is spoken of or not. How many times I have heard the words, "Remember me, Reverend," from persons who had little or no experience talking about prayer. The wisdom literature of the Bible can remind us that, more often than not, our work involves dealing with people who talk of practical, everyday things more than they talk about their relationship to God. The Bible's wisdom literature and the work of the chaplain are similar in that both spend most of their time addressing the way things are in the world of everyday life. Our relational wisdom involves recognizing that we can talk seriously about life and its meaning without talking explicitly about relationship with God.

Wisdom for the chaplain does not grow out of her association with health care or the psychological knowledge of the physician or psychoanalyst. It comes instead from the power of relationship to reach out and affirm the humanness of the separated ones— those trapped in loneliness, confusion, and often, powerlessness. It is also found in the ability to perceive complexity and important relational dimensions in the most ordinary conversations and prayers.

The chaplain's wisdom, today, also involves the recognition

that we who offer a religiously motivated care must do this in a world in which care is understood in a different way. In a world where it is assumed that care can be managed, religiously motivated care—pastoral care—becomes more important than ever before. In my book on pastoral counseling (Patton, 1983) I used the term, "relational humanness," to describe what should be offered to persons in pastoral care and counseling. I think that is a particularly fortunate term today. In a health care world that seems to have become more cost-conscious than person-conscious, people need to experience their humanness in relationship.

The institutional world in which the chaplain works is populated with all kinds of specialists. At one level the chaplain is understood to be a specialist in religion, or, more generally, in spirituality. Certainly, the chaplain is trained in religion and now, to some degree, in ethics, but I would argue that the chaplain's specialty is not so much her religious knowledge as it is her relational wisdom. Whereas most specialties within the institution involve particular knowledge and skills applicable to the patient as an individual, the chaplain's focus is broader. It involves the patient's relationships with family, the institutional staff, persons within the community, and with God. The chaplain's ministry also involves the staff and the similar relationships in their lives. I believe that relational wisdom is a specialty that Joan Hemenway fully embodied.

Relational wisdom involves both how we understand our fellow human beings and how we engage them in relationship. Essential for the chaplain's relational thinking is a holistic view of human being that grows out of the religious tradition that she represents. The modern era of pastoral care education began with the holistic theories of personality first published in the late 1930s. It was broadened by the systemic and relational theories of the person that flowered in the 1950s and 60s. Certainly, the other specialists within the institution believe that the patient or resident is more than a diagnosis or problem, but the chaplain is one who most fully represents and embodies a relational view of human being in her work with staff, with patients, and with families.

The chaplain's relational wisdom is informed both by a variety of psychological theories of the person and by the religious tradition that most of us represent. That religious tradition assumes that humankind was created for relationship with God and other human beings. The chaplain is a reminder to patients, family members, and staff that persons live in a web of relationships. She is there so that they may call upon her to use her relational wisdom to sort out what needs to be said and done in those relationships. She reminds those around her of the importance of relationships, and her training and continuing education is designed to enable her to offer wisdom about how persons can best deal with those relationships.

Postmodern and culturally-informed thinking has warned us about developing norms for human relationality that are informed primarily from one culture, race, gender, or other influencing factor. We have learned to attend to the particulars in any situation and to avoid generalizations based on an unacknowledged perspective of our own. In recent years, we have been influenced in our caring by what I have called the communal-contextual paradigm for pastoral care and its critique of individualistic and mono-cultural thinking and acting. Nevertheless, in all their culturally and gender-conditioned different ways human beings are relational, and the chaplain is a reminder of this and a specialist in working with these relationships.

I do not argue for any one psychological theory for developing and maintaining relational wisdom, but I believe that reading, study, and reflection on ministry should continually be informed by sound relational theory—family studies, group theory, system and organizational theory, and ethical and theological understandings of relationships. I offer here a few examples of some theories that have consistently informed me in my work.

An early and lasting influence is the work of Harry Stack Sullivan. Although Sullivan wrote with a terminology that has not endured, he said many things that were later developed in family systems and psychoanalytic object-relations theory. His theories, which grew out of his early work with deeply disturbed schizophrenic patients, in some ways parallel those of Anton Boisen. He affirmed the humanity of those who seemed so different from others with what he called his one genus hypothesis: "We are all more

208

alike than otherwise." In his relational wisdom there was an affirmation of the humanity of the other and, in that, an offering of security that allowed the other—patient, staff member, or member of the community—to be what he or she was.

Sullivan believed a helping person ought to be an "expert in interpersonal relations." This expertise included attention to the ordinary that was characteristic of Dicks, and the concern for depth found in Boisen. Sullivan's expert was, first of all, extraordinarily perceptive in responding to anxiety and noticing the detail of the anxiety involved in relationships. Second, he could offer enough security to the other to allow him to explore what needed to be understood in his immediate predicament and his life as a whole. The third characteristic of Sullivan's expert was "realness." He was available and genuine—the way Nathaniel is described in the Gospel of John—one in whom there is no guile. His communication was simple, in contrast to much of the communication experienced in a health and welfare institution. Having dealt with terribly anxious persons who confused their speech to deal with their anxiety, Sullivan sought to deal with his patients in a down-to-earth, understandable way. A chaplain's relational wisdom, characterized by sensitivity and the ability to offer a trusting relationship, is exhibited in a similar way.

A second influence in my understanding of relational wisdom involves a continuing study of the three fundamental life relationships that grow out of our experience in being a family member and later extend into all areas of life. I have argued that ethically all persons are expected to care for their generations: the family members in the generation before them—the parental generation; their own generation, composed of brothers and sisters and other peers; and the generation that comes after them, their children or the children of others. I believe that one cannot be fully human without caring about and for all three of these relationships. Using a different terminology to describe them, in our institutions we are called upon to deal with relationships to authorities, with peers, and with those for whom we are an authority or to whom we offer care. Parenthetically, I believe that much of the strength of Clinical Pastoral Education has been its constant examination of those relationships in the process of supervision.

Many of us assume that our relationships with persons in authority are the most difficult to deal with, but I am convinced that it is necessary to examine all three types of relationships and how they are interrelated. How is the staff member with whom we are consulting dealing with peers, with patients, with supervisors, and how does it relate to her life experience insofar as that is available to you and her? If we learn to explore those three relationships for ourselves and for others, we develop competence in the specialty of relational wisdom.

Relational wisdom requires developing a theory for group work that is developed through study and experience. Among the many valuable theories about participating in and leading groups, Joan Hemenway's *Inside the Circle* (1996), has been a helpful resource for pastoral practitioners. Most helpful to me have been theories that emphasize that groups have two essential needs—accomplishing a task and satisfying the emotional needs of the group members. If we fail to achieve some balance between these two needs we will have a difficult time in our group leadership. Moreover, we need to be aware of how these needs are expressed by the group members and by us, the leader or supervisor. Recognizing and balancing these two basic needs has enabled me to survive and even thrive in many different kinds of groups.

In summary, I have argued that within an institution populated by specialists a competent chaplain is best understood as a specialist in relational wisdom. That specialty within religion is at the heart of chaplaincy's meaning and in keeping with most religious traditions. Relational wisdom, in the tradition of Dicks, Boisen, and Joan Hemenway, is an important contribution to the life of an institution, to patients or parishioners, families and staff.

One of the ways that many of us have learned about relational wisdom is through the study of pastoral events, often in the form of a verbatim. I close this paper with two such events, shared in seminars by two former students who have given permission to use them for teaching purposes. The first event is with a patient in a psychiatric unit. The other is with a family member in a county hospital waiting room.

Chaplain Rosie was called to the psychiatric unit to talk to a young woman about her own age who was suffering from, among other things, an agitated depression. The conversation went something like this:

Chaplain: They told me that you feel very depressed.
A: Yes, I'm so tired, so exhausted. I wish I could die. I'm so tired I want to rest.
C: Rest?
A: It's too much for me. I mean, everybody expects me to do something. I do a lot, but not enough.
C: Why do you have such high expectations of yourself?
A: I'm a perfectionist. You see for the last month I have felt like Amy Christ.
C: Amy Christ?
A: Yes, like Jesus Christ. I know it sounds crazy, but in my mind I am God's begotten daughter.
C: Oh.
A: Like Jesus.
C: How like Jesus?
A: He was perfect.
C: So you have to be perfect too.
A: Yes.
C: But we are humans. We can never be perfect.
A: That's what makes me feel so bad.
C: You know, I don't think you're God's only begotten daughter. I'm his daughter too. You're important to him, but you're not the only one.
A: If I'm not the only one, I don't have to be Amy Christ.
C: You don't. You're Amy Adams.
A: So, instead of trying to live like Amy Christ I should just try to be Amy?
C: Yes. Sometimes that's not easy. [Perhaps having heard Martin Buber's story about Moses she says:] There's a story I remember in which someone said, "I'm not afraid that in the last days God will ask me, 'Why didn't you live like Jesus?' I'm afraid God will ask, 'Why didn't you live like yourself?'"

A: Like Amy.

C: Yes. Like Amy.

A: That feels better. I like the story.

(As we walked back to the nurse's station Amy said to the staff there, "We decided that I am not Amy Christ," and everyone smiled.)

In our relationships we are reminded again and again that both we and the patient are, as Sullivan expressed it, "more alike than otherwise." We don't have to be God's only begotten daughter—Amy Christ—just Amy, and that may be enough.

The event of another student touches on relational wisdom in another way. This student chaplain describes an encounter with a tired young mother dealing with her grief in a hospital waiting room:

While she picks her nose and rebukes her children for being rude, she sheds some tears in remembrance of the many family members she has lost in this very hospital and with a desperate look on her face says that "It isn't always true that God gives us only what we can bear. Sometimes he gives us more and we have to shut up and deal with it anyway." She then explains to her curious child that I am the chaplain—a good person who is here to "help us with our grief—like when papa died and the chaplain who was here then gave us Kleenex and we took the whole box home."

Relational wisdom sometimes means giving a family a whole box of Kleenex to dry their tears.

References

Hemenway, J.E. (1996). *Inside the circle: A historical and practical inquiry concerning process groups in clinical pastoral education.* Decatur, GA: Journal of Pastoral Care Publications, Inc.

Patton, J. (1983). *Pastoral counseling: A ministry of the church.* Nashville: Abingdon Press.

CHAPTER 15

CPE and Spiritual Growth[2]
George Fitchett

Introduction

When CPE goes well it is a profound, life changing experience. A recent student summarized her experience of a basic quarter saying:

I have had a wonderful time at Rush. I cannot remember a time in my life when I have been challenged by my work and at the same time, so fulfilled by it. At the end of each day I have people and conversations that have added dimension to my life. (All students' quotes are used with their permission.)

Another student in that training group wrote:

CPE offered me a more powerful way inside myself. The depth and completeness astounded me. To see myself reflected in my colleagues and patients, to find myself starkly revealed against the hospital background was more intense than expected, more wonderful and awe-full than expected, and more catalytic to change than expected.

[2] Reprinted with permission from the *Journal of Supervision and Training in Ministry*, (1998-1999), 19:130-146. With Volume 27, 2007, the Journal was renamed *Reflective Practice: Formation and Supervision in Ministry*. An earlier version of this paper was presented at the annual meeting of the Australia New Zealand ACPE, Melbourne, Australia, June 30, 1998. The author would like to express his gratitude to his Australian, New Zealand, and American colleagues who commented on earlier versions of the paper and to the students who gave permission for their stories to be included here.

At the end of their year of training, several residents from a recent training group also commented on the significant changes that had taken place for them. One man wrote:

> "Never underestimate the energy of this chaplain." I take that as the staring point of this evaluation of myself and my experience this unit. I have had a taste of the switch from analog to digital and from copper wiring to fiber optics in my inner connectedness. The psychic, spiritual, and physical energy boost that has taken place over the past two units has been very exciting for me.

A woman in the group wrote:

> The past quarter has been so filled. I can't believe it. I don't know how to hold everything up. I was surprised about my own pastoral care. I have found a way to reflect on visits which helps me much more than verbatims. I need to include the scene, the smells, the feelings. I found a new awareness of different levels of interaction. It has also given me more ground to reflect on how God happens in these encounters. I was so surprised when George brought in a candle [and lit it] after I read one of these stories to him in supervision. I think I had not recognized at that time that I have found my own way of being a pastor, in what I am doing and also in how I am writing about it, allowing readers to enter the experience.

Another woman in the group wrote:

> I wish I had the right words. Words that would convey the wholeness of the last twelve months. My feelings are mixed. The sadness and pain of letting go. Gratitude. Affection. Joy. Hope. Fear. Longing. I feel I have made progress. This experience has been transformative. I can see myself becoming the pastor I'd hoped to be, comfortable with my own authority, certain of my love and concern for others, and hopeful that redemption will arise out of suffering. I have grown to trust my pastoral skills and instincts.

214

Our standards say that our work is about assisting students with growth in personal and professional identity, knowledge, and skills, but growth or changes in those areas, as important as they may be, would not evoke words such as these about the impact of the CPE experience on the students' lives. I believe that one reason why CPE has a reputation for being a profound, life transforming experience, one reason why the experience of CPE leads students to write comments such as those above, is that CPE, at its best, is an experience of spiritual growth; it is an experience that touches and transforms our soul.

In this paper I will begin by sharing a personal story which CPE helped me to see was an important formative spiritual experience. I will place that experience in the context of a theory of spiritual development and identify three features of CPE that I believe contribute to its potential to facilitate spiritual growth. I will then illustrate and expand on this theory with stories from several CPE students. I will conclude with a discussion of the implications of this for CPE supervision.

Baptism in the Flushing Reformed Church

I was raised in the Reformed Church in America, a moderate to conservative denomination of Dutch-descended Calvinists. Fifteen years ago I left the Reformed Church and joined the Religious Society of Friends, the Quakers. Recovering memories of the baptism liturgy in the Flushing Reformed Church, the church in which I was raised, helped me understand why I felt the need to leave the Reformed Church and find a new spiritual home.

Excepting the annual Christmas pageant, there was nothing about worship in the Reformed tradition, in the imposing sanctuary of the Protestant Reformed Dutch Church of Flushing, New York, which made it appealing to the spirituality of a child. It was worse than unappealing. It was torture. A friend tells a story that gives a good illustration of the particular manner in which this torture was carried out. He recalls the first time as a child he attended a performance of the oratorio "The Messiah." As the choir repeated the verse, "All we like sheep have gone astray," over and over, my friend recalls a great despair gripped his soul. He knew the Oratorio was based on the Bible. He knew the Bible was a huge book with many verses. He put two and two together and realized that if each verse were repeated as many times as this verse was he would be sitting there for the rest of his life.

Long choral works with many verses repeated over and over and over again were some of the sacred acts that were performed in the sanctuary of the Reformed Church of Flushing. Long sermons and prayers that lasted forever were also. As a child, sitting through these services effectively began the lesson that faith was composed of self-discipline, of repression of the natural tendency to wiggle, talk, gaze about, or otherwise behave like a child. It set the stage for understanding God and what you did in God's house. It was like being at the home of a distant relative. You wore uncomfortable clothes and behaved unnaturally and were scolded for being yourself.

The arrival of Spring brought some hope for a break in this annual liturgical calendar of torturous self-control. In the Spring, proud families brought their newborn infants to the church to be baptized. The whole tone of those Sundays seemed different. The windows seemed to let in more light. The members of the congregation seemed to let slight smiles break the solemnity of their expressions.

On those Sundays I eagerly awaited the time when the pastor would come down from the pulpit and stand with the family around the baptismal font. In large part, the excitement of these times stemmed from an uncertainty about how the infant would take to this encounter with God's grace, and how the family and pastor would take to the infant's reaction. The times when the babes slept peacefully through the whole event spoke to us of the soothing, maternal aspects of God, but offered little relief from the agonizing liturgical year.

The best times were when the infants cried. It was even better if the infant was quiet right up until the moment when the minister gently sprinkled the water of blessing on their foreheads and then let out with anguished wailing. What excitement there was in watching the scene that followed. The pastor would sputter as he tried to find the closing prayer and recite it over the noise of the screaming child. Embarrassment would be written all over the faces of the infant's parents, undone that their precious one should be so misbehaved in God's house. Anxious grandparents would reach for the babe, offending the parents and insuring an increase in their anxiety and thus in the child's anxious crying.

As soon as the Amen was out of the minister's mouth, the offending infant and embarrassed parents would be ushered out the side door. The elders and pastor would quickly restore order and proceed with the rest of the service. But the return to the weekly liturgy did not dampen my joy in knowing that a new recruit had made their protest against our common liturgical oppression known in no uncertain terms.

As I grew older and began to hear and understand the words which were spoken in the baptism liturgy, my hope that our side might eventually win diminished sharply. It was clear from the liturgy that the church took this business of self-discipline seriously. The very first words of the baptism liturgy effectively set the mood. Whatever smiles might be found on the faces of the congregation, as they resonated with the pride and joy of the new parents, were quickly wiped away as the minister began reading. Whatever lightness and light had been brought into the sanctuary by the infant was soon darkened by the church's teaching. The liturgy begins with the following words:

The principal parts of the doctrine of holy Baptism are:

> *First.* That we, with our children, are conceived and born in sin, and therefore are children of wrath, insomuch that we cannot enter into the kingdom of God, except we are born again. This the dipping in or sprinkling with water teaches us, whereby the impurity of our souls is signified, and we are admonished to loathe and humble ourselves before God, and seek for purification and salvation without ourselves (Liturgy of the Reformed Church in America, 1940).

I had seen the joy and delight which the infants had brought to the faces of their parents and to the congregation around me. But the liturgy contradicted what I thought I knew from experience. Nothing could be more pure than an infant brought into the church to be baptized, but the church declared it was otherwise. "We are admonished to loathe and humble ourselves before God, and seek for our purification and salvation without ourselves." In our Reformed tradition, nothing was left to our faulty imagination. Lest the family or congregation lose sight of what this smiling infant was really like, the very first words of the liturgy were there to remind us.

These first words of the baptism liturgy became symbolic of what was for me destructive in the Reformed tradition. They were words that directed me to loathe myself and seek to understand myself "without" myself. I later realized, in part through CPE, in part through therapy, for me to be saved I had to begin to free myself from the faith which these words proclaimed. I had to leave the sanctuary of the Flushing Reformed Church to see if the sacred, as I was coming to know it from my experience, could be found dwelling in another place.

Spiritual Growth and CPE

There are many theories of spiritual growth or faith development available to help us interpret our own spiritual stories and our students' (Ivy, 1997, pp. 32-45). One of the ones I like the best was described by John Westerhoff (1976, pp. 79-103). Westerhoff sees the pilgrimage of faith proceeding through four styles. The first style is *experienced faith*. It is the non-verbal experience of the trustworthiness of existence formed in infancy and childhood by our interactions with primary caregivers. The second style is *affiliative faith*. It refers to the beliefs and practices we develop through participation in the religious life of our family. The third style is *searching faith*. It is a time of questioning the faith of our family. It is a time of experimenting with alternative beliefs and practices, and hopefully a time of renewed connection with our own experiences of the holy. The fourth style is *owned faith*. It is a time when, through the process of searching, we have formed a faith where our beliefs are rooted in our experiences and our rituals and practices give expression to those beliefs and experiences.

The importance of community in the first two styles is obvious. 'Good enough' parenting provides a positive foundation for experienced faith. Abusive or neglectful parenting plants seeds of despair or chaos. In the stage of affiliative faith, the family and/or primary faith community communicates foundational beliefs and morals, and introduce the rituals which teach and reinforce them.

The role of community for the second two styles is no less crucial, but generally more problematic. For most people, the style of searching faith is experienced as a time of un-faith. Key figures from the period of affiliative faith usually disapprove of the questions and behavior that constitute searching faith. Our exemplars in the affiliative period were rarely people whose stories of searching faith, if they had one, were told. Sustaining the search in this period is a demanding process. Some searchers foreclose its uncertainty with a new affiliation. Others adopt the identity of non-believer and assume the search is ended. A community which values and tolerates people in the midst of searching faith is rare.

Such communities, when they are found, are often the communities that also welcome people with owned faith. They find themselves enriched, not threatened, by the diversity of beliefs and practices of a group of people with owned faith.

My experience of CPE was one of being part of a community of people in the process of searching and owned faith. Consequently my experience of CPE had a significant impact on my spiritual growth. The CPE experience, and especially the relationships with peers and supervisors, provided me with an important antidote to Calvinist self-negation. By suggesting that experience and process could be trustworthy, CPE also exposed me to a radically new theology of inspiration.

As I reflect on my CPE experience and the experiences of my students, three features of the CPE experience seem to play an important role in facilitating the kind of spiritual growth Westerhoff describes: questions, answers, and community. First, CPE is a time of encounter with major questions about life, death, self, and ministry. Second, in CPE the answers to these questions are not simple or clear and the sources of authority for answering them are complex. Third, when CPE is at its best, as students experience these questions and search for the answers, they are supported in gracious and caring relationships with peers and supervisors (Palmer, 1998). Let me tell the stories of several students to illustrate the different ways CPE influences the spiritual growth of students at these different points in their faith development. As most students comes to us during the affiliative or searching phases of their faith development, the stories and discussion focus on those two phases.

Baptism in The Royal Children's Hospital

David Dawes (1997), chaplain and supervisor in training at the Royal Children's Hospital, Melbourne, Australia, has written the following:

Gilbert was anxious, anxious to do the right thing by the program, by me, and by the church. The following dialogue named a conflict right from the start. This conversation occurred during our first supervisory conference after Gilbert had an opportunity to explore the hospital and the wards to which he was to provide ministry.

G.1   So do I start on call this week?

D.1   I was thinking maybe next week after you have had some time to get used to the hospital and become familiar with it and the issues of pastoral care to sick kids.

G.2   Yeah. What are the main things that the on call chaplain gets called to?

D.2   We primarily get called to crisis events such as death, immanent death, distressed families who have just received poor prognosis, and we get called to baptize sick or dying children. And occasionally we are asked to baptize children who are already dead.

G.3   You wouldn't do that. You'd offer them a blessing.

D.3   Ah, no. I am prepared to baptize. I have baptized a

small number of kids who have been brought into Emergency already dead. Any child who appears to have died from Sudden Infant Death are automatically brought into here.

G.4   Yeah, but the child is dead; baptism is for the living.

D.4   The parents are living and are going through the worst time of their lives. I don't want to add to their horror by adhering to a strict interpretation. I've baptized children who are alive only because of the machines they are on and as soon as they are extubated they are no longer alive.

G.5   So it is a pastoral response, meeting the needs of the parents?

D.5   Yeah, but it is also a theological response because God is not offended by my action. Well, I don't think he is.

G.6   You've given me something to think about.

This was one part of a discussion that had a profound impact on Gilbert causing him to have a few sleepless nights wrestling with the issue. It was revisited in each of the next three supervisory conferences.

Gilbert wrote in his journal:

My preparation for ministry has involved a theological understanding of Baptism of the living. In fact in the UCA [Uniting Church of Australia] Baptism of the dead is considered an inappropriate practice. For me it was a simple straightforward stance which afforded no great difficulty.

There is a sense in which our 'alienation' from God is *past* (Gilbert's emphasis) because of what Christ has done for us. But I have to say that Christ has done for us something for which our Baptism changes nothing (i.e.) God's love for us in Jesus Christ is undeserved, free and for all and is not dependent on *Baptism*. Paul's word in Romans 8 'nothing can separate us from God's love...not even death'. And yet, the pleading heart of Mum and Dad for their child (dead) is a confronting pastoral issue.

In supervision, my response to Gilbert was to affirm that it is his decision and that I would support either decision for either decision was appropriate. I told Gilbert in our third supervisory session, before he went on call, that in the event of him being called and requested to baptize a child who had died I was able to be called. Gilbert continued to wrestle with the theological and pastoral issues raised by either decision.

Several weeks later, in the early hours of the morning, Gilbert had the opportunity to confront, in the practice of ministry, the conflict that until now had been academic. Gilbert was called to the Neonatal Unit where a family whose six week old daughter was on the cusp between life and death requested that she be baptized. Gilbert spent a long time with Rebecca's parents and was prepared to wait until the mother Sarah's sister and husband arrived before baptizing Rebecca. Gilbert said in our supervisory session later in the day:

G.7 Once I had decided for myself that Rebecca did not have to be alive for me to be able to baptize her, the pressure just slipped away. I was able to be present with the family with no need to rush.

D.7 So you decided that for you to baptize Rebecca she did not have to be alive?

G.8 Yes and I felt my need to rush just fall away and I was able to sit and be with Sarah and Alan without putting any further pressure on them.

D.8 It sounds like your decision was freeing?

G.9 Yes it was.

D.9 Were you worried about the church?

G.10 No. I was more concerned about being there for this couple.

D.10 Congratulations, it feels like a celebration.

G.11 Yes. Yes it is and it has been a long and painful journey. But when I was there with Sarah and Alan all I could think about was being there for them, caring for them.

Gilbert was now able to be present to the family and able to meet their needs for he was able to let go of his anxiety of doing the right thing by the church and was able to be pastorally present to the family. He was able to claim his responsibility to provide ministry to this family as he best thought fit. Gilbert later wrote of this baptism in his Final Evaluation:

> Sitting with the parents, watching the struggle of staff to save their daughter and hearing their story of pain during the past year, especially the last six weeks since the premature birth of their child. I was asked to baptize the baby and did so. Before doing this though I spoke to the parents about alerting other members of the family they may want to be present. For the first time in my life I faced the issue of pastoral ministry and where it diverged from book learning. In deciding to baptize I decided I would do this, in the context of this particular pastoral situation, even if the baby died before other family members could arrive. By arriving at this decision, I took away the division that threatened to be a barrier to my being present to the family.

Gilbert's Experience of Questions, Answers, and Community

In Gilbert's story we see all three spiritually formative features of CPE at work. First, pediatric hospital ministry raises profound questions for Gilbert, questions about baptism, sacraments, and Christology; questions he may never encounter in the classroom, and perhaps not in the parish. Is it permissible to baptize a dead child? Is baptism necessary for us to be saved? How do you balance the importance of correct ritual and doctrine with the pastoral needs of anxious parents? These were abstract questions that confronted Gilbert as he began CPE. The questions caused Gilbert some sleepless nights and he raises them again in the next three supervisory conferences. The questions became a pressing issue requiring him to make some important choices when he was called to be with Rebecca and her family.

Second, CPE does not offer any simple answers for the questions Gilbert encounters. You wouldn't baptize a dead child, would you? Gilbert asks his supervisor? Yes, David says, I would. Well, you'd really only do it to comfort the family, right, Gilbert asks? Well, yes, David answers. But I don't think "God is offended by my action," he adds. David's responses to Gilbert's questions gives Gilbert "something to think about." Where can he go for the answers? He considers doctrine and scripture, but the answers there aren't clear. His supervisor shares his position but doesn't insist that Gilbert agree with it. His CPE experience forces Gilbert to face the complexity of this question and the absence of clear, simple answers to it (Anderson & Foley, 1998, pp. 128-134; Dawes, 1997, pp. 147-160; Smith, 1998-1999, pp. 25-35).

But CPE also provides Gilbert with a supportive community as he wrestles with this issue. In this story, that support is evident in David's relationship with Gilbert. David gives Gilbert time to become familiar with the hospital before he asks him to be on-call. David listens as Gilbert wrestles with the baptism question, wrestles with it for several weeks. David assures Gilbert, "that it is his decision and that [he] would support either decision for either decision was appropriate," and that he could be called if there was a request for baptism that Gilbert wished to refer. Finally, after Gilbert's ministry with Rebecca's family, and decision to be present with the family, David senses the importance of the moment and affirms Gilbert's decision, "Congratulations, it feels like a celebration." I would propose that, in part, it was David's gracious, supportive relationship with Gilbert that allowed Gilbert to enter into the questions raised by the baptism issue and not defend against them. And that this relationship also allowed Gilbert to respond compassionately and graciously rather than rigidly to the needs of this distressed family.

From the limited material we have about Gilbert, it isn't clear to me where he is on his spiritual pilgrimage. My guess is that he was primarily working out of an affiliative faith. His CPE experience and specifically his wrestling with the issue of baptism may have challenged that faith a little, but probably not enough to push him into an extended time of searching faith. In terms of spiritual growth, the primary result of Gilbert's experience in CPE, at least as we know it, was to help him move toward a more compassionate balance between law and grace, between obedience to the formal teachings of his church and the pastoral needs of those to whom he ministered.

Finding Grace, Voice, and Liberation

In contrast to students like Gilbert, for whom CPE is a time of moderate spiritual growth, there are other students, and they are obviously the students with whom I identify most strongly, for whom CPE is a time of intense spiritual struggle and search for an owned faith. Let me illustrate this with the words of several women who have been in our training program.

Jean wrote:

> One of the biggest areas of growth that has been clarified for me this quarter is regarding my need for definition, for direction, for right answers, for success. I want to know what my assignment is, how to do it, and then to do it well. I have known this about myself, but it became problematic this quarter. I have been able to talk about the strengths of that way of being, but it has caused a lot of distress this quarter. As my verbatims clearly showed, I was continually feeling that I wasn't doing the pastoral care work right and I had difficulty just being with people even though that is what I most want to be able to do for myself and have others do for me.
>
> A theme that also seemed to come out of supervision and verbatims is what a heavy burden these expectations become. So, I would like to find some ways to lighten the load, to be responsible, but not to get drug [sic] down by these expectations that are coming from my past and from myself.

Earlier in this evaluation, Jean addresses a key theological issue that seems to be linked to her sense of heavy burden. "In my basic quarter of CPE, grace became an important theological theme for me as I struggled with some of the issues I currently struggle with—wanting to do things right and follow the plan or the rules. I have not been too aware of grace this quarter, which has probably made those frustrating times even more difficult."

Another student Grace wrote:

> Once again [this quarter] I was told I was being hard on myself—a response that surprised me because I didn't see it. The conversation has left me pondering once again the meaning of self-acceptance. JoAnn [one of my supervisory colleagues] pushed me to accept what I keep trying to change —to accept myself in this way seems to be "settling for what is" with an unwillingness to change.
>
> I have been trying so hard to "get rid of" what I don't like about myself that accepting those characteristics I am ashamed of or thinking about God's accepting me as I am now instead of as I hope to be someday just hasn't ever occurred to me. I really have spent my life trying to "be" better hoping that someday I would "be" good enough. To move out of this mode feels somewhat like putting down my armor—to quit fighting—myself. Even in the writing of this I can feel my heart softening—what would it mean to quit fighting, to relax, to just be who I am and to say— thank you. It would be grace.

Grace has struggled with this issue a lot. In her evaluation of the previous quarter she acknowledges the spiritual dimension of the struggle even more explicitly.

> I am beginning to realize that much of what I am learning can not be forced. It is a process of learning to trust myself and the spirit of the divine within. It feels very risky, very new. I want to go where the spirit leads, yet I am afraid and find it hard to let go as much as I say I want to do so.

One of the keys to the process of liberation Jean and Grace are describing is being able to name the bondage they are experiencing. To do that, a student must find her voice. That was also an important goal for Cathy:

> I have already mentioned the issue of 'voice.' Just last week, George helped me to see that this included the voice of pain and sadness as well as the voice of strength. It was important for me to be able to 'give voice' to my feelings of

heaviness and weariness and to share them in the group instead of stoically holding them myself. I have also learned how essential it is to speak with my voice rather than attempting to assume the voice of someone else, and to be aware of when and how I can be tempted to give my voice away. Having a voice also relates for me to coming out of hiding, being willing to be visible, to acknowledge the light.

Reflecting on her year of CPE, Linda is even more explicit about what it has meant to find the voice to name her experience:

What would it mean to be known? That's the question which has echoed through my mind and through my experience of these last four quarters. I began the year with a commitment –to you and to me. A commitment to speak the truth. But I had missed a step. To speak the truth I would first have to know the truth. I would have to believe it. You have heard me talk about how difficult and painful the year has been in many ways. The pain comes from knowing the truth about myself. There are many things about myself, my talents and abilities, which I appreciate, many ways in which I love myself for who I am and who I am becoming. In general, I like being me. I like who I am. But there are other ways I have refused to know myself, other parts of who I have been or who I am that I have not admitted to myself until recently. I have had to know myself differently than I allowed before. Today, I know myself as the child of alcoholic parents, as once anorexic, as sexually traumatized, as a victim of my mother's depression. It may sound strange, but I have lived most of my life not facing these realities and all that they imply. The stories I have shared with you hurt. Sometimes I can barely utter the words. I've heard them come out of my mouth before, but now, with you, they sound different. They fill my head and I know they are my words. They are me, who I have been, who I am, who I fear. Eating disorder—alcoholism—starvation—depression—abuse. Words that are mine in one way or another. Words I have come to know. But even now, knowing brings a certain liberation. I am beginning to imagine letting go of the past in a deeper, more complete way. I know better who I have been and because of it, who I am capable of becoming. I am not fully liberated. One theme we have heard in evaluations so far is that one is never fully liberated from the burdens acquired in childhood. I still feel very close to the past, to the old hurts, but not confined to them. I can imagine freedom now, even where I have not yet achieved it.

For these women, finding a voice lets them tell their story, lets them name their reality, lets them know themselves and be known to others. This time of searching is a time when old images and ideas are collapsing. Grace, a former doctoral student in theology, finds an important parallel process occurring for her.

I have struggled significantly with my faith and continue to grapple with images of God that are not helpful. I know what it means to "have the rug pulled out from under me," to have all that I had put together in my head pulled apart. This has helped me to be with others who find the world, as they have known it, falling part. I know the importance of "finding one's own way" and am grateful for those who have accompanied me. As a chaplain I try to do the same, accompany the other with respect for their process, their wisdom.

For some students, the images and methods of their affiliative faith block the path forward into searching faith and must be torn down. Sophia tells about her struggle to write her final theology of pastoral care.

I am sitting at the desk, unable to get my thoughts together. This is supposed to be my big thing. The result of one year of searching for my passion and my voice. The search for my truth, for what I believe in. It should all come together and make breathtaking sense. And I panic because I will never be able to do that. In my mind, "Theology" becomes again a systematic answer. I thought I was over that. But the very idea of theology implies so much of the tradition I studied, of the God I grew up with. The word God carries associations and values that I can't get out of my mind, lest out of my feelings. God is linked with fear, power, feeling never good enough, focusing on my short-comings. As much as I try, God keeps showing up as a male figure—Like a weed it grows back, saying, You ain't gonna get rid of me! The Weed-God, He-God, the system of the father's father's. I try to cut it back, because it is not good for me. But it keeps growing.

When she abandons the systematic method of the father's fa-ther's and takes up her own method something different happens:

Because I can't write, I take refuge in the watercolors. Maybe they can help me out of my frozen state. The next day, the colors dry by now, I glance over to the picture, and what I see is incredible. I can feel my heart beating. I am so surprised and in awe: there she is, a woman imprisoned, naked, her hands tied in the back, trying to get free.

Theology Go to Hell! You are the stepfamily, the enemy that strips off my clothes, ties me down and locks me in a cell. I am not doing this again to me. Not this time. I don't want to do theology. I don't want the Weed-God He-God.

I want to thrive.

The truth is in me. I just have to take time for her. She comes in dreams, in paintings. She comes in pieces. She does not have to be consistent. She makes me alive. Her names are: beauty, creativity, I am who I am.

The quotations from these students tell the story of what it is like to be in a time of searching faith. For these women, the three spiritually formative features of CPE, questions, community, and answers, were important aspects of their search. Unlike Gilbert, these women did not need CPE to put them in touch with profound questions about life, self, faith, or ministry. They were experienc-ing the pain of their questions, the bondage of old ideas and images of themselves, of ministry, of God. For them, CPE was a place where they found a voice that enabled them to name their pain and bondage, a voice that enabled them to raise questions about the suffering they experienced, the burdensome expectations to be per-fect, the struggle for self-acceptance, the pain of hiding and then naming the truth of one's life.

The community these women found in CPE played an essential role in their time of searching faith. It helped them find their voice and name their experience. It sustained them in their lament, in their pain and questions. It encouraged them when they were hesitant or resistant to naming their bondage. It celebrated with them when the searching led to liberation and new life. While the quotations I have shared here do not capture the key role of the peer group for each of these women, it, as well as competent and compassionate individual supervision, was an essential element in their experience.

For each of these women, CPE was also a place that recognized there are many right answers to life's deepest questions. It was a place that recognized that theology could be written or painted. It was a place that affirmed that the best answers to the questions with which they wrestled, were the answers that were in harmony with the truth of their experience, answers that affirmed the presence of the divine spirit within them. "The truth is in me," Sophia wrote. "I just have to take time for her."

For some students, like Gilbert, CPE is a time of modest spiritual growth. For other students, such as Jean, Grace, Cathy, Linda, and Sophia, CPE is a time of intense spiritual searching. CPE's attitude toward questions, answers, and community makes it an ideal context to support students who are in that phase of their spiritual growth. My goal in CPE however, is not to keep students in an endless process of searching faith. My hope is that by providing students like Grace, Linda, and Sophia with a community that understands and supports their time of searching faith, it will develop into something like the owned faith Linda described. "This experience has been transformative. I can see myself becoming the pastor I'd hoped to be, comfortable with my own authority, certain of my love and concern for others, and hopeful that redemption will arise out of suffering." Like many of our students whose time of searching faith in CPE is followed by owned faith, since completing CPE, Linda and Sophia have returned to their respective faith groups and are in the process of becoming ordained.

Implications for Supervision

So What? What are the implications of these ideas for our work as supervisors? Let me answer that by referring to the three key spiritual features of CPE.

Regarding the role of questions, for students in a time of affiliative faith, such as Gilbert, the confrontation with issues of life and death, and ministry often raises significant questions. It is important to trust such students to select, from among the many questions arising from this experience, the one or ones that they are ready to address. As in other matters, pressing these students to address some other question or issue of obvious importance to us is only likely to create defensiveness and not facilitate learning.

Students who are in a time of searching faith are likely to bring significant questions with them. CPE need only be a place that welcomes their engagement of them. Some students who come to CPE may be in the process of a transition from affiliative to searching faith. Asking deep questions about their affiliative faith may feel strange and uncomfortable to them. It may feel like unfaith, like betrayal. It takes little more than helping them name their questions as an essential component of the process of growth in faith to help them move into the searching process.

Regarding answers, CPE's central gift, for me and for so many students, is captured in the well-worn phrase, trust the process. I've come to believe that the best theology is sung and regarding answers, I love the hymn, "Lead on O Cloud of Yahweh. The journey is our home." Regarding answers, I feel some affinity with Roy Bradley's emphasis on "keeping the mystery present" to our students (Bradley, 2000, p.1.). Our best gift to our students is like David's gift to Gilbert, clarity about our own perspectives, and support and encouragement to help our students find the answers that have the authority of their experience.

Regarding community, I feel affinity with Bradley's emphasis on "redemptive relationships." Regarding community, I would emphasize that part of what has made CPE redemptive for me and for many of our students has been its ability to be welcoming and inclusive of many different people: women and men, lay and ordained, gay and straight. Community is what makes CPE a place where spiritual growth can take place. Our programs, our peer groups, our supervisory relationships must be places where students feel welcomed, respected, and safe. When these things are present, the rest of the process almost takes care of itself.

But unfortunately, we cannot take respect and safety in relationships in CPE for granted. As I was writing it, I shared some of my ideas for this paper with a good friend and respected teacher of pastoral care. I told him I was going to make a case for CPE as a place of spiritual formation because in CPE anxious students experienced gracious relationships with peers and supervisors that enabled them to grow in awareness of God's gracious love for them. "That wasn't my experience in CPE," he reminded me. And I remembered his story about how, years ago, as an eager but anxious and awkward young seminarian, his CPE supervisor and peers criticized and humiliated him week after week. Fortunately, I believe we have outgrown the worst of our confrontive and "boundary-less" days in CPE. But if CPE is to be a place for spiritual exploration and growth, we must insure it is a place where students feel respected and safe.

Conclusion

What a gift it is to be a CPE supervisor and to be with students on their spiritual journeys. I can't imagine doing any other work. Here is what Grace said at the end of a quarter last year:

> How different life is becoming! There are hints that I am on my way to that more gracious, grace-filled space. Choosing to come to Rush was the first big step in that process. I feel some shifts happening in my family relationships, some new spaces opening up within me. I am more aware that my anger is often a means of defense/protection. I am learning about my need/right to create boundaries for myself. I am becoming aware of my tendency to take things personally which aren't personal. I am also discovering some areas that are particularly "charged" for me, places

that have me hooked. The learning has been difficult but worthwhile. My imagination is being stretched—because there are new moments where I can just be in the midst of what is and say with genuine gratitude—Thank you!

But my favorite image of a student's spiritual growth, of her owned spirituality, comes from Sophia, who after wrestling with the Weed-God He-God writes:

> I am making myself a dress. I have been wearing a lot of grays and blues, hiding myself. I was wearing what I thought I was supposed to wear. To fit in. If I am in the image of God, I want to be worthy of her. I want beautiful fabrics and warm and strong colors. I want to shine. I want to honor the body I am given, the talents that I have, the things I don't like about myself. It is hard to believe that she is ok with all of that, but she somehow *is* in all of that. Of course, impatient as I am, I wanted the dress to be finished within two days. But after two sewing machines failed, it is still in pieces, in the making. And that is actually as well. That's the place where I am at.

> I am bringing her alive, and I think she is quite excited that she appears!

> *There will come a day, when all dry bones will be alive again. The hearts will beat. And all will wear red golden clothes. They will enjoy each other's beauty.*

As I supervise, I think of the work I do as supporting my student's spiritual growth, as enjoying their unfolding spiritual beauty. In this paper I have tried to describe the kinds of spiritual growth that I have seen and how I think CPE facilitates that growth.

References

Anderson, H. & Foley, E. (1998). *Mighty Stories and Dangerous Rituals*. San Francisco: Jossey Bass Inc., Publishers.

Bradley, R.B. (1997). What are we doing in supervision? In R.B. Bradley (Ed.), *Clinical pastoral education beyond 2000* (18). Heidelberg, Victoria, Australia: Austin and

Repatriation Medical Center.

Dawes, D. (1997). A response to baptismal demands and requests. *Ministry, Society and Theology, 11*(2), 147-160.

Ivy, S.S. (1997). Spiritual assessment as a tool for the pastoral supervisor. *Journal of Supervision and Training in Ministry*, 18, 32-45

Liturgy of the Reformed Church in America (1940). New York: The Board of Publication of the Reformed Church in America.

Palmer, P.J. (1998). *The courage to teach.* San Francisco: Jossey-Bass Inc., Publishers.

Smith, T.M. (1998-1999). Pastoral and ritual response to perinatal death: A narrative of a departmental policy change. *Journal of Supervision and Training in Ministry*, 19, 25-35.

Westerhoff III, J.H. (1976). *Will our children have faith?* New York: The Seabury Press.

CHAPTER 16

The Concept of Circle and Group
in the African-American Community
Teresa E. Snorton

J oan Hemenway's *Inside the Circle: A Historical and Practical Inquiry Concerning Process Groups in Clinical Pastoral Education* emphasizes the importance of the small group (circle) in the CPE process. She writes specifically about the small group manifested in CPE as the Interpersonal Relationship Group (IPR, IPG, etc). For Hemenway, CPE group work seeks to facilitate individual insight and growth within the group context, with the group playing a specific and active role in the student's quest for deeper awareness and professional formation for ministry. While Hemenway uses the metaphor of a circle to address a specific aspect of group process in CPE, it is also a good metaphor for understanding the broader interpretations of group and community in African-American life and how those may carry over into a CPE experience.

CPE evolved out of a particular cultural context–Western, Protestant, Anglo-European-American–so it should not be surprising that a particular world view and cultural ethos is embedded in the CPE process as a whole. While this inherent world view is the foundational backdrop of the action-reflection model, as CPE students become more diverse, it is important to recognize whether the values and interpretations of CPE are congruent or incongruent with the world views of students from other diverse backgrounds. Hemenway's emphasis on the importance of the small group is an important segue into understanding the world view of African-American students when it comes to small group process. For example, Hemenway's contributions to CPE have led to a deepened acceptance of the purpose of small group in CPE as facilitating individual learning and growth. Moving beyond that understanding, in the African-American context personal growth is understood not as a goal itself, but small group work is viewed as one of the steps towards enhancing the entire village/family/community. For most African-American students in CPE, group process will not only be understood as the IPR group, but experienced every time the peer group gathers: verbatim seminar, worship seminar, didactics, etc.

Circle, in the African-American context is not merely a physical construct determined by time and space, but also a symbolic construct determined by covenant and connection. In other words, the cultural ethos of the African-American student is such that one is always a part of the community/group, bound to the community/group, and expected to keep the community's/group's best interest in mind, even when the community/group is not present. In supervising African-American students and students of African descent it is essential for the CPE supervisor to grasp such fundamental differences between Western thought and African thought when it comes to group process, as well as when accepting African-American students and building the CPE curriculum.

In most native African cultures, there are definitions and paradigms that dictate every phase of group and community life. In the African-American experience in America, the impact of slavery, racism, and Jim Crow on the formation of safe community adds greater complexity to these definitions. These factors must be considered and understood in order to be sensitive to the dynamics of African-American definitions of group, ministry, self-disclosure, transformation, and other commonly accepted phenomena of the CPE process. In forming a coherent, systematic definition of group and community from the African-American perspective, there are three basic concepts that form a perimeter—world view, relational values, and religiosity/spirituality. Each is discussed in the following paragraphs reflecting on the CPE experience. These discussions are intended to be descriptive, but in no way representative of the experience of every African-American student. It is also important to note that these same concepts can be applied to other cultural and ethnic groups, or parallel similar constructs in other cultural groups and for their students in CPE.

World View

World view is understood as "the most basic and comprehensive concepts, values and unstated assumptions about the nature of reality shared by people in a culture.... Existential assumptions provide people with a sense of order and meaning" (Hiebert, 1990, p. 1338). One's world view determines the variables through which reality is accepted and interpreted, and thus the way the individual "knows" (epistemology). Towards this end, it is critical for CPE supervisors to understand the difference between "constructed" versus "mechanistic" views of reality. In historic African life, symbolic meaning of sacred principles (constructed) rather than human principles and laws (mechanistic) was the primary epistemology (Sindima, 1990, pp. 137ff). This trust of the symbolic is rooted in the premise that all life is interconnected—the land, the people, and all of creation.

This interconnectedness is not accepted because of principles of science and technology (mechanistic), but because of beliefs of creation relationships that span multiple generations. The ritual life in many African countries relates to symbolic seasonal celebrations in which life is sustained (or not) because of the maintenance of balance (or lack of balance) within creation. The notions of interconnectedness and balance can be better understood through the concept of *Ma'at*, an underlying, widely accepted aspect world view in Africa. In historical Egypt/Africa, *Ma'at* was both a goddess of truth, justice, and order and a codified system of principles and laws. "To the Egyptian mind, *Ma'at* bound all things together in an indestructible unity: the universe, the natural world, the state, and the individual were all seen as parts of the wider order generated by *Ma'at*" (Budge, 1969, p.418). Contemporary beliefs around the concept of *Ma'at*, include order, truth, justice, harmony, reciprocity, righteousness (propriety), and balance as principles for living life together and for honoring the Creator. Group life is the arena in which these principles are practiced. The wellbeing and future of the group is dependent on each person participating in the maintenance of group life, not for self-enhancement but for the good of the whole.

The remnants of such a world view can still be seen in African-American life. Symbolic "knowing" through intuition, emotional expression, and spiritualism are valued just as much as facts and figures, mental acuity, and cognition. In addition, there is a strong tendency to believe that beyond the written and the spoken, there is symbolic meaning that must be discovered and experienced through relationship. The Eurocentric trust in the written word over the symbolic expression contradicts the core of a symbolic/relational world view. Thus, trusting relationships with the educator/supervisor, the institution, and the peer group are prerequisite to effective learning.

In the CPE group setting, African-American students may be more interested in the discovery process (observing and engaging with others in order to construct meaning) than in the process of self-disclosure through written learning contracts, reflection papers, and verbatims. Some African-American CPE students may find it difficult and restrictive to utilize written forms of reflection, not because they lack the intellectual ability to do so but because in their world view knowing comes symbolically (i.e., "It felt like the right thing to do." "We had a connection." "The Lord led me to pray for her.").

Permitting, perhaps even encouraging, the symbolic reflection on experience in CPE may be one way to begin to include the African-American student in the "circle." This sense of inclusion is critical since many CPE groups continue to reflect "disjunctive" rather than "serial socialization" (Griffith, 1979, p. 471), meaning there is still the likelihood that there is only one African-American student in the group at any given time, even in CPE programs that have histories of being inclusive. According to Griffith, when a student is the "first" or the "only," the socialization experience "is disjunctive because training programs reflect a mentality which does not allow for the uniqueness of the black experience, often rendering improbable any true interaction between the system and the black resident" (Griffith, 1979, p. 472). In *Racial and Ethnic Identity: Psychological Development and Creative Expression*, Griffith and other contributors explore the dynamic nature of identity formation and the impact on creative expression and learning when a member of the group differs culturally from the group invested with power within a society (Griffith, 1994). The experience of having one's world view validated and valued (not just recognized) by the CPE group can help ameliorate some of the disconnect for African-American students. ACPE Supervisor Osofo Atta writes "adjusting to valuing another world view might bring a bit of fuzziness to the lens we are accustomed to wearing. It is the CPE supervisor's ability to sit with this 'fuzziness' that helps to create a more rich and authentic learning experience for all involved" (personal communication, 2008).

Relational Values

The second concept to be aware of when supervising African-American students is that of "relational values." In historic African life, "bonded" or "relational" values took precedent over the individual and his/her rights and desires. Village and family or tribe took precedent over personal preferences. African-American students may come into the CPE group seeking to form and maintain relationships rather than to utilize critique and confrontation that may be perceived as destructive to the bonding process and maintenance of relationship. While CPE group supervision commonly embraces critique and confrontation as part of the learning process, the African-American student often experiences this as "counter" to the learning process. "Being in the hot seat," "in the fishbowl," or other descriptions of ways in which the CPE group is often is experienced can, for the African-American student, be a signal that community is deteriorating. Direct attention to one's shortcomings (or growing edges) is a cultural taboo, as the entire community sees its role as minimizing and compensating for, rather than focusing on, such deficits. The African-American student can sometimes be labeled as a "rescuer" or as "resistant to feedback," yet from another cultural lens that same behavior could be understood as kind, as preserving the dignity of the other, and even as pastoral.

African-American theologian J. Deotis Roberts points out the significance of group consciousness in the African-American value system. He writes, "The sense of wholeness is characteristic of the cultural heritage of African Americans. This affirmation of group 'belongingness' or solidarity carries over even to those who are outside the group—namely the unchurched or non-blood related African Americans. This group solidarity also extends to whites who are genuine in their friendship. This characteristic of the Africentric spirit is illustrated in wholesome relationship within the African American family and church" (Roberts, 2000, p. 85). Being and staying connected is a crucial value for the African American. This connectedness can not be overridden by individual needs and personal desires. In fact, in the African-American community the greater value is the denial of one's personal needs, desires, or fulfillment when it brings overt benefits to the community. This may be acted out the in CPE group by the African-American student's refusal to confront, to express anger or tears, or to challenge the authority of the supervisor.

There are a number of other books written about the role of community and relationship in the life of the African American that could be helpful to the CPE supervisor in understanding these dynamics. Dr. Barry Hallen (2001), professor of Philosophy at Morehouse College, examines the historical formation of community in African society and its contemporary interpretation in Western society. African-American theologian Howard Thurman (1971) provides a theological foundation for the African Diaspora's concept of community. Communications professor Richard Allen (2001) looks at the African retentions as well as the social forces in America that have shaped the individual and collective sense of self among African Americans. Becoming familiar with such texts gives the CPE supervisor a template to interpret and evaluate the African-American student's participation in CPE group.

Religiosity/Spirituality

The third concept of "religiosity" makes it critical for CPE supervisors with African-American students to understand that CPE is often regarded in the African-American culture as an extension of "church" and "church work" and not just as education. One's religion and spirituality are most often wrapped together in the black culture. Church and religion are highly regarded as the "cultural womb" for individuals and the community. Michael Dash (2007), Associate Professor of Ministry and Context at the Interdenominational Theological Center in Atlanta writes: "The general understanding of self and community exists at a different level for African-Americans. African-American heritage reflects a concept of community, 'village,' relationship to one another and support for one another, which became the foundation for African-American religiosity. The historical circumstances and conditions reinforced the ways in which African-Americans communicate, relate to themselves and support their sense of relationship among others." He continues, "Religion, understood as being one with life, is not an isolated part of the community's life, but permeates every facet of the community's existence" (p. 21). In addition, for most African Americans, "religiosity" is both connected to a particular faith tradition, creed, or denomination, as well as to core "spiritual" beliefs that may exist outside of their chosen organized religion.

For many African-American students in CPE, the group is "church" and becomes the opportunity for a "more perfect" village to be created by a community of pastoral caregivers. This is where the African-American student may struggle with conflict, confrontation, regression, and other interpersonal dynamics that seem incongruent with religion and spirituality. These dynamics may be resisted, ignored, or even denied by African-American students. In their internal processes, these dynamics may be renamed in ways that seem to suggest the student is using religious language (i.e. "the devil is trying me") to avoid taking personal responsibility for his/her growth. In addition, the "secular" is often interpreted through the eyes of "religion," expressed in God-talk and references to scripture and bridged to the "sacred" through prayer in black culture. African-American students may not understand why the group or supervisor suggests that these behaviors could preclude rather than facilitate good pastoral care. Such misunderstanding and misinterpretation can become yet another experience of being outside, rather than inside, the circle for the African- American CPE student.

Conclusion

As one takes these alternate theoretical concepts into consideration, it is apparent and important that methodologies that are culturally sensitive or culturally specific also be embraced as models for creating group life in CPE and for managing group dynamics. It is critical for the group and the supervisor to respect cultural boundaries on self-disclosure in order to create trust. Clear communication about the value of the communal CPE learning experience as a step towards the supervisor-student alliance and the peer-peers alliance of trust is vital. The supervisor would be wise to observe and name any dynamics of exclusion that occur, as well as to encourage and structure various and rotating student groupings to keep exclusion issues from becoming a barrier to the African-American student's group experience. Finally, when the student experiences confrontation or critique, the supervisor should be intentional in overtly or symbolically re-integrating the African-American student back into the group as an affirmation of the group as a whole.

In group settings, the CPE supervisor should balance community-building and confrontive encounters. In recognition of the symbolic knowing that is central in the world view of the African American, CPE programs should also begin to utilize reflective processes in addition to the written tools of verbatims and case studies. Finally, concepts and markers of one's religiosity could be incorporated as a part of the reflection process when using verbatims. For example, asking an African-American student to identify a Bible story or hymn that represents the pastoral encounter being presented offers great promise that the student will access a deeper and more authentic level of theological reflection than when the reflection questions are weighed towards the social sciences. Creating a context where the world view, relational values, and religiosity of the African American student will be embraced rather than diminished or dismissed will continue to create a dynamic of "inside the circle" that Hemenway would have agreed is vital to group life in Clinical Pastoral Education.

References

Allen, R. (2001). *The concept of self: A study in black identity*. Detroit, MI: Wayne State University Press.

Budge, E. A. W. (1904,1969). *The gods of the Egyptians: Studies in Egyptian mythology* (Vol. 1). New York: Dover Publications.

Dash, M. and Chapman, C. (2007). *The shape of Zion*: Leadership and life in black churches. Eugene, OR: Wipf & Stock Publishers.

Griffith, E. E. H., Harris, W. H., & Blue, H. C. (Eds.). (1995). *Racial and ethnic identity: Psychological development and creative expression*. New York: Routledge.

Griffith, E. E. H., & Delgado, A. (1979). On the professional socialization of black residents in psychiatry. *Journal of Medical Education, 54*, 471-476.

Hallen, B. (2002). *A short history of African philosophy*. Bloomington, IN: Indiana University Press.

Hemenway, J. (1996). *Inside the circle: A historical and practical inquiry concerning process groups in clinical pastoral education*. Atlanta, GA: Journal of Pastoral Care Publications.

Hiebert, P. (1990). Worldview. In R.J. Hunter (Ed.), *The dictionary of pastoral care and counseling* (pp. 1338-39). Nashville: Abingdon.

Roberts, J. D. (2000). *Africentric Christianity: A theological appraisal for ministry*. Valley Forge, PA: Judson Press.

Sindima, H. (1990). Community of life: Ecological theology in African perspective. In C. Birch, W. Eaken & J. B. McDaniel (Eds.), *Liberating life: Contemporary approaches to ecological theology* (pp. 137-47). Maryknoll, NY: Orbis Books.

Thurman, H. (1971). The search in identity. In W. E. Fluker & C. Tumber (Eds.). *A strange freedom: The best of Howard Thurman on religious experience and public life* (pp. 273-294). Boston: Beacon Press.

CHAPTER 17

Contextualizing CPE: Developing a Jewish Geriatric
CPE Program
Mary Martha Thiel

> All the world is a narrow bridge.
> The main thing is not to be afraid.
> -Rabbi Nachman of Bratslav

Origins and Aims of the Program

In 2005 Rabbi Sara Paasche-Orlow, Director of Religious and Chaplaincy Services at Hebrew SeniorLife/Hebrew Rehabilitation Center (HSL/HRC) in Boston, invited me to develop a Jewish Geriatric CPE program. Sara wanted to expand the limited spiritual care services throughout the Hebrew SeniorLife (HSL) system. CPE was an option that could expand pastoral care coverage significantly with the addition of just one staff person. Sara herself had done CPE in a Roman Catholic setting. She had appreciated much of that experience, but was clear that much of her experience in Jewish end of life care and in the Jewish Healing movement had remained unconnected to her CPE education. Her vision was to build a model Jewish CPE program that could have national and international impact on the training of Jewish chaplains. A gifted leader and fundraiser, Sara was already at work building a donor base of individuals and foundations, drawing in many of the most qualified Jewish teachers from the East Coast Jewish community and engaging HSL administration and staff in owning the program. This program would never have come to be without Sara's creativity, drive, and ability to energize diverse constituencies around a compelling vision. I accepted her invitation with both trepidation and excitement, and we joined resources in our commitment to make HSL's CPE program of the highest quality. Indeed, I believe it is the sparkle of excellence that has helped our program over some of the bumps related to the acceptance of a Jewish CPE program with a Christian supervisor.

This endeavor began at a time when ACPE was placing great emphasis on cultural competencies in CPE. In the 2005 Standards, many new standards were added which required programs to explore the impact of culture on pastoral dynamics. New focus was put on exploring one's own culture as well as the culture of the other. The development of CPE programs in Asia and Africa and with Native Americans in the United States had stimulated conversation about translating CPE into other cultural vernaculars. The time was right for contextualizing a CPE program to the particular American subcontext of Jewish pluralism in a geriatric setting.

Jewish chaplaincy is currently in ascendancy. Not quite twenty years old, the National Association of Jewish Chaplains (NAJC) has taken its place alongside the National Association of Catholic Chaplains (NACC) and the Association of Professional Chaplains (APC) as a professional chaplaincy organization with high standards for certification and continuing education. Like NACC, its religion-specific nature speaks to the importance of a minority religious tradition having a hand in forming and supporting its chaplains. Unlike NACC, NAJC does not have its own accredited CPE centers to train Jewish chaplains in specifically Jewish understandings and approaches to pastoral care. Most Jewish chaplains have done their CPE in Christian or interfaith settings, then translating and integrating their learning within their Jewish tradition.

The aim of the HSL program was to allow Jewish students to learn pastoral care skills from within a Jewish worldview. As one student writes, "After having been the only Jewish person in a peer group with a non-Jewish supervisor, it is an incredible relief not having to try and translate my theology, background, language, etc., for others." Students going into the congregational rabbinate would find their CPE directly applicable to their context. Students going on to be Jewish chaplains would benefit from having had at least part of their CPE in a tradition-syntonic context, the way most Christian chaplains do. After listing many Hebrew concepts explored in class, one alumnus wrote, "I now think one couldn't be a

Jewish chaplain without Jewish CPE. Sure, I knew those words before, but I learned how they applied to spiritual care and I came to truly understand them – in my *kishkes* (gut)! They framed the work for me. They inspired and often sustained me. This could not have happened in an interfaith setting." Non-Jewish students who choose our program have a cultural immersion experience as a member of a minority group and often become aware of the power of minority status in group and interpersonal dynamics.

Our program is currently a satellite of the Beverly Hospital/Northeast Health System CPE Center, offering Level I and II CPE. In the next few years we hope to become accredited as an independent CPE center and to develop a CPE supervisory education program.

Setting of the Program

Hebrew SeniorLife's precursor organization began just over 100 years ago in a single family home to house indigent Jewish elders. With much growth since, HSL now has seven campuses throughout the greater Boston area, and an eighth underway. The largest of the campuses, Hebrew Rehabilitation Center (HRC), like many such large Jewish organizations across the country, provides housing and health care for persons who cannot afford care in a more luxurious setting. It is a chronic care hospital. The average age of our residents is just a few months shy of 90. The food is kosher. HSL is Jewish in its name, mission statement, funding, and resident/patient base. It stands in the high Jewish tradition of caring for the elderly.

More so than any other CPE program of which I have been a part, the HSL program is deeply connected to the wider Jewish community. This has many benefits. HSL allots two slots in each CPE unit to Jewish chaplains employed in other organizations to do the clinical component of CPE in their own settings through a site contract. This allows us to support the education and credentialing of other Jewish chaplains and to impact the quality of Jewish pastoral care in our region more broadly. Boston's rabbinical school, Hebrew College, has adjusted the schedule for fourth year students so that they can take an extended unit of CPE, allowing for a strong relationship between our program and the school. The program is donor funded, and we are blessed with generous donors who are drawn to support a distinctly Jewish endeavor. The local Jewish community often provides free housing to rabbinical school students who come to our program from out of town. The wider Jewish community is proud of the program, as evidenced in articles published by the local Jewish media and in receiving in the 2008 JASA (Jewish Aging Services Association) award for best new program. In the ACPE context, while envisioning the program, I wrote to the Jewish supervisors I knew personally, and each one was supportive and helpful. In just two years Hebrew SeniorLife is challenged with a demand for its CPE program which outstrips its capacity.

Ninety per cent of the 600 chronic care residents at HRC are Jewish. Fifty percent of the approximately 100 acute care patients are Jewish. These Jewish residents and patients fall across the Jewish affiliation continuum. The others are mostly Roman Catholic, reflecting wider Boston's demographics, and a few are Protestant. On occasion HRC will have a resident/patient from another religious tradition.

CPE students are most typically assigned to two units at HRC so that they have the opportunity to learn different skill sets. Pastoral care of nonverbal persons in advanced dementia is significantly different from pastoral care with cognitively intact residents whose bodies require chronic hospital care. Students provide pastoral care to residents, families, and staff. They lead regular religious services (Jewish or Christian, according to their own identity), memorial services, welcome the Sabbath on their units, and/or teach classes. Some help prepare individuals for Bat Mitzvah celebrations.

Particular populations of HSL residents have been impacted by their Jewish identity in especially definitive ways, inviting CPE students to learn, serve, and reflect on diverse aspects of being Jewish. Not only were the Shoah survivors impacted by the Holocaust, but we see the multi-generational impact on their children and their children's children. Two units provide housing and healthcare for Russian-speaking Jews dislocated from the former Soviet Union and other countries in its sphere of influence. Students assigned to these units engage the challenge of providing pastoral care to Jews who often have had almost no religious education or ritual experience.

HRC staff supports this program enthusiastically. Representatives from medicine, nursing, social work, therapeutic recreation, pastoral care, and palliative care serve on the Professional Advisory Committee and/or teach in the program. Each clinical assignment includes working with an identified liaison from that unit's team. Liaisons help orient students to the unit, provide initial referrals, and serve as resource persons to the students. Not quite two years into the program, it is hard to imagine the interdisciplinary care web at HRC without the Chaplain Interns. The health care staff is proud that the religious and spiritual needs of residents are being so enthusiastically tended.

The Students

Most of our CPE students have come from across the Jewish continuum: Orthodox, Conservative, Reform, Reconstructionist, Renewal, and secular. Some are rabbis, cantors, or rabbinical students. Some are already working as Jewish chaplains. Some are lay by choice. Our rabbinical students come from the local Hebrew College and other rabbinical schools across the country. This pluralism invites dynamic conversation about Jewish observance, authenticity, gender, power, ordination, culture, theology, and spirituality. As one alumnus reflected, "Authority and authenticity were wild currents."

In keeping with ACPE Standards, the program is open to students from any religious tradition. I am very clear with potential students about the Jewish identity of the place and the program. I have accepted more non-Jewish students than have chosen to come. I continue to think our program is an excellent placement for a non-Jewish student, especially one working at Level II. There are few contexts in which Christian students can learn so quickly about the experience of being a minority, and a feared minority at that—important learning about sociologically induced vulnerability for any professional chaplain.

The Curriculum

Our aim is to contextualize our CPE program to our specific setting. Most ACPE programs reflect to some degree the Protestant culture of the origins of the clinical pastoral education movement, with characteristic emphases on personal relationship with God, personal authority, psychological differentiation from family of origin, and developing autonomy of spiritual and professional functioning. Some Catholic ACPE programs have contextualized the CPE tradition to their settings to emphasize such themes as spiritual formation, preferential option for ministry to the poor, and dialogue with the historical tradition and religious authorities of the Church. CPE Standards are flexible enough to allow for deep contextualization of programs, a real strength as our organization seeks to shift the foundations of our pastoral supervision to a multicultural and multi-religious world, a challenge lifted by Joan Hemenway (2000). We see our CPE program as standing in what Teresa Snorton calls the movement "to lift up the needs of those who represent a point of view not always regarded as the norm, to advocate for programs, ministries, policies, and procedures that are inclusive of those often left out or overlooked..."(Hemenway, 2000).

Calendar

The broader American culture operates on a calendar that largely accommodates the Christian calendar. At HSL, we work our schedule around the Jewish calendar. This means allowing students time to prepare for Jewish holidays in addition to being off on the holidays themselves. It means building some curriculum around memorial days, such as Tisha B'Av (remembering the destruction of the Temple) and Yom HaShoah (remembering the Holocaust). It means not requiring students to travel on Shabbat to fulfill worship leadership or on-call functions, if their level of observance precludes this.

Approach to Learning

Perhaps the most fun and most difficult part for me of developing the Hebrew SeniorLife CPE program has been trying to understand and then bring Jewish learning process and culture into the program. Stepping outside of one's own culture is difficult! Instead of morning prayer or devotions, which I had always enjoyed in other CPE programs I have led, we have built text study into the curriculum, often employing the traditional process of studying in *chevrutah* (pairs). This Beit Midrash (house of learning/ text study) component is led by the students, the Director of Religious and Chaplaincy Services, or by a guest presenter. Texts are from Hebrew Scriptures, Jewish liturgy, Talmud, or other traditional Jewish resources. They are chosen for their direct applicability to patient/resident care and/or their guidance in approaching the many issues facing our patients, families, staff, and chaplains. Text study as prayer is an identifying feature of Jewish culture, and it creates and deepens community just as devotions do in Christian circles. Students can fill their worship/teaching requirements at HSL by participating in Shabbat worship services and/or teaching classes for residents, families, or staff.

In addition to Beit Midrash, we have a component called Iyun Ruchani (spiritual reflection). This is an opportunity for the students to generate short prayers, readings, *niggunim* (wordless meditative tunes), or meditations that apply to the work and might be used in various chaplaincy settings.

An interesting cultural realization for me has been that I need to allow more time for discussion in a group of Jewish students than in a Christian or heterogeneous group. Whether the students are engaging with a Limud (didactic) presenter, or discussing Experience of Religious Themes essays, the conversation is fast paced, intense, thorough, and lengthy, reflecting the chevrutah style of text exploration that is so much a part of Jewish tradition. I have adapted the CPE schedule here at HSL to provide for this deeply embedded cultural pattern. It has been fascinating for me to observe a student I taught previously in an interfaith setting now in the HSL program: in this Jewish setting she is much more participative, uses much more Hebrew interspersed in her conversation, and is much more fully herself and at ease. She comments, "For me both models of CPE were valuable. The collegiality and learning of Jewish peers is sustaining and nourishing. Issues requiring technical expertise can be addressed. Interesting professional connections are made."

I have adapted many of the learning tools I have used previously in CPE to incorporate Hebrew names and concepts. I observe that Jews need Hebrew to express themselves theologically. The words "ministry" and "faith" have largely dropped out of my teaching here, as being much more meaningful to Christians than to Jews. I have kept the phrase "pastoral care" even though it is deeply Christian in connotation because so far in Jewish literature, despite other suggestions having been made, "pastoral care" is still the term most widely used. A Christian concept dear to me, vocation or call, is introduced to HSL students as Vocation/Commandedness, reflecting a significant difference between Christian and Jewish approaches.

Content

In this setting, geriatric and Jewish content intertwine. Our Limudim (didactics) follow a natural pattern. We start with aging, looking at psychological, physical, spiritual, and sociological issues, with a particular focus on the American Jewish community. We consider spiritual assessment tools appropriate to this setting. We move on to illnesses of aging, highlighting Alzheimer's disease and other dementias, since a majority of our residents have some level of dementia. Then we turn to issues of end of life, life review, ethical wills, palliative care, end of life decision-making across

Jewish pluralism, Jewish approaches to afterlife, and pastoral care at the time of dying. We then focus on issues of bereavement: memorial services and ritual practices, supporting family members, supporting residents who have lost adult children, and working with diverse needs in interfaith families. Toward the end of the unit we consider a variety of special issues, tailored to the particular students and their clinical assignments. These might include working with residents from the former Soviet Union, Holocaust survivors, or persons with psychiatric illness other than dementia. We look at Jewish approaches to healing, leadership, and authority. I often use poetry, narrative, or fiction to deepen students' understanding of the circumstances of their residents. We look at Roman Catholic and Protestant pastoral care, rituals, and theologies of suffering so that the students can grow in meeting the needs of their Christian residents. We consider how institutions such as ours manage the challenges of balancing mission and money. We look at preparation for chaplaincy certification.

In a typical intensive summer unit, the students are in group activities four mornings a week, Monday through Thursday. These sessions include Text Study, two Limudim, Covenant Group, Verbatim Seminar, Verbatim as a Theological Event Seminar, and an Experience of a Religious Theme Seminar. In the afternoon, the students are on their units doing clinical work. Friday is set aside as an entirely clinical day, reflecting the importance of helping residents prepare for Shabbat. Students greet Shabbat on each unit, participate in a Sing In Shabbat! program, and help residents attend the Kabbalat Shabbat service in the synagogue. Thus, the rhythm of each week is in keeping with the Jewish calendar. The students graduate on Thursday rather than Friday, in order that our celebration does not upstage Shabbat.

Final Evaluations and Outcomes

Except for minor changes in language ("pastoral caregiver" rather than "minister," for example, or "theology" rather than "faith"), the final evaluation formats my students and I use are similar to those I have used in other settings. My evaluation of each student includes comments on their clinical work, relationships with peers, relationship with supervisor, progress on each learning goal, and progress on the outcomes set by ACPE for their level of CPE.

I have paid particular attention to program evaluations, as I view the students as important coaches in refining our program. The students do written program evaluations at the end of their unit, engage verbal exit interviews with members of our advisory committee, and are asked to do written program evaluations a year after the completion of their unit with us. These sources of feedback have led to adjustments in both process and content, just as they do in any good CPE program.

The CPE Supervisor

With less then a dozen Jewish supervisors in ACPE at the time, and none in Boston, Sara faced a real challenge in finding the right person to start up HSL's Jewish geriatric CPE program. A key donor knew about my longstanding professional commitment to interfaith chaplaincy and suggested considering me for the job.

As a non-Jew, I felt understandable trepidation at the prospect of taking on such leadership. More surprisingly, at the same time I felt called to the work (such a feeling of "calling" is an aspect of my Christian worldview).

Several themes of my own life story have resonance. First, my parents were from vastly different countries, cultures, and first languages. My American mother's ancestors came to these shores on the Mayflower. My Estonian father was twice a refugee from the tragedies of European history, his life one of multiple dislocations and great grief. So my experience of the world has always been marked by difference and diaspora. Although my social location provides me many aspects of privilege, as a lesbian I also experience a powerful lack of privilege. This has often placed me internally "on the margins." I know the place of fearing others' judgment and having concerns about safety. Had I lived in Nazi

Germany alongside a number of today's HSL residents, I, too, would have been put on transport trains and sent off to the unimaginable. Similar to many Jews, the grounding and rejuvenation I feel when I'm with "my own" is no small thing. This experience gives me a bridge of empathy for the oppressed status of Jews and their need to have contexts in which they can be unrestrainedly Jewish.

Interestingly, I have also been fortunate to have rich exposure to the Jewish community throughout my professional formation. I was the Christian minority of one among the majority of Jewish students who majored in the History of Religion at Bryn Mawr College. My seminary, Union Theological Seminary, collaborated with Jewish Theological Seminary. A Conservative rabbi was a peer in one of my CPE residencies, and all the pastoral care departments I have worked in have had wonderful Jewish chaplains from whom I have been pleased to learn. In my personal life I am part of a "Daughters of Abraham" group of observant Jewish, Christian, and Muslim women who meet monthly to share food, discuss a book about our faiths, and deepen friendships (www.daughtersofabraham.info).

How does this work in Jewish CPE fit into my own faith identity as a Christian and United Church of Christ minister? First Church in Cambridge, Congregational (UCC), of which I am an active member, includes in its covenant a commitment to "love...our close and distant neighbors as ourselves; to seek peace through justice and equity for all people; to foster community across every barrier and division." CPE supervision has a natural affinity to this covenant, made even deeper in the context of a Christian supervisor supporting Jewish students. Our congregation's commitment to social justice has much in common with the Tikkun Olam (repair of the world) emphasis of parts of the Jewish continuum. In the language of my Christian faith, I feel called to and prepared for this work of Jewish CPE.

The work has deeply impacted me, forcing me to be clearer about who I am as a Christian, helping me understand ever more deeply the roots and rich resonances of Judaism with my own faith, heightening my awareness of the hegemony of Christian language and culture in the wider American context, and strengthening my commitment to push the horizons of my own worldview.

Challenges

My religious identity is also a challenge in supervising Jewish CPE. ACPE's other two Jewish CPE sites (Hebrew Union College—Jewish Institute of Religion in Cincinnati, and occasional units through The HealthCare Chaplaincy in New York City) have Jewish supervisors. When we started CPE at HSL, I was quite conscious of the downsides of my not being Jewish: I did not have a Jewish education; I was not socialized to Jewish culture; I could not read or speak Hebrew; I had not read most of the Jewish pastoral care literature, and—no small thing—I am part of a culture that has repeatedly had devastating impact on the history of the Jewish people. Although I have done a huge amount of reading and study in these two years, I still do not teach Jewish content sessions, but bring in wonderful Jewish teachers to do that.

In time, the students have helped me see upsides of my not being Jewish in this setting. First, I am not aligned on the Jewish pluralist continuum. This gives me a certain freedom to facilitate conversations among the students about their sometimes deep Jewish differences. (An alumnus wrote, "To explain and clarify positions under the direction of a safe and neutral person, allowed everyone to listen with a more open attitude.") Second, I am an available resource on Christian pastoral care and beliefs. It has been a surprise to me how little many of the Jewish students know about Christian theology and practice. I had assumed that as a non-dominant group, they would have learned some of the dominant culture for survival, as so many non-dominant groups become bi-cultural to survive and thrive. What I hadn't realized was the level of taboo and fear blocking that learning. The Limudim on Roman Catholic and Protestant approaches to pastoral care and prayer have been enthusiastically received by the students. Finally, there is something moving for the students in my commitment to learn about their world and support them within their own framework, while still being grounded in my own. This is teacher as curriculum. Just as I model welcoming my learner status to support them and their learning needs, they learn in order to support and provide for the spiritual needs of the residents in their care.

Another set of challenges of having an all or mostly Jewish group of students exists around confidentiality and multiple relationships. The Jewish community in Boston is small enough that many students have known each other for years, and sometimes in multiple roles. It is impossible to know beforehand all the previous relationships among members of a group. In my last group, seven of eight had prior relationships! This heightens the challenge around developing peership among individuals who may, for example, have been rabbi and congregant earlier in their lives, and ramps up the risks around breaches of confidentiality. And as one alumnus put it, "Unlike the traditional interfaith CPE, where people scatter far afield, we all return to the same community."

CPE: Universal or Particular?

As mentioned above, I believe our ACPE Standards provide an elasticity that allows for real creativity and particularization of CPE programs, while holding useful parameters of pastoral formation, competence, and reflection.

Michelle Oberwise-Lacock has developed a CPE program for Native American pastors, as part of the United Methodist Church's Course of Study. Noting that oral tradition is a core part of Native American tradition, she has developed ways to let some verbatim learning be oral rather than written. She draws on literature by Native Americans and others outside the Anglo European traditions. By focusing on Story Theology, her program is able to integrate and work with the Native American community's historical, communal, and individual grief. Pastors representing many tribes come to her program, bringing diverse perspectives along the Native American continuum. This program is another example of contextualizing CPE within Standards to serve an often marginalized group.

My work with Sister Sheila Hammond at Massachusetts General Hospital (MGH) to develop a CPE program for health care professionals reflected this same impulse: to work within Standards to serve a particular constituent group of students who could then serve spiritual needs of a population not currently being reached with current pastoral staffing. This program, still thriving at MGH and replicated at several other CPE centers, has been described elsewhere in the literature (Todres, Catlin & Theil, 2005).

As I talk with CPE supervisor colleagues about my work at HSL, I encourage them to think about ways to contextualize their programs to the cultural realities of their students, staff, and patients. At MGH I had a medical historian talk about the cultural struggle in that institution between those who honor science only and those open to less quantifiable approaches to healing. At a hospital in Salem, Massachusetts, I invited a priestess to present a didactic on Wicca so that students could be sensitive to patients from that tradition.

Conclusion

Contextualizing CPE is a challenging but richly rewarding process. Working outside one's own cultural comfort zone, while difficult, is increasingly important in our multicultural world. I welcome conversation from colleagues interested in engaging the challenge in a Jewish context or in their own, that together we in CPE may "foster community across every barrier and division."

Postscript

Reflecting the very *chevrutah* model of learning out of which Hebrew SeniorLife's Jewish CPE program was born, Rabbi Sara Paasche-Orlow contributed this Postscript.

When we invited Rev. Mary Martha Thiel to come and help us create a CPE program at HSL I felt trepidation and knew that I was breaking very new ground. By virtue of our collaboration, we were declaring that there is a way to take a Protestant founded concept and, as part of a multi-faith journey together, to re-invent it to serve a patient cohort with vastly discrepant beliefs and cultural biases to a mainstream Protestant and Catholic milieu. This was evidenced the first time I attempted to introduce our new "Reverend Chaplain" to a group of our residents: we quickly ended the encounter as some became irritated and expressed fear that our Jewish Chronic Care Hospital would no longer remain Jewish, but be "Christianized." By contrast, our prospective students did not seem at all bothered by a Christian supervisor; in fact, only the excellence of her leadership, not its religious basis, was relevant to them.

Albeit brief, my own experience with CPE involved important learning about the different Christian movements, Christian theological concepts, interfaith dialogue, and self-exploration in the context of a Christian cultural norm. I in no way regretted the experience and the exposure, but it was clear to me that there was a huge amount of territory that could be explored and developed in a Jewish setting. What I learned from my involvement in Jewish end of life care and in the Jewish Healing movement remained unconnected in many ways to my CPE training.

Mary Martha and I then spent a summer reviewing the basic concepts integral to CPE and trying to see them through diverse Jewish eyes. What is the role of prayer in Jewish culture? How can the intensity of Jewish textual learning be worked into the strength of CPE education? Do concepts like "calling," "ministry," "faith," and "forgiveness" belong in a Jewish program? What are the core theological concepts related to Jewish identity that should be essential to the program? There were many moments of revelation in this process and in the units that followed as groups responded to our efforts and added their own voices to our ongoing process.

We made the decision from the outset that along with my teaching role in our groups and collaborating on the curriculum, we would bring in the most qualified Jewish teachers from the East Coast Jewish community to complement Mary Martha's group and individual supervision. I drew on a large network of close colleagues and friends who have gone out of their way to support this program conceptually and contribute to the depth of the learning.

This process has worked because we have managed to maintain open minds to all the possibilities and to feel like every day is an opportunity to invent and to learn. Our long term care residents have influenced the content of the program as their lack of interest in God, their post traumatic Holocaust stress, and their secular Jewish attitudes have pervaded the group learning.

The HSL administration has welcomed this program with open arms and, in addition, the embrace the chaplains have received from Social Work, Nursing and Medicine has strengthened the role that pastoral care can play throughout out facility.

I grew up in a mixed marriage family—a culturally Christian father and a Jewish mother—and chose to pursue ordination and communal life in the traditional world of Conservative Judaism. Conservative Judaism puts learning at the center of the spiritual encounter and relies on the engagement with text and observance of *halakha* or *mitzvoth*, (Jewish law, the rabbinic and biblical rules that guide daily life) to create a sense of belonging and closeness to God. While I have spent many years in pluralist Jewish community, and look at the world now through trans-denominational Jewish eyes, there is still this bias toward text and lived experience that I see reflected in our program.

Mary Martha has helped our institution, our Jewish community, and our community of funders and students realize a program that is fully responsive to Jewish theological and cultural perspectives and in tune with our patient body. It is with excitement that we offer this model to others, and we look forward to influencing the face of Jewish chaplaincy across America and in Israel.

Acknowledgements

Special thanks to Rabbi Sara Paasche-Orlow, Jane Hodgetts, Rabbi Susan Harris, Nancy Cahners, Rev. Michelle Oberwise-Lacock, Rev. John Pearson, George Fitchett, Rev. Kitty Garlid, and Rev. Angelika Zollfrank for their assistance with this essay.

References

Hemenway, J. E. (2000). The shifting of the foundations: Ten questions concerning the future of pastoral supervision and the pastoral care movement. *Journal of Supervision and Training in Ministry*, 20, 59-68.

Todres ID, Catlin EA, Thiel MM. (2005). The intensivist in a spiritual care training program adapted for clinicians. *Critical Care Medicine*, 33(12), 2733-6.

CHAPTER 18

The Lost Art of the Apology:
An Educational Tool in CPE
Paula J. Teague and Stephen L. Dutton

We are delighted to contribute to this Festschrift in memory of Dr. Joan Hemenway. She was our friend. In our professional roles, Dr. Hemenway supported us in her inimitable style of both holding and challenging. She encouraged Paula to pursue an MBA and use it to educate potential chaplains and pastoral care department leaders about management. And she was quick with a pat on the back for Steve as he pursued ACPE certification. This article is a way to demonstrate where our efforts have taken us as recipients of Joan's care and push!

Two Vignettes

Joyce is a 55 year old Euro-American Roman Catholic laywoman. She is part of a resident group in a CPE program and is functioning with Level II ACPE outcomes. Joyce is bright, articulate, and values responsibility. Joyce was on-call and received a page to minister to a family of a patient who was on a ventilator and unable to communicate. The patient had two significant persons in his life, and both were battling for control and supremacy in decision making. Joyce realized there was a full fledged war taking place and tried to find a way to mediate the differences. Both rejected Joyce's efforts and dismissed her from the case in a loud and judgmental fashion. Upset and feeling rejected, Joyce came to her CPE supervisor's office for support and advice only to find the supervisor otherwise occupied. Feeling more and more upset, Joyce paged her CPE supervisor to say that she was in a jam and asked for time. The supervisor took time to meet with her quickly and when he heard that the patient and family had been upset with Joyce, he focused on that aspect of the situation. He made it clear that Joyce and he could further discuss this in a regular individual supervisory session. Two days later Joyce came to her supervisory session upset and angry about what she perceived as the supervisor not responding to her feelings of hurt and rejection. Joyce's working hypothesis was that the supervisor was too busy for her, too focused on patient care, and not willing to give her the time she had needed. In short, the patient's family had rejected Joyce and so, she believed, had the CPE supervisor.

Mike is a 50 year old African American who has been a pastor for 20 years. Mike has built his career on being well liked and respected. Mike is in his first unit of CPE. It seemed to Mike's CPE supervisor that Mike's smiling could give a mixed message in interactions with peers and patients. Mike used humor, snappy comments, and sarcastic interactions in his pastoral care. When Mike presented in a verbatim seminar this interactive style was evident in his ministry to a family. The CPE supervisor commented on this dynamic and wondered aloud about the impact on the family. Mike said that he was being labeled in a prejudiced way. Mike's peers were divided about their perceptions that Mike's attempt at the use of humor and sarcasm in a patient encounter could have a positive pastoral outcome.

Both of these vignettes are composites of situations that have occurred with CPE students over the years in our practice. What the vignettes have in common is a good faith effort to act in the role as CPE supervisor and pay attention to many layers of dynamics and systems. In each the student characterizes the CPE supervisor's actions as missteps or mistakes and at least at this stage not as ethical violations. The vignettes also have in common the fact that the CPE supervisor had alternatives and could have chosen differently within a set of acceptable options. And finally, the students are responding to the impact of the CPE supervisor's actions on them and not on the CPE supervisor's underlying intent.

This paper proposes that apology is a supervisory intervention that in both cases could re-establish supervisory trust, provide modeling for pastoral care situations, and open the supervisory relationship to a deeper learning liaison. In this essay, we will present some background on the role and impact of apology in our personal histories and then offer a theoretical basis for the intervention that we call the Five Cs. We will then return to Joyce and Mike to illustrate how the Five Cs could be a useful supervisory tool.

Background

In many institutions where CPE takes place there is a clear imperative to own mistakes when they happen. No matter the care, they still happen. In a reflective article about making an apology to a patient when the physician had prescribed the wrong medication, the physician says, "The moral imperative to be honest with patients about an error is clear. Patients want to know the truth and hate being lied to most of all" (The Apology, 80).

It is hard to apologize. It is so easy to subtly blame others, focus on intent rather than impact, and to phrase our errors without the key letter, I.

Paula's first unit of CPE was in 1979. She came to that experience as a 23 year old who would say "I am sorry" to almost everybody for almost anything. Within a very short time Paula was confronted with the fact that she had apologized to a patient for something she had not done. A patient had told Paula about a horrific situation and Paula had said "I am so sorry." Paula's CPE supervisor asked her what she had had to do with the patient's situation. Wasn't the apology somewhat arrogant? After all, did Paula think she was responsible for a medical situation and family crisis? Was Paula not allowing this patient to be angry or genuine in relationship to whoever was responsible? For Paula the fact that this attempt to be kind and empathic could be so interpreted was a new perspective. Paula began to reflect on her quick "I am sorry" and realized that her apologetic stance was related directly to self deprecation and low self esteem. Paula realized that when she did make a mistake she had a terrible time saying these same words that came so easily at other times. Shame and embarrassment at a mistake made it difficult to own responsibility. To break the habit of saying an inappropriate "I'm sorry" she had to deal with her feelings of being a bad person.

Steve's history is somewhat different. He grew up in a family where mistakes could mean grave punishment and shaming. Making a mistake was an anathema and when one did, it was best to cover it up and disavow it. To come to the place of owning a mistake meant working with his historic feelings of fear and shame. In Steve's supervisory CPE education his supervisor was open about the need for apology in the supervisory relationship. Steve experienced his CPE supervisor offering apology and thus modeling a different approach to mistakes than his childhood authority figures. This relational experience was complemented by the theory from self psychology that holds that it is a basic human reality that disappointment and hurt can be experienced in relationship even when there are good intentions. For Steve, a different experience of the place of apology in CPE has been a crucial piece of personal healing and the basis for the theoretical material that is presented here.

Theories that Help

Four theories aid our understanding of the role of apology in the supervisory relationship: the Twelve Step program of recovery, Object Relations Theory, Self Psychology including intersubjectivity as espoused by Pamela Cooper-White, and current theories in business.

The Twelve Step Program: The Twelve Step program of recovery from addiction began in the 1930s with the ground breaking experiences of Dr. Bob Smith and Bill Wilson. They developed an approach to recovery that included working through a series of steps. These steps are a living approach and are available for reworking as new life experiences and challenges arise. Step nine says "make direct amends to such people wherever possible, except when to do so would injure them or others" (Alcoholic

Anonymous (AA), p. 59). The list of persons who have been harmed in some way by the addict's behavior is developed over a period of time through extensive self examination. The process of making an amends is presented as crucial to recovery (AA, pp. 77-84).

Recovering people have written about the process of differentiating between situations where they have no control and situations within their influence. They are encouraged to focus on the latter. Within those boundaries, what actions were wrong or hurtful or inappropriate? Once it was clear what those things were, an individual needs to make amends directly to the wronged party except when to do so would inflict more hurt. Apology is important. It counters shame, which could drown even the best intentions. In its clearest form, apology has no strings or expectations attached. It simply is an apology.

Object Relations Theory: Object Relations theory tells us that it is important to remember that in the supervisory relationship there is a power differential. The dynamics of this power differential mean that there are times when the student will experience the supervisor as an authority figure and project false expectations onto the supervisor. The CPE supervisor carries the power and the projection that he or she is always on top of things and able to make the appropriate response. Like the adult student's early childhood authority figures, the CPE supervisor will be human and will disappoint. The key is how the supervisor as the person in authority handles this disappointment. This supervisor must give the message that while mistakes may happen there is the option for relationship and healing.

Winnicott(1987) describes the ability to manage these natural disappointments as part of relationships where the goal is to be "good enough." That is not to say that disappointments should be fostered or simply accepted as part of the relationship. However, they are to be expected, and it can be healing when the person in the seat of power acknowledges that there has been a mistake or disappointment. This can allow the person in the student role to experience the CPE supervisor as good enough. If the supervisor is attentive to both the power differential and the student's need for

267

the supervisor to be aware of his or her own mistakes, the student can experience a good enough authority relationship that, while not perfect, does not cause further wounding.

It has been our experience as supervisors that even very small disappointments need to be addressed. This includes being late for sessions, rearranging schedules, forgetting some small fact, etc. Students who experience a CPE supervisor able to own the impact of even these small disappointments can build a trusting relationship that allows the student to share his or her own humanity.

Self Psychology: Heinz Kohut, the creator of Self Psychology, builds on the understandings of object relations, and offers a theory of human development that describes how personality structures are built in the relationship between the child and caregiver. Self psychology delineates further what the object offers to the growing child (Wolf, 1988). Along with many of his disciples who have contributed to the growing influence of a psychology of the Self to the healing arts, Kohut believes that the therapist in the therapeutic setting must be ever attuned to the inevitable disruptions that occur. Then, at the time of the disruption, it is important for the therapist to restore the alliance by acknowledging the client's perception of the therapist's failure as real (Wolf, 1988). So in the supervisory alliance of the CPE supervisor with Joyce and Mike described above, it was important for the authority figure, the CPE supervisor, to own the mistake, acknowledge the disappointment, and communicate this to the student. In doing so the student's self esteem and competence are affirmed. The supervisor has recognized the student's experience and acted in a way that the relational response of an acknowledgment is received by the student. The student's perceptions are verified and esteem is built. In doing so the supervisor has acknowledged the student's difficult perceptions of the CPE supervisor: the CPE supervisor is human and has made a mistake that hurt or injured the student. Although the CPE supervisor has disappointed, he or she has the opportunity to mitigate this disappointment by supporting the authentic experience of the student.

The process of offering an apology impacts both the student and the supervisor. The work of Pamela Cooper-White focuses on intersubjectivity, a growing discipline from the theories of self psychology. In her books, *Shared Wisdom* and *Many Faces*, Cooper-White suggests that in interpersonal professional relationships like CPE supervision, there is no such thing as objectivity. Rather, there is subjectivity contributing to the relationship. Intersubjectivity examines the different subjectivities brought to the professional relationship. What this theory offers to us as we think about apology is the idea that the CPE supervisor, as well as the student, is impacted by situations and can be both affected and changed. Subjectivity itself can create situations that are either hurtful or mismanaged so that an apology is in order.

Business Practice: Business practice can inform our understanding of apology in CPE supervision. In 1982, seven people died from cyanide that had been inserted into Tylenol tablets by a person who was found to have no relationship to Tylenol (Retrieved March 8, 2008, from http://www.jkador.com/ASimpleApologyNoSuchThing.htm). James Burke, CEO of Johnson and Johnson at that time, made a decision to assume immediate responsibility for the situation and gave directions that no one should take Tylenol. The cost to the company was estimated at $100 million. What seemed like a huge loss at the time, has paid off in the respect and profitability of Tylenol since that time.

At the time that Burke apologized and with such cost, there was very little study of the apology in the business world. Today, there are various principles from business that can inform CPE supervision.

Writing for *The Harvard Business Review,* Barbara Kellerman (2007) quotes Nicholas Tavuchis, sociologist and researcher in the arena of apology and reconciliation, who notes that apologies speak to acts that cannot be undone "but that cannot go unnoticed without compromising the current and future relationship of the parties." Kellerman goes on to say that in applying this general principle: "leaders will publicly apologize if and when they calculate the costs of doing so to be lower than the costs of not doing so. More precisely, leaders will apologize if and when they calculate that staying silent threatens a current and future relationship between them and one or more key constituencies" (p. 75).

Kellerman also writes that apologies should serve two purposes. The first is an *individual* purpose where the leader made the mistake and an apology will facilitate forgiveness and forward movement of the group or project. The second is an *institutional* purpose where a leader takes responsibility for a group for whom he is responsible so that the group can maintain its cohesion and external reputation. The leader may also make an institutional apology when a group makes a mistake which impacts another group, so that the injured parties can experience repair. Finally, a moral purpose can be achieved by a leader when he or she experiences genuine remorse so that the leader can engage in a process of confession and forgiveness (p. 76).

When a mistake causes a serious breach, a root cause analysis is often initiated. The root cause analysis is a process in which tools are brought to bear in order to increase customer trust and satisfaction. In the root cause analysis process there is a disciplined *drill down* to the systemic mechanism in place that caused the mistake. The purpose of the drill down is two fold: (1) so that an individual is not held solely accountable for the catastrophic event and (2) so that the root cause, the systemic inefficiency that supported such an event is changed (Andersen & Fagerhaug, 1999).

In recent years the intent of root cause analysis has been expanded to the concept of 'just culture" (Patient Safety and the 'Just Culture,' 2001). Championed by David Marx, a lawyer who in 1997 developed a research and consulting practice focusing on the management of human error through the integration of systems engineering, human factors, and the law, 'just culture' presents what some believe to be a theologically astute system . As an advisor on patient safety to the Agency for Healthcare Research and Quality he teamed with Harold Kaplan of Columbia University in authoring the document "Patient Safety and the 'Just Culture': A Primer for Healthcare Executives." In this system he proposes that to err is human and the process of rebuilding trust comes only through justice. A 'just culture' is a proactive learning culture where mistakes are not only to be fixed but are recognized as opportunities to improve our understanding of risk.

In the field of service recovery, accountability for behavior substantially mitigates risk. Further, human risk behavior is distinguished by three subsets of intent. First, there is human error that is the product of a current system design and the task is to console the initiator of the event. The second is at risk behavior or unintentional risk-taking which is managed through coaching; that is removing incentives for at risk behaviors, creating incentives for healthy behaviors, and increasing situational awareness. Third is reckless behavior or intentional risk-taking. This category of human error is managed through remedial action and punishment. Marx and Kaplan's description of intent seems to take seriously the theological consideration given to aspects of the apology and to repentance in terms of healing. Understanding the level of risk behavior and the appropriate response according to the level will also be applied as modeling for CPE students. By learning more about levels of risk taking and appropriate response, the CPE student transfers this educational event into practice in ministry.

The business practices of owning mistakes and understanding risk taking behaviors have been further developed by Stone, Patton, Heen, & Fisher (1999). They posit that any problem or difficulty has many contributors and that ownership of one's "contribution" is the work an individual can do and offer in a relationship. So rather than blame or fault finding, contributing factors are defined and ownership of each one is attributed. As we all know, it is rare when there is a singular cause of a problem, even if it appears to be only one on first examination.

The Content of the Apology

We have described the theoretical background advocating for the use of an apology. What then is the content of the apology? In this section, we want to frame an apology that can be used as a tool in CPE supervision.

A variety of writers have discussed the use of apology in the world of business. One comes from a web source discussing the Tylenol decision. "A good apology must be seen as genuine, as an honest appeal for forgiveness. Such apologies are usually best offered in a timely manner, and they consist of the following four parts: an acknowledgment of the mistake or wrongdoing, the acceptance of responsibility, an expression of regret, and a promise that the offense will not be repeated" (Retrieved March 8, 2008, from http://www.jkador.com/ASimpleApologyNoSuchThing.htm).

In the health care setting apology is an option when mistakes have been made or when patients or their families have been inconvenienced. Service recovery is a skill that many hospital employees are asked to master. Service Recovery is initiated in order to win back the confidence of the consumer when a breakdown in care or service has occurred. The skills of positive service recovery can be easily remembered with the acrostic H.E.A.R.T. (Retrieved on June 29, 2008, from http://www.baymed.org/documents/Orientation/stars.pdf):

> Hear the person's complaint, for as long as it takes. That is, "hear them out!"

> Empathize, that is, listen in order to understand the experience of the other, what the experience has cost them how they feel about what has happened.

> Apologize; this is not an admission of guilt but an assertion that you are personally sorry that the patient or patient family member is disappointed.

> Respond and take responsibility, do what you can to help alleviate the disruption.

> Thank, meaning, do what you can to support the fact that the patient brought this to the attention of the health care team.

This simple art of apology communicates care and is a sound method to repair the breach of trust that has occurred in the encounter.

272

In summary, we posit that in CPE an apology is a multi-faceted response to both a dynamic in the power differential and a thoughtful, well-timed intervention designed to build trust and transparency and enhance the learning relationship. We believe an apology is characterized by humility, reassurance, commitment to relationship, and recognition that intent does not equal impact.

Proposed Tool: The Five "Cs"

We propose following five steps to craft a supervisory intervention in order to reclaim the lost art of the apology:

1. Culture
2. Contribution
3. Claiming
4. Convinced Conversation
5. Continuing Consultation

Step One: Culture

To meet the ACPE standard for CPE supervisory practice, a program must provide a culture of learning for the CPE student. Part of the culture of learning is the ability of the CPE supervisor to normalize making an apology. This happens in balance with holding true assignation of responsibility and the support for inner struggles with self esteem or self deprecation. From object relations theory, Winnicott's imaging of the good enough supervisor, student, etc. could be explored and defined. When is making a mistake simply a part of the normal learning process and when is it unacceptable?

We advocate for building a culture with a demarcation of error akin to the work of Kellerman sited above. It seems crucial to delineate between system error, unintended mistakes that need coaching and can be made by student or supervisor alike, and more deliberate or knowing errors such as a breach of confidentiality or abuse of power. Building such a culture accomplishes two goals. The first is to provide a sense of safety for a student in a learning process where mistakes can become learning opportunities. The second is to provide a structure for addressing serious errors.

Step One builds on the theory of self psychology including intersubjectivity. In this initial intervention the student will be encouraged to build his or her own wisdom as the CPE supervisor builds a relationship of trust. It is important that this step include genuine intention about a culture where apology can be offered as well as a culture where a student can express hurt and/or anger in the supervisory relationship and be assured that this will be explored.

Step Two: Contribution

A tool called a "fishbone diagram" because of its resemblance to a fishbone when completed, is used in business for defining the contributing factors to a problem.

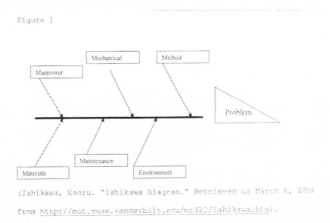

Figure 1

(Ishikawa, Kaoru. "Ishikawa Diagram." Retrieved on March 8, 2006 from http://mot.vuse.vanderbilt.edu/mt322/Ishikawa.html).

This tool assumes that any problem or mistake has multiple contributing factors and that individual responsibility is a part of the problem and not the entire problem. Ishikawa divided the contributing factors into six categories including materials, manpower, maintenance, environment, machine, and method.

Figure 1 shows the fishbone outline. The method for doing a fishbone is to define the problem through the center line and begin to build the "bones" with contributing factors.

For the purposes of the Five Cs, the categories we are proposing are systems issues, individual mistakes and misperceptions, cultural influences and other issues of diversity, personal history, external factors, and CPE culture.

The primary tool in the fishbone exercise is listening, unearthing the feelings and thoughts that surround the problem. The CPE supervisor has to be willing to take a step back and to hear without judgment or defense the feelings that are being stated. This acknowledgement of the problem will help to develop a variety of contributions.

For example, let us apply the contribution step to Joyce's case. Clearly there are many contributing factors in the situation. It is a good exercise with the student to start to brainstorm all the contributing factors with little discussion about the pros and cons of the different issues. Figure 2 illustrates a possible diagram. When the fishbone is full of contributing factors, it becomes easy to identify the ones within the control of the student and CPE supervisor and those that are simply out of their control. Sometimes the participants can impact a culture or system change when the contribution of each has been identified.

We believe that the joint exercise of building a fishbone either with the individual student or with a CPE group helps to take the issue out of the personal realm of blame or shame. We want CPE students to learn about themselves in the context of reasonable responsibility, opportunity for learning and change, and collaborative interchange toward professional growth.

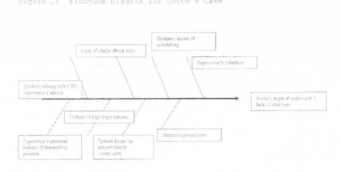

Figure 2: Fishbone Diagram for Joyce's Case

Step Three: Claiming

After the fishbone exercise has been accomplished and there is a full sense of exploration, it is time to claim what belongs to the CPE supervisor. This step requires a willingness to be surprised and open to new information. The work of Cooper-White is particularly helpful here in that she describes intersubjectivity partially as this kind of openness on the supervisor's part. This step is a dialogical process and needs to steer clear of shame and self deprecation. It requires an honest assessment of one's own responsibility for actions that may have added to perceptions of miscommunication. With Joyce, as the situation was unpacked it became clear that the perception of being "too busy" was a contributing factor for the problem with the student. Sometimes a contributing factor can be a behavior; sometimes it is a perception that has been created through non-verbal, non-specific behaviors that leave a vacuum open to interpretation.

Step Four: Convinced Conversation

In the Society of Friends (Quakers) the term "Convinced Friend" (Faith and Practice, Philadelphia Yearly Meeting, 1998, p. 216) refers to someone who is led in a spiritual sense to a place of

276

alignment or attunement with Quaker values. This person may have begun their journey from many different points of view, values, and perceptions.

We assert that "convinced conversation" is similar. Like the Quaker exercise of coming to a spiritual place of convincement or truth, a convinced conversation is a sacred or spiritual journey toward alignment or attunement. This process makes space for the awareness that the CPE supervisor can apologize from a sense of integrity and thoughtful reflection. Like any confession, this convinced conversation is not to be taken lightly nor quickly offered.

It is important not to move to the convinced conversation until the previous steps have been discussed so that the apology is neither over- nor understated and is a clear response to behavior. The Twelve Steps of Alcoholics Anonymous emphasize this as well. The apology is only as good as the process and no step should be omitted. The apology is about the impact and not the intent of the behavior. It encompasses the various ingredients of the apology that were discussed earlier including: acknowledgement of the individual contribution, acceptance of responsibility for that part of the problem, regret, and assurance that this will be addressed for the future.

It seems important that apology be shared when it is appropriate. With Joyce, the supervisor apologized for disappointing the student, for the contribution to the perception of being "too busy," and for lack of clarity about other resources available to the student. The student was encouraged to express what she had learned as a way to own her behavior and move forward from her mistakes. The reconnection between Joyce and her CPE supervisor also gave Joyce an opportunity to reflect on authority and authority relationships. Joyce could brainstorm about other options and skills for obtaining advice when a situation had gone sour. And she could learn how one's personal history impacts events and sometimes creates obstacles to achieving what one needs to function professionally.

Step Five: Continuing Consultation

This is an easy step to omit and if that happens, there is a potential loss of solidification of learning on the student's side and the normalizing of difficulties and the need to monitor change. Systems changes, perception modification, and culture shifts do not happen all at once.

This fifth step is achieved by continuing to check in with the student about perceptions, new insights, and other reflections. And the CPE supervisor is also continuing to reflect. We believe that the five step process as outlined above leaves room for the CPE supervisor to gain personal insight and to achieve deeper competence in the practice of CPE supervision. A heartfelt apology needs to be supported by colleagues and peers. We believe this is a good working example of intersubjectivity.

Mike and the Five Cs

Let us apply the tool to Mike's case that involved his perception that his supervisor was making racial stereotypes about him. Here it is important to realize that this intervention happened early on in the student's CPE process when trust had just begun to be developed.

Step One: Culture

In order to effectively work with Mike, the CPE supervisor would need to build a culture where examining contribution and responsibility was normalized. As discussed earlier, building a culture includes the theoretical understanding that an apology is not a simple intrapersonal interaction. Because of the power differential between student and supervisor, an apology becomes a tool which the supervisor can use to help the student increase self reflection and self esteem, and a sense of trust in the his or her perceptions and in the supervisory relationship. This can be accomplished in the orientation, in didactics about difficult conversations, and in the style of examining verbatims and ministry events.

Mike would be learning about a group context where there are different opinions and perceptions that could potentially be helpful to his learning process. And the CPE supervisor would be modeling apology and responsibility in the small things that occur early in a CPE unit.

Step Two: Contribution

Once Mike had identified that there was a problem in the feedback that he had received, it would be important to begin to develop the fishbone (Figure 3). Various contributions could include: a culture of conscious and unconscious racism and stereotyping, a history of racist comments that have inflicted pain, projections from personal history of pain in all the participants, fear of offending others and using humor or sarcasm rather than direct feedback, and the CPE culture which offers critique and is unfamiliar in a beginning first unit.

In this case the fishbone could be continued over time so that the heat of the moment could pass and the learning from that experience could continue. Differences in the group perception could also make for a group experience of exploring values and perceptions in a safe context.

An important aspect of the contribution step is the time to listen and to unpack all that is happening both cognitively and affectively.

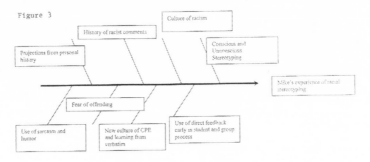

Figure 3

Step Three: Claiming

In this process the CPE supervisor would own that prejudice and stereotyping are beliefs that sometimes translate to behavior. This direct apology agrees with the theory of building an alliance through ownership of mistakes and hurtful situations. The transfer of a comment about sarcasm and humor to a generalization about black men could be an unintended impact of the reality of the power differential and underlying stereotyping. The CPE supervisor would want to stay with the impact rather than intent of the comment. So the ownership is about how, to Mike the comment was experienced as racist. It is important to emphasize that while the apology may feel personal for the supervisor, it must be genuine and focused on the supervisory role of maintaining a learning alliance with Mike.

Step Four: Convinced Conversation

This example is particularly poignant for us as we have encountered such circumstances in our practice. Our intention has been quite the opposite of racism. And yet, because of our personal histories and upbringing, and the reality of white privilege, we have been confronted with racism as a blind spot with unintended impact on others.

Mike's CPE supervisor would want to engage in a convinced conversation openness and willingness to be led to an understanding of the impact of the comment on Mike. This is a sacred process in that the CPE supervisor is willing to learn about Mike's experience, validate that experience, and explore his or her own blind spots in terms of racism. Ultimately the CPE supervisor would apologize for a comment that Mike considered racist and for the impact of the statement that was hurtful or experienced as stereotyping. The supervisor would ask Mike whether he has received and heard the apology, and the supervisor should be able to let Mike know that this aspect of racism will not occur again.

While the apology is important in and of itself, the process that has led to this point reconnects Mike with his CPE supervisor in an alliance that can provide opportunities for even greater learning and growth for Mike. Mike may or may not be able to reflect on his contribution to the problem in this setting and if not, this can be a topic for a later time.

Step Five: Continuing Consultation

In Mike's case one aspect of follow up would be in the verbatim itself. The role of humor and sarcasm in patient care could be explored in a more general way so that the opportunity for learning about an intervention would not be lost.

Another piece of follow up is the relationship with peers where there is a difference of perception. In our practice this is a worthy topic for interpersonal relationship group or group process. However this unstructured group experience is established in the curriculum, difference of perception and personal history and understandings can be explored.

Finally, the relationship between the CPE supervisor and Mike needs to be nurtured after such a breach of trust. It is the hope of the CPE supervisor that a convinced conversation can reconnect and validate Mike's experience for a long term positive impact. However, this cannot be taken for granted and checking in with Mike about his on-going perceptions is important.

Conclusion

In summary, the art of the apology as outlined in the Five Cs is a supervisory tool that will positively impact the student's trust of the supervisor and the ability of the student to use and engage the CPE process faithfully. It will also relate to theological considerations and implications for ministry, and interface with business practices in many CPE institutions.

We realize that we have focused here on errors in supervisory practice that fall within the acceptable parameters of CPE supervisory relationships. We have not dealt with the apology when there has been an ethical violation of some kind. That is a topic for another paper.

In this paper we have attempted to explore the ways that the Five Cs can be a tool in CPE supervision. Case material was examined through our individual personal journeys, theories from Twelve Step programs, Object Relations theory, Self Psychology, and business practice. We have proposed the Five Cs which we believe can be used to enhance the CPE learning relationship.

References

Alcoholic Anonymous World Service Inc. (2008). Retrieved from http://www.aa.org/bigbookonline/en_tableofcnt.cfm

Anderson, B. & Fagerhaug, T. (1999). *Root cause analysis:Simplified tools and techniques.* Milwaukee: Quality Press.

Cooper-White, P. (2004). *Shared wisdom: Use of the self in pastoral care and counseling.* Minneapolis, MN: Augsburg Fortress.

Cooper-White, P. (2007). *Many voices: Pastoral psychotherapy in relational and theological perspective.* Minneapolis, MN: Fortress Press.

H.E.A.R.T. Retrieved March 11, 2008, from www.baymed.org/documents/orientation/stars/.pdf3

Ishikawa, K. (1969). *Ishikawa Diagram*. Retrieved May 16, 2008, from http://mot.vuse.vanderbilt.edu/mt322/Ishikawa.htm

Ishikawa, K. (2005). Retrieved May 16, 2008, from http://www.envisionsoftware.com/Management/Fishbone_Diagram.html

Kellerman, B. (2007). When should a leader apologize? And when not? *Harvard Business Review*. [Electronic version].

Marx, D. (2001).Patient safety and the 'just culture:' A primer for health care executives.(Pamphlet, Columbia University). http://www.mers-m.net/support/Marx_Primer.pdf

Rothman, M.D. (2007). The apology. [Electronic version] *Yale Journal of Biology and Medicine*. 80.

Phildelphia Yearly Meeting of the Society of Friends. (1998). *Faith and Practice.*

A simple apology-no such thing. (2008) Retrieved on March 11, 2008, from http://www.jkador.com/ASimpleApologyNoSuchThing.htm

Stone, D., Patton, B., Heen, S. & Fisher, R. (1999). *Difficult conversations.* New York: Penguin Books.

Winnicott, D.W. (1987). *The child, the family and the outside world.* New York: Perseus Books Reprint Classics in Child Development.

Wolf, E.S. (1988). *Treating the self: elements of self psychology.* New York: The Guilford Press.

ACKNOWLEDGEMENTS

We are grateful for the many people who helped the idea of this festschrift become a reality. We appreciate the commitment of all of our contributors, especially as it was expressed in their hard work and timely responses to our timelines. We have been fortunate to have wonderful assistance in the production of this volume, including typing and formatting by Alisa Damholt and Emily Ostegaard and copy editing by Margaret M. Brennan. Our colleagues at the Journal of Pastoral Care Publications, Inc., Orlo Strunk, Jr., Managing Editor, and Terry Bard, Associate Managing Editor, have provided helpful encouragement and guidance since the idea was first presented to them.

Many colleagues in ACPE have also played important roles in supporting this project. We are grateful for all who contributed to the fund that has helped produce the volume, and especially to the members of the Board of Representatives of ACPE for their generous support. Teresa E. Snorton, ACPE Executive Director, in addition to contributing a chapter, has been a special source of support.

Jennifer Allcock, Joan's partner, has been enthusiastic about this project since it was first discussed with Joan in their living room. We are grateful for her generous support and for her assistance in providing important biographical details for Joan's life and work.

We also appreciate the encouragement and support of our colleagues, friends, and families. A special word of thanks goes to Peter Garlid, for his excellent idea and on-going support.

CONTRIBUTORS

Yvonne M. Agazarian, Ed.D., CGP, DGAGPA, FAPA. Self-employed in Philadelphia, Pennsylvania. Yvonne has developed the Theory of Living Human Systems and its System-Centered Practice and founded the Systems-Centered Training and Research Institute. She has authored and co-authored seven books and is in private practice teaching and training in Systems-Centered methods. Joan was the first person she knew who not only understood but also wrote about Yvonne's theory. Joan joined SCT in training and became a well-loved member of several training groups. To Yvonne Joan also was a great, warm, and valuable friend.

Stephen L. Dutton, D.Min., AAPC Fellow, ACPE CPE Supervisor, is Manager and Program Director, Clinical Pastoral Education, Christiana Care Health Services, Wilmington, Delaware. Steve's current professional focus is the utilization of creative arts, especially fiction and poetry in teaching pastoral care to CPE students. He serves ACPE on the Accreditation Commission and is the Chair of the Eastern Region Accreditation Committee. Steve currently studies Freud and neo-Freudian authors as they may contribute anew to the Clinical Pastoral Education movement.

Steve met Joan Hemenway when he entered ACPE supervisory education. Joan contributed to Steve's CPE practice through her group theory and courageous interactions with others. Steve's chief regret with Joan is that they never attended a baseball game together. Stephen is married to Paula Teague, the co-author of his contribution to this volume.

George Fitchett, D.Min., Ph.D., BCC, ACPE CPE Supervisor, is an Associate Professor and the Director of Research in the Department of Religion, Health, and Human Values, Rush University

Medical Center, Chicago, Illinois. Since 1990 George has been involved in research examining the relationship between religion and health in a variety of community and clinical populations. George is the author of *Assessing Spiritual Needs* (Academic Renewal Press, 2002). Joan was an editor of the Augsburg Press series in which the book was originally published. George also knew and respected Joan as a colleague and leader in CPE and consulted with her when she was looking for a publisher for her book, *Inside the Circle*.

Susan P. Gantt, Ph.D., ABPP, CGP, is a psychologist and Assistant Professor in Psychiatry at Emory University School of Medicine, Atlanta, Georgia, where she coordinates group psychotherapy training. She is the Director of the Systems-Centered Training and Research Institute. She is a Diplomate in Group Psychology through the American Board of Professional Psychology and co-author of the books *Autobiography of a Theory*, *SCT in Action*, and *SCT in Clinical Practice* with Yvonne Agazarian. In private practice she works as a licensed practitioner in systems-centered group, couples, and individual therapy. She consults to organizations, and is a trainer, supervisor, and conference director in Systems-Centered Training in the United States and Europe. Joan and Susan met in the context of SCT.

Catherine F. Garlid, M.Div., BCC, ACPE CPE Supervisor, is the Director of Spiritual Care and Pastoral Education at Greenwich Hospital in Greenwich, Connecticut. She supervises students in a community based CPE program that is a satellite of the program at Yale New Haven Hospital. Kitty did her CPE residency with Joan Hemenway in 1981-82. Having collaborated many years later with Peg Lewis and Joan in the establishment of the Pastoral Education Consortium of the Yale New Haven Health System, Kitty trained with Joan in that program where she was introduced to Systems-Centered Training. Kitty joined an SCT training group in 2005 to explore further integration of CPE and SCT.

Peg Lewis, M.Div., BCC, ACPE CPE Supervisor, is the Director of the Department of Religious Ministries at Yale New Haven

Hospital in New Haven, Connecticut. She was very pleased that, under the leadership of Joan Hemenway, Yale New Haven Hospital was able to offer five years of Supervisory Education. In addition to administrative and pastoral responsibilities, Peg feels fortunate to be able to supervise summer unit students and extended units of CPE for Healthcare Professionals. Her supervision is increasingly influenced by the theory and practices of Systems-Centered Training.

Ted Loder, M.Div., served for nearly thirty-eight years as Senior Minister of the First United Methodist Church of Germantown in Philadelphia, Pennsylvania. The church is notable for being in the forefront of social action for justice and peace, artistic endeavors, and community development. Loder is the author of several books including *Guerrillas of Grace* and most recently, *The Haunt of Grace*, and *Loaves, Fishes and Leftovers: Sharing Faith's Deep Questions.* Joan was a colleague and friend for over forty years.

John Patton, M.Div., BCC, ACPE CPE Supervisor, is Professor Emeritus of Pastoral Theology at Columbia Theological Seminary, Decatur, Georgia, and author of a number of books in the field of pastoral care and counseling. In retirement he continues a part-time practice of Marriage and Family Therapy at the Samaritan Center of Atlanta and serves as a supervisor of lay ministry in his local United Methodist Church. He has served as a pastor of United Methodist churches, as director of chaplaincy services at Emory University and Grady Memorial Hospitals in Atlanta, and as Executive Director of the Georgia Association for Pastoral Care. He is a Diplomate and past president of the American Association of Pastoral Counselors and a Supervisor with the Association for Clinical Pastoral Education and the American Association for Marriage and Family Therapy. He and his wife Helen, who was also a friend of Joan, have been married for over fifty years and have four children and ten grandchildren.

Bob Raines, M.Div., is an ordained minister in the United Church of Christ serving three congregations. He was a Fulbright

Scholar to Clare College, Cambridge University, England. Bob served as the Director of the Kirkridge Retreat and Study Center and is the author of thirteen books including *New Life in the Church, Creative Brooding, Going Home,* and *A Time to Live: Seven Tasks of Creative Aging.* Joan and Bob were friends for 45 years. They enjoyed being back in close touch in recent years as neighbors in the town of Guilford, Connecticut.

A. Meigs Ross, M.Div., BCC, ACPE CPE Supervisor, is the Coordinator for Clinical Pastoral Education at the New York Presbyterian Hospital System in New York City where she supervises all levels of CPE. She served as a CPE supervisor and Director of Clinical Pastoral Education at the HealthCare Chaplaincy for several years where she was instrumental in developing a new curriculum for clinical pastoral educators. The curriculum included courses in supervision and group leadership that integrated systems theory. Meigs began her study of Systems-Centered Theory with Yvonne Agazarian in 2002 where she and Joan Hemenway studied together as colleagues. Meigs met Joan in 1994 at a workshop that Joan was teaching on process groups in CPE. Joan was a valued consultant for Meigs in her journey toward certification as a CPE supervisor and was her respected colleague and friend.

Teresa E. Snorton, D.Min., BCC, ACPE CPE Supervisor, is the Executive Director of the Association for Clinical Pastoral Education, Decatur, Georgia. Formerly she served as the Executive Director of Clinical Services and Administration at the Emory Center for Pastoral Services in Atlanta, Georgia, and the Director of Pastoral Services at Crawford Long Hospital. She has been an adjunct instructor of Pastoral Care at Candler School of Theology at Emory University since 1991. Teresa is an ordained minister in the Christian Methodist Episcopal Church. She and Joan collaborated closely, particularly during Joan's terms as ACPE President-Elect and President, and shared their mutual dedication to the work of ACPE.

Paula J. Teague, D.Min., MBA, BCC, ACPE CPE Supervisor

Manager, Clinical Pastoral Education Program and Course Director for the Institute for Spirituality and Medicine at Johns Hopkins Hospital, Baltimore, Maryland. Paula has been an ACPE CPE supervisor since 1989. In May 2008, she received her MBA from Johns Hopkins University Carey School of Business. Paula's current focus is the integration of the MBA with its focus on leadership, best business practices, and strategic planning with clinical education. Paula hopes that her efforts will benefit pastoral care givers as well as hospital practitioners. Paula met Joan Hemenway in 1993 when she moved to the Eastern Region of ACPE and was privileged to be in a professional peer group of women for over ten years which included Joan. Joan was a good friend, professional colleague, and mentor. Paula is married to Stephen Dutton, the co-author of her contribution to this volume.

Mary Martha Thiel, D.Min., BCC, ACPE CPE Supervisor, is the Director of Clinical Pastoral Education at Hebrew Rehabilitation Center/Hebrew SeniorLife, Boston, Massachusetts, and member of the CPE supervisory education staff at Beverly Hospital/Northeast Health Systems, Beverly, Massachusetts. She helps coordinate the curriculum for the Institute of Pastoral Supervision, one of the Northeast Region's supervisory education consortia. Mary Martha was instrumental in developing the CPE for Healthcare Professionals model, and is involved now in adapting the CPE process to a Jewish context. Joan Hemenway was Mary Martha's field education seminar leader at Union Theological Seminary, and then a consultant to her during Mary Martha's supervisory education.

Audun Magne Ulland, Cand. Philol., Cand. Theol., BCC, Licensed Group Analyst, is Vice President at the Board of the Norwegian Association of Group Psychotherapy and a Training Teacher at the Norwegian Institute of Group Analysis. He has served as a minister in the Norwegian Lutheran Church and for 13 years as a chaplain at Oslo Hospital, Psychiatric Hospital. Since 2006 he has worked as a group psychotherapist at the Unit for Group Psychotherapy, Lilleström Psychiatric Centre, Akershus

University Hospital near Oslo, Norway. He was Joan's student in a CPE program at Bridgeport Hospital in 1998. Later Joan and Audun became dear friends.

Angelika A. Zollfrank, M.Div., BCC, ACPE CPE Supervisor, is the Director of Clinical Pastoral Education at the Massachusetts General Hospital, Massachusetts. She supervises basic and advanced CPE students, including groups of Healthcare Providers in CPE. Since 2003 Angelika has been involved in training in the context of the Systems-Centered Therapy and Research Institute (SCTRI). Her ACPE theory papers integrated some Systems-Centered concepts into a CPE supervisory theory. She has been interested in applying Systems-Centered Practice to CPE. Joan Hemenway was Angelika's supervisor during her supervisory training and introduced Angelika to SCT. Both shared their love for group work in CPE.

Articles

1. Agazarian, Y.M. (1992). Systems-Centered group psychotherapy - How to develop a working group.

2. Gantt, S.P., & Agazarian, Y.M. (2004). Systems-Centered emotional intelligence: Beyond individual systems to organizational systems. organizational analysis, 12 (2), 147-169. doi:10.1108/eb028990